AF575466

HOW TO DRAW NEARLY EVERYTHING

VICTOR PERARD

DOVER PUBLICATIONS, GARDEN CITY, NEW YORK

This big book by Victor Perard is the choice of the most important material from ten of his amazingly successful books for students and artists. Added to these already published pages are fourteen new plates showing how to draw cats. The combination therefore contains what the student needs, with or without a teacher, to begin the successful drawing of people, of nature, and of the animals most often wanted in pictures, in a wide variety of mediums.

The selection has had the effect of concentrating emphasis on essentials and on principles, hence the material offered is well within the capacity of the most untaught beginner. Nevertheless — and the sale of hundreds of thousands of Mr. Perard's books in their original editions proves it — these simple and straightforward instruction materials have lasting value even to established illustrators and artists.

THE PUBLISHERS

Bibliographical Note

This Dover edition, first published in 2012, is an unabridged republication of the work originally published by Pitman Publishing Corporation, New York, in 1949 under the title *How to Draw: Figures, Children, Faces, Expressions, Flowers, Trees, Houses, Landscapes, Sea and Sky, Dogs, Horses, Cats.*

Library of Congress Cataloging-in-Publication Data

Perard, Victor Semon, 1870–1957.
[How to draw]
How to draw nearly everything / Victor Perard.
p. cm.
Originally published: New York : Pitman, 1949.
ISBN-13: 978-0-486-49848-5 — ISBN-10: 0-486-49848-4
1. Drawing—Technique. I. Title.

NC730.P46 2012
741.2—dc23

2012013292

Manufactured in the United States of America
49848407
www.doverpublications.com

FIRST OF ALL

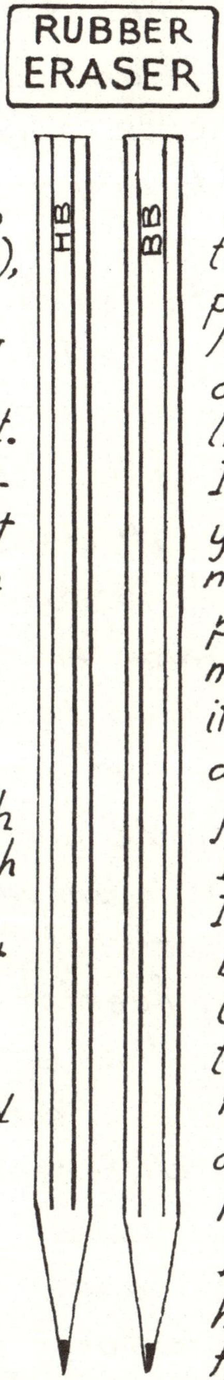

Art is the finest way of doing anything. Pencil drawing is one of the fine arts and the student should master its technique.

It is important to have the right tools to work with – a medium-hard pencil (HB), a softer one (BB), an eraser, a writing pen and ink, plus a white pencil to draw on black paper.

Materials should be treated with respect. Learn to use your pencils deftly with varying pressure to obtain the dark and light tones. Keep your drawing neat and aim at a professional appearance.

Before starting to draw, analyze your subject carefully. Ask yourself what are the principal lines of action. Study the proportions, that is, the length and width compared to the height. Observe from which side the light is coming.

The shadows come where the rays of light are witheld by the protruding forms of the object.

The shading serves to give depth and thickness, and by varying the intensity of the tints gives the impression of the object as it appears to the eyes.

Once you have analyzed the object you intend to draw the next step to consider is the placing of the drawing properly on the paper. To do this, sketch with your finger on the paper an imaginary outline of the picture you are about to draw; at the same time try to visualize the completed picture. This is an essential part of your art training.

Now take up your medium-hard pencil and draw very lightly the essential lines of the subject you have selected. If you draw with heavy black lines you kill your vision of the picture, and not only are mistakes registered on the paper but they are also impressed on the mind. With a well-prepared drawing and its essential lines, begin to draw with some decision; this helps to strengthen the judgment.

Do not sacrifice accuracy to speed. If you hurry you give out knowledge but do not take it in.

After becoming proficient in copying, try to compose pictures of your own in order to cultivate creative ability and the facility for recalling passing impressions.

It would be of further benefit to see how well you can redraw a picture from memory.

RUBBER ERASER

HB

BB

Further Comment

The feeling for art goes to waste unless backed by knowledge with which to work. To draw well is less a natural ability than the result of acquired training. Most gifted students lack the patience to study and try stunts to escape work, thus enabling students with less natural facility and more method and application to outclass them.

The advantages to be gained from studies direct from nature are best secured after a certain degree of elementary training in copying is obtained. Facility can at first be gained by copying, and there is no fear of becoming only a copyist if the student understands the principles upon which the original drawing is based.

A grave mistake is haste, not giving sufficient consideration to the subject before commencing the work. Haste is liable to produce inaccuracies which would necessitate corrections and erasures and mar the pleasure derived from the study of art.

Drawing teaches the eye to observe and the hand to co-ordinate with the mind. Training the eye and hand to co-ordinate gives quite a thrill when mastered. Without order and method the work is uneven in quality, good one day and bad the next. In starting a picture it is well not to get interested in details too soon; a more forcible style is maintained by keeping the whole drawing under way rather than by finishing in detail one part at a time.

The first line in a drawing should be the most important and the last of least value. The problems are somewhat different in every picture, which makes for one of the fascinating aspects of the study of art.

With proper training there should be no waiting for inspiration; preliminary and memory sketches should be made to force inspiration.

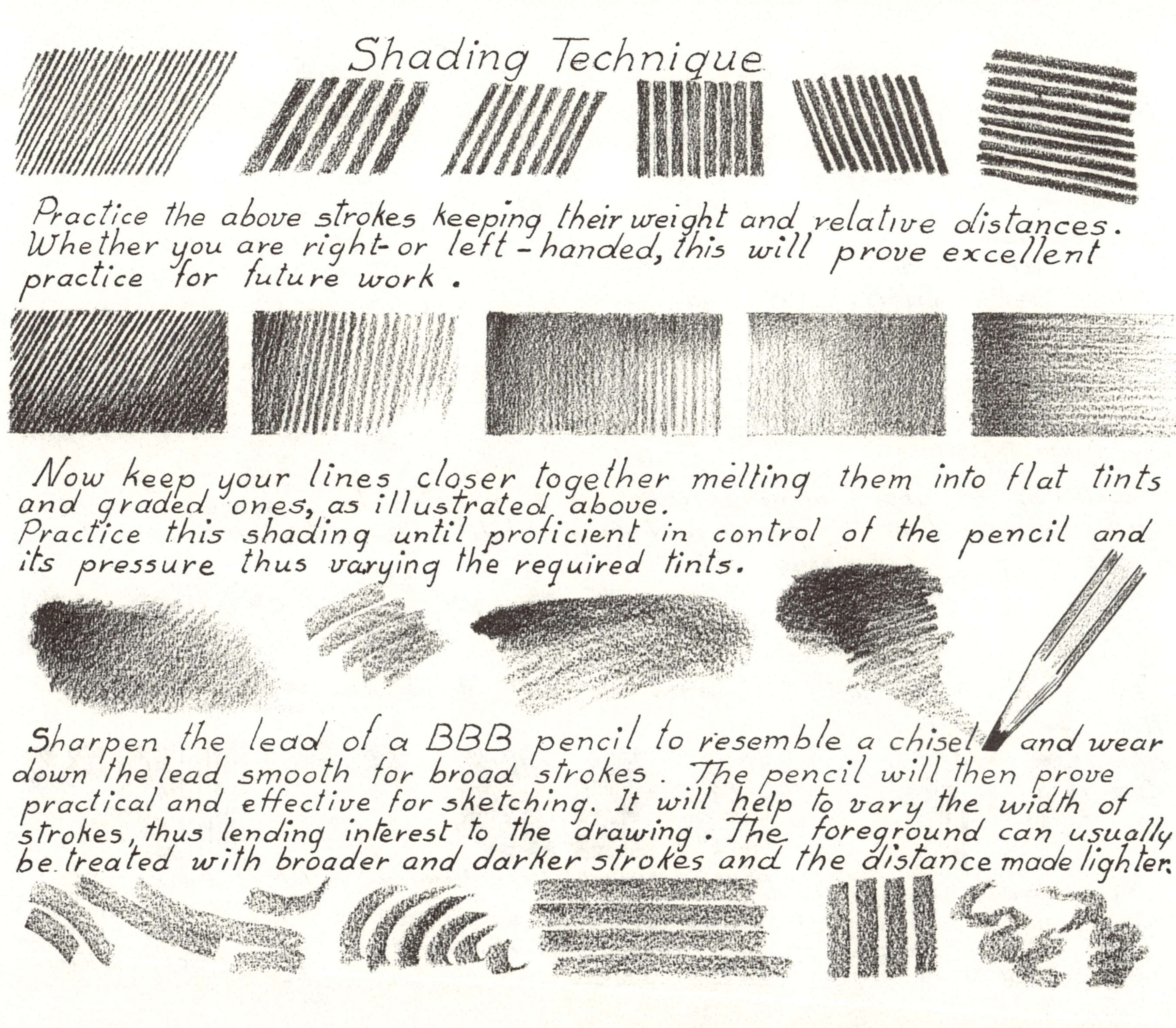
Shading Technique
Practice the above strokes keeping their weight and relative distances. Whether you are right- or left-handed, this will prove excellent practice for future work.
Now keep your lines closer together melting them into flat tints and graded ones, as illustrated above.
Practice this shading until proficient in control of the pencil and its pressure thus varying the required tints.
Sharpen the lead of a BBB pencil to resemble a chisel and wear down the lead smooth for broad strokes. The pencil will then prove practical and effective for sketching. It will help to vary the width of strokes, thus lending interest to the drawing. The foreground can usually be treated with broader and darker strokes and the distance made lighter.

Pencil, Pen and Brush Technique

The materials needed are graphite pencils HB and BBB, a soft rubber, a pliable pen, black ink, sable brush No.1 and a drawing pad 8"x12".
Too many tools make for confusion. A few, well cared for and used with judgment, can supply unlimited means of artistic expression.
The harder pencil HB is usually used to start a drawing as its lines are lighter and details can be indicated for a bolder technique later with the softer pencil BBB. Drawings made entirely with the HB pencil have a tendency to be hard and to have insufficient variety of tones.

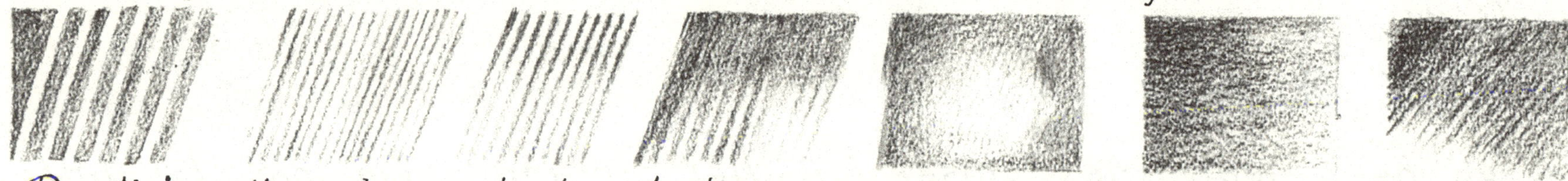

Practicing the above shading technique by varying the pressure of the pencil, will give control of the pencil and its possibilities for obtaining light and dark tones.

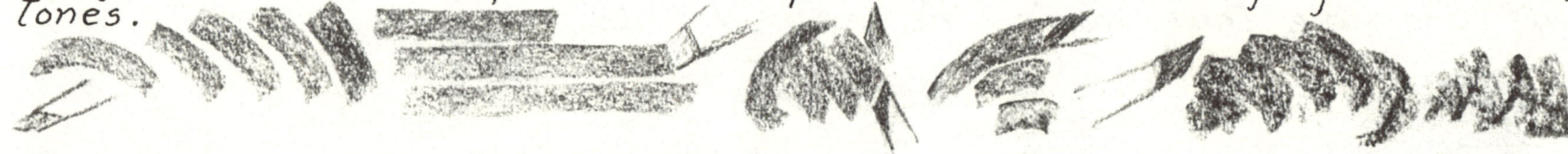

For broad strokes with the pencil, the lead should be worn down to a chisel form.

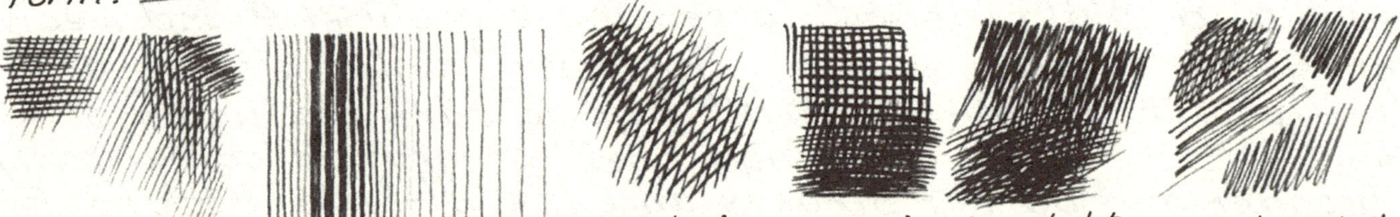

Different directions From dark to light. Flickering Formal For a dark tone Back and forth

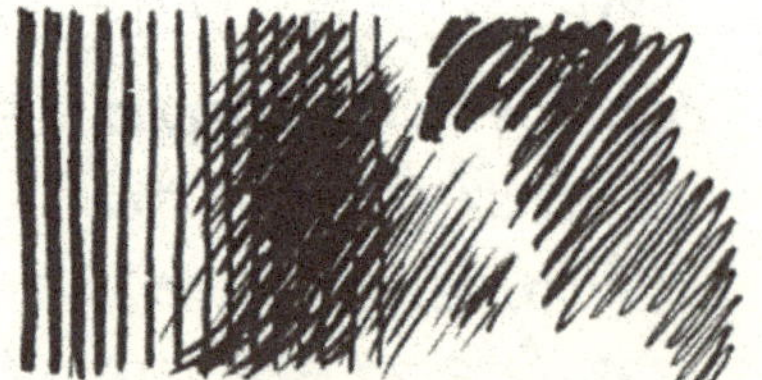

Brush strokes

The lines are softer and richer but more difficult to control.

It is useful to learn to use the pen in different directions and to cross hatch at various angles. Practicing these strokes will give control of the pen and added freedom.

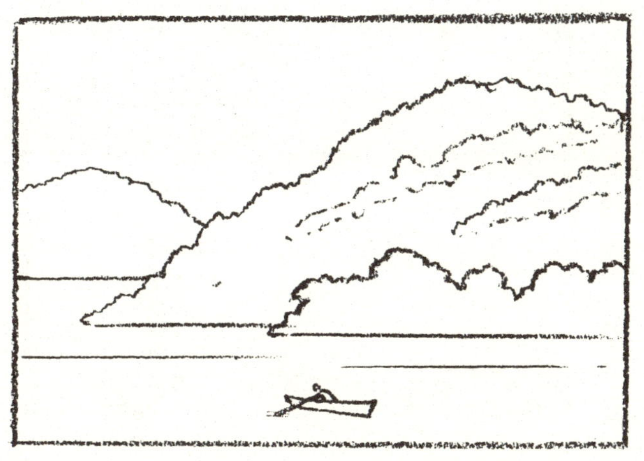

Fundamental Outline

The first and all-important concern of the artist is to see the forms before him in simple outline at first, avoiding interest in detail.

This method should be closely adhered to in future work.

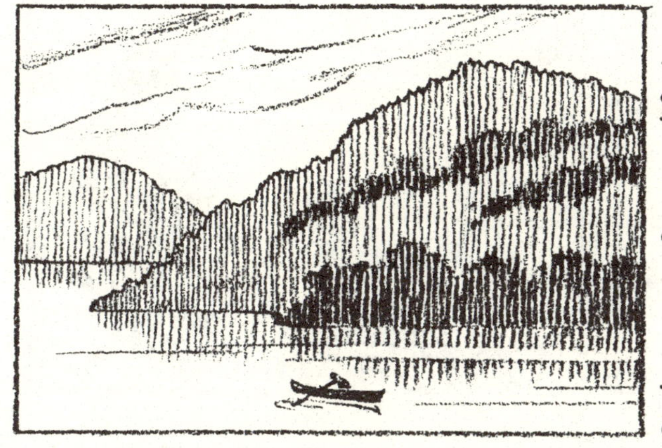

<u>To shade distant landscapes</u> with vertical strokes gives solidity, keeps the mountains in simple masses. The distant mountain is silhouetted and shows no detail except for a slight broken line to indicate trees on the mountain top.

The same broken line is used on the nearer mountain, but with more detail and the nearer mountain is shaded to suggest that it is covered with trees in the distance, middle distance and foreground.

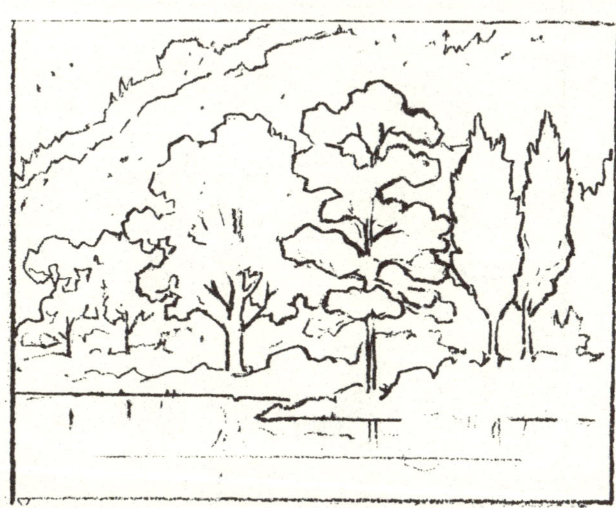

The group of trees on the right is nearer and so begins to show the shape of the shadows made by the foliage. These should be mapped out and seen as a pattern giving a feeling of design.

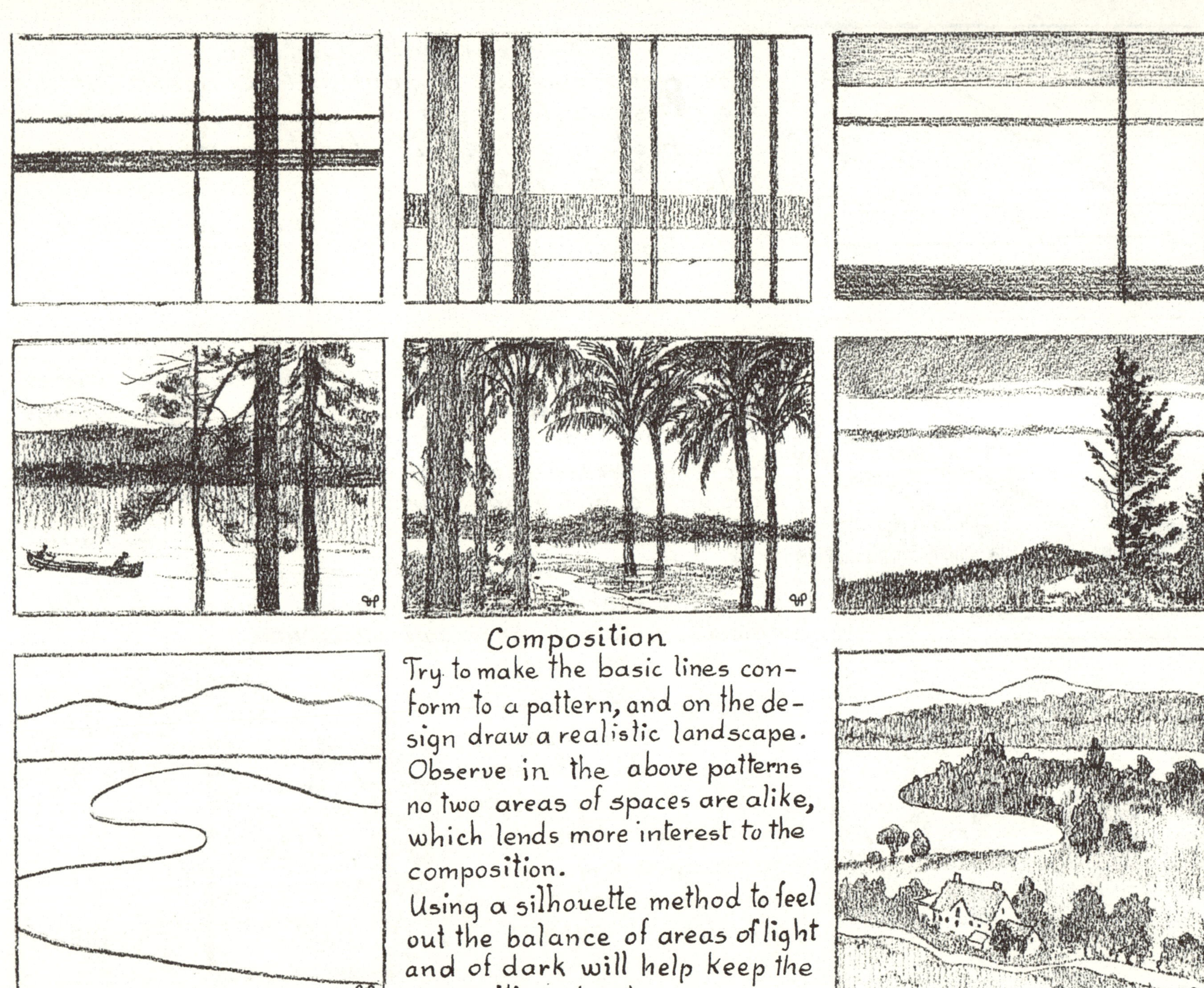

Composition

Try to make the basic lines conform to a pattern, and on the design draw a realistic landscape. Observe in the above patterns no two areas of spaces are alike, which lends more interest to the composition.

Using a silhouette method to feel out the balance of areas of light and of dark will help keep the composition simple.

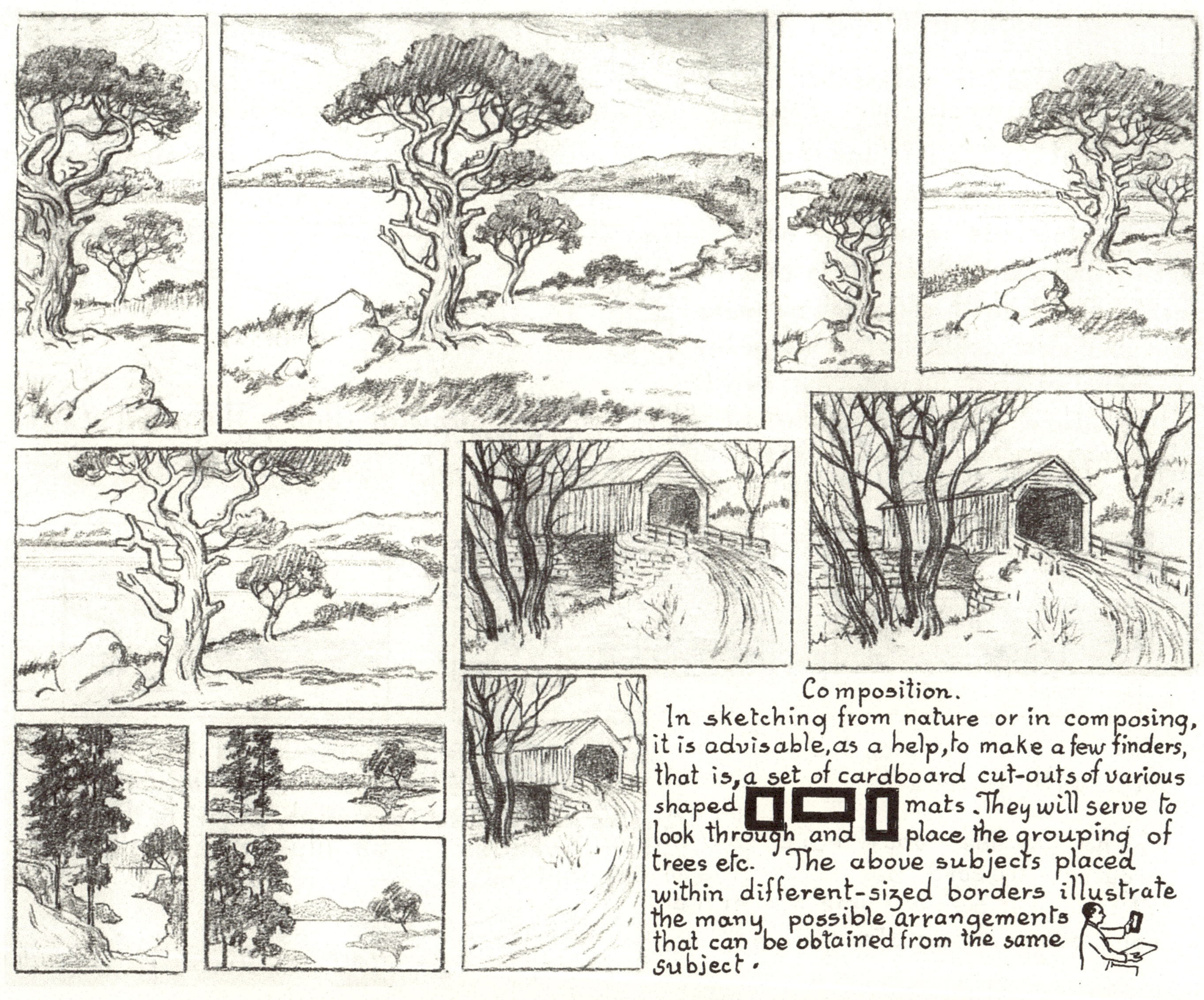

Composition.

In sketching from nature or in composing, it is advisable, as a help, to make a few finders, that is, a set of cardboard cut-outs of various shaped mats. They will serve to look through and place the grouping of trees etc. The above subjects placed within different-sized borders illustrate the many possible arrangements that can be obtained from the same subject.

Perspective

Perspective is the representation of the diminution of objects to the eye as they become more or less remote to the observer. It is an important and indispensable auxiliary to the artist. As a test take a ruler and measure a person forty feet away and as he approaches see how much larger he appears. This will show the difference in size of things remote or near.

Point of sight

When the eye is directed to any scene in nature it embraces no more than what most agreeably fills its power of vision without turning the head.

The picture would naturally be embraced by a circular limit. The point of sight is always within the picture because that is where the eye is placed.

The line of the horizon is always on a level with the eye of the observer.

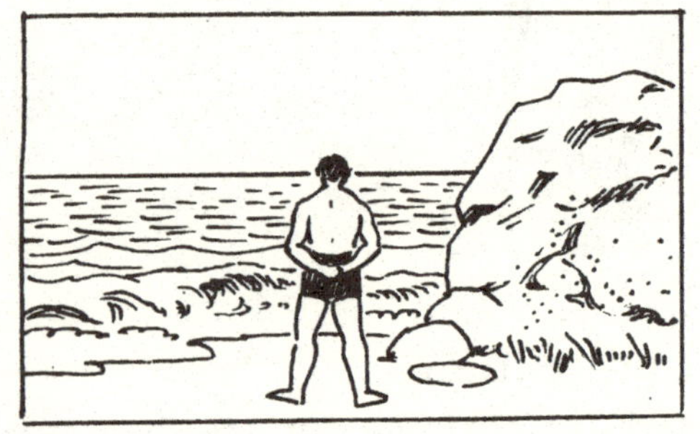

The horizon line is on the level with the eye.

The horizon line would have the curve of the earth but so little of it is seen at a time that it can be drawn straight.

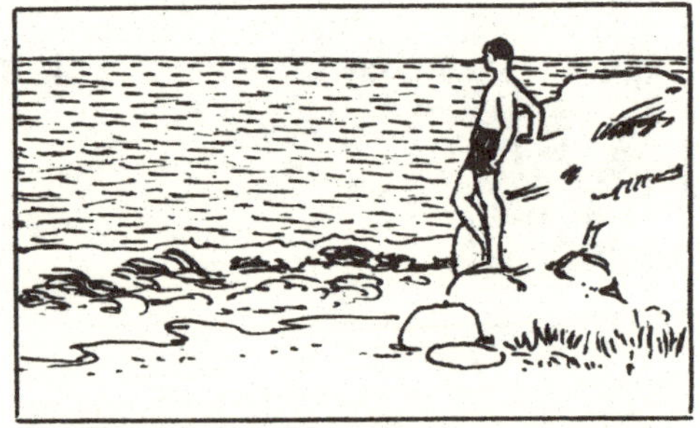

The horizon line is still on a level with the observer's eye but as he has climbed to a higher level, the line of the horizon is higher.

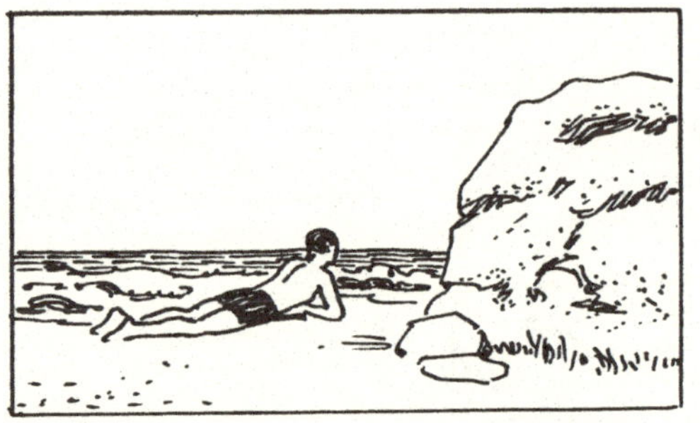

By assuming the onlooker's position, the horizon line is much lower to the eye, as illustrated above.

PERSPECTIVE

Looking through a window with square panes of glass would give upright lines and horizontal lines to help in seeing how much of an angle the lines would take to reach the point of sight. To this point of sight the lines that are parallel converge and terminate.

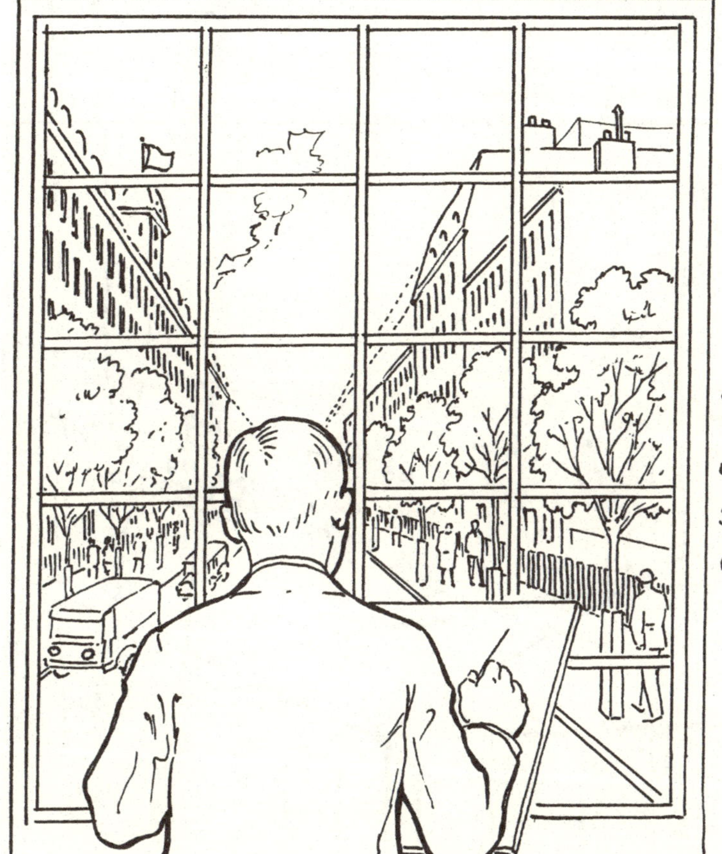

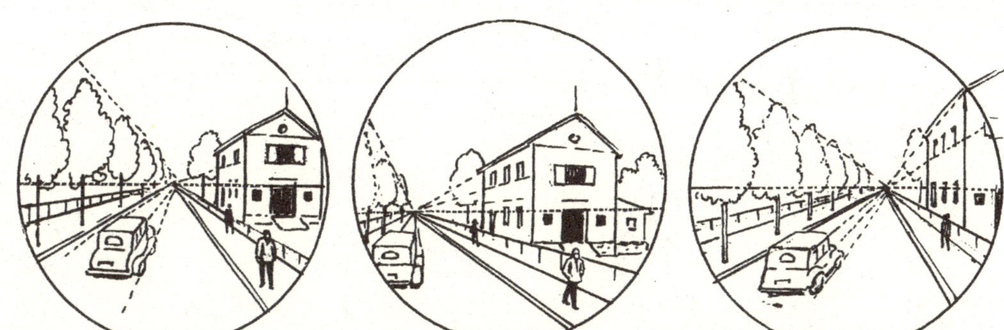

The point of sight need not always be in the center of the picture. It may suit the composition better to shift it to one side or the other on the horizon line to obtain a more pleasing arrangement.

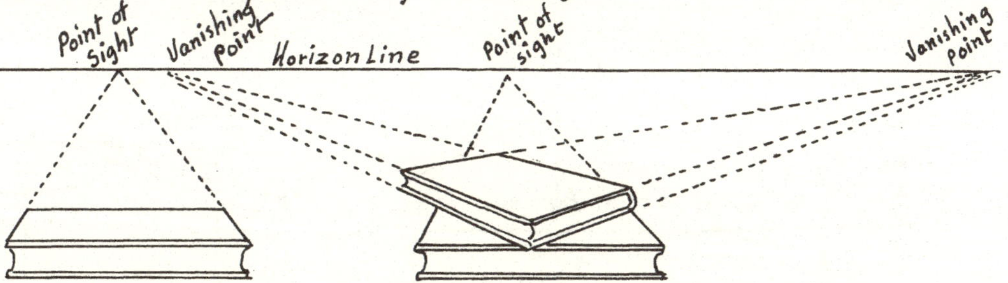

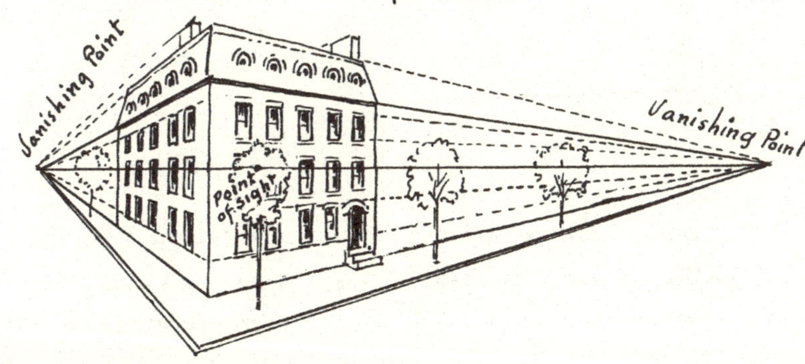

Aërial Perspective has reference more particularly to atmospheric conditions by which objects more or less remote are affected as to color, light, shadows and gradation of tints according to their distance.

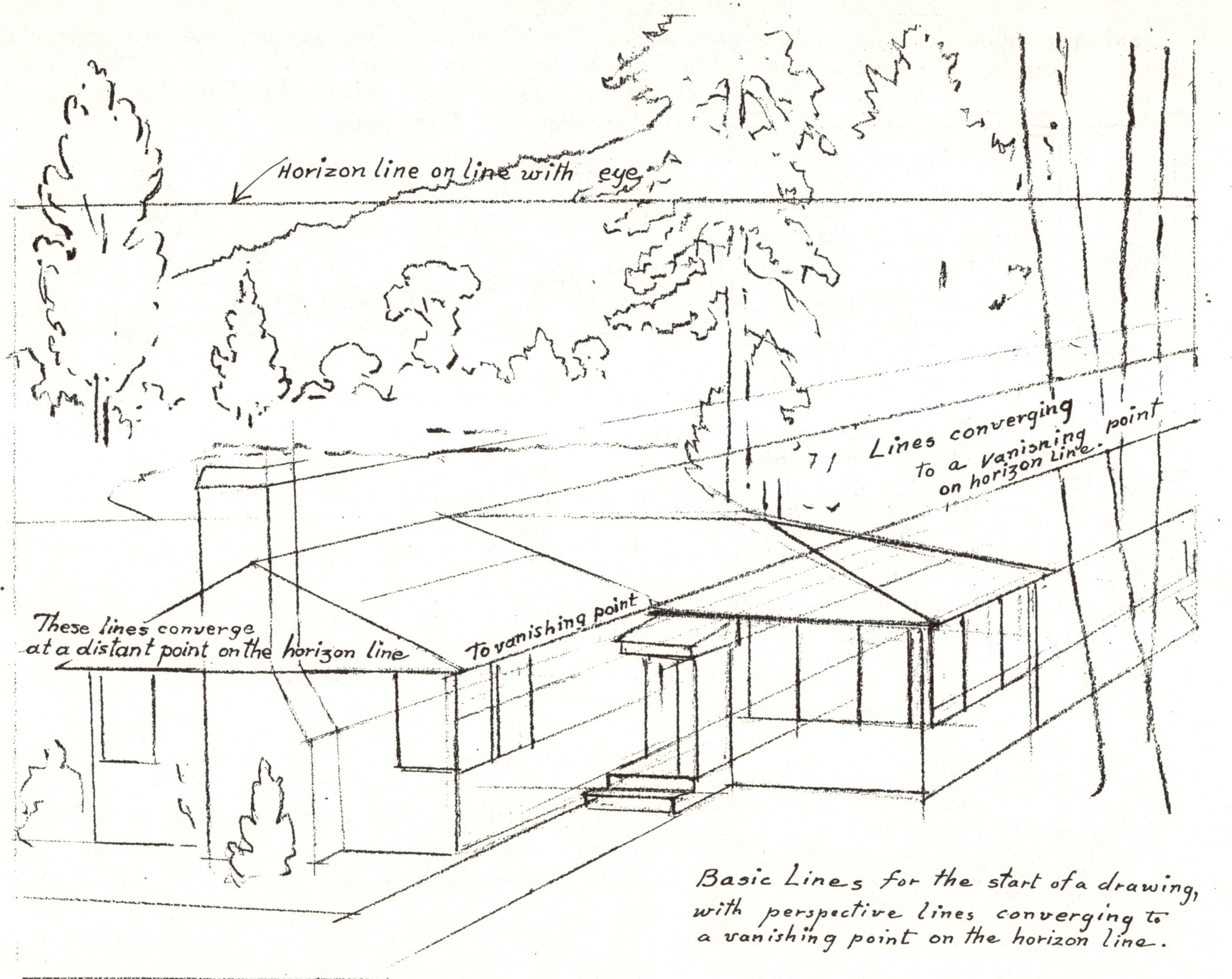

Basic Lines for the start of a drawing, with perspective lines converging to a vanishing point on the horizon line.

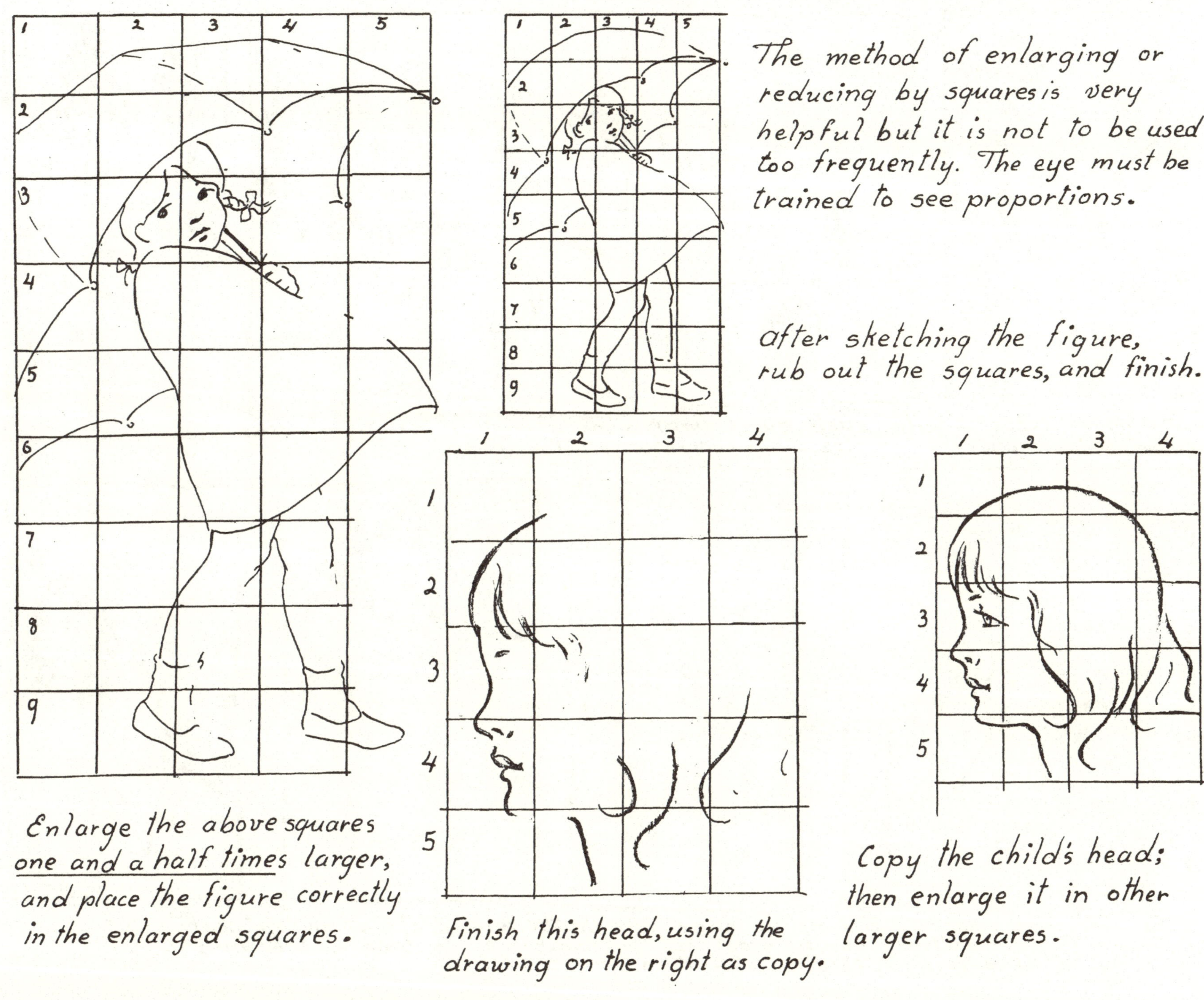

The method of enlarging or reducing by squares is very helpful but it is not to be used too frequently. The eye must be trained to see proportions.

After sketching the figure, rub out the squares, and finish.

Enlarge the above squares <u>one and a half times</u> larger, and place the figure correctly in the enlarged squares.

Finish this head, using the drawing on the right as copy.

Copy the child's head; then enlarge it in other larger squares.

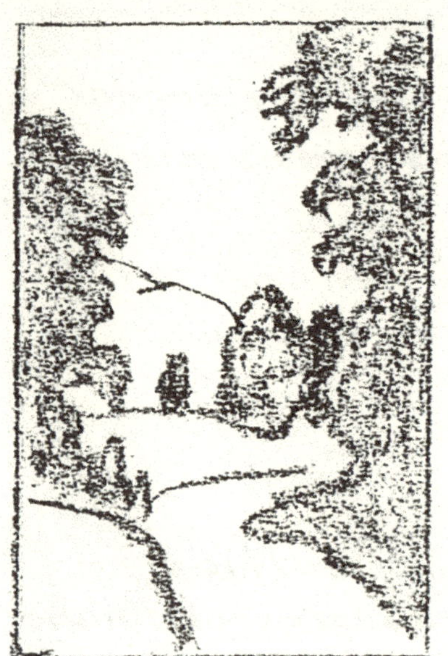
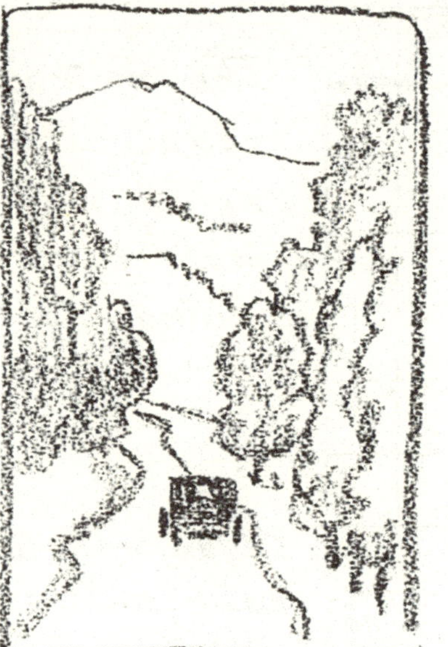
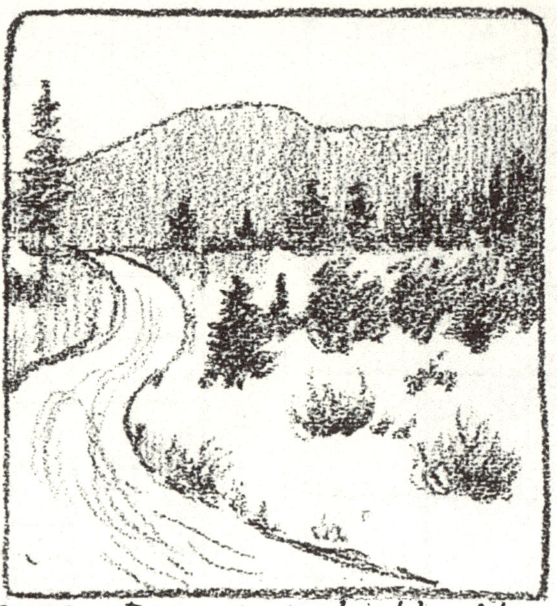
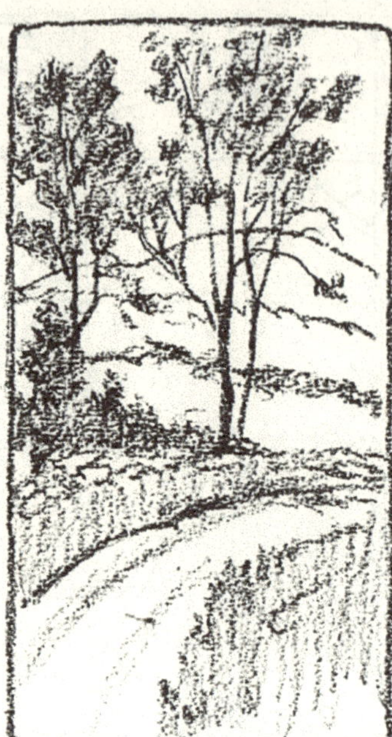

Filling note-books with such quick impressions stores up valuable ideas for future pictures. Use a very soft pencil for speed.

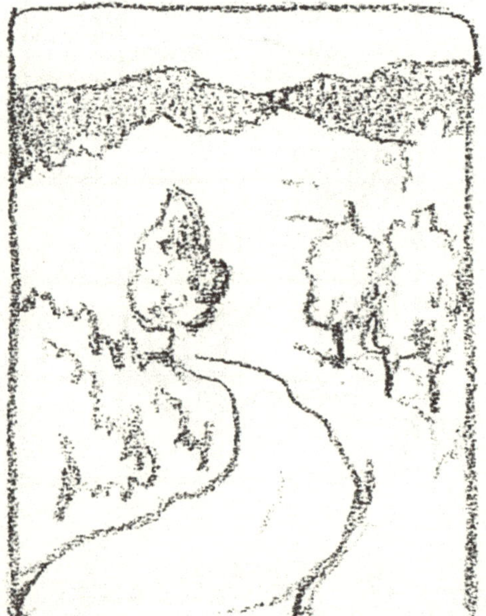
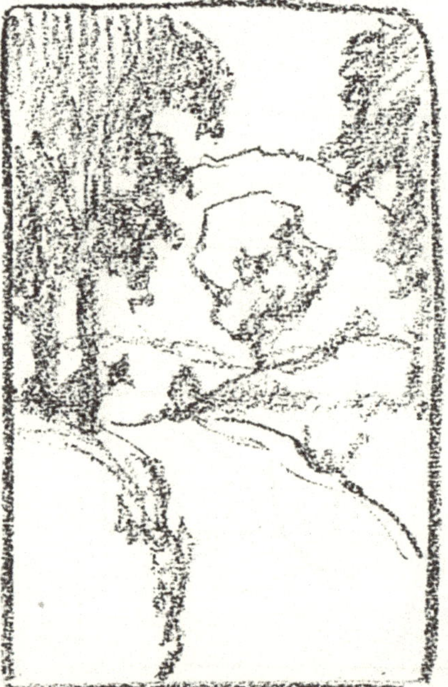
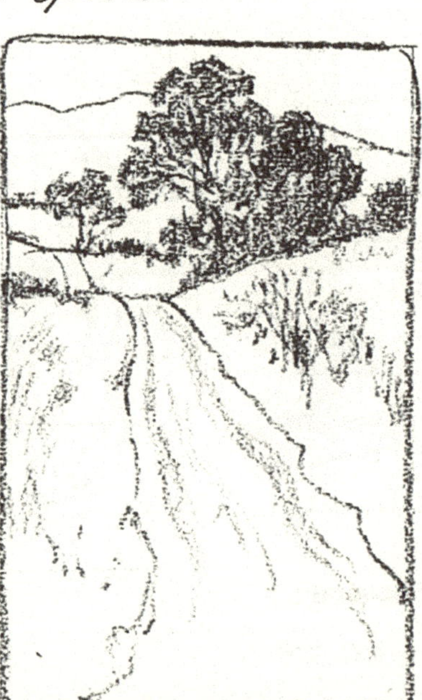
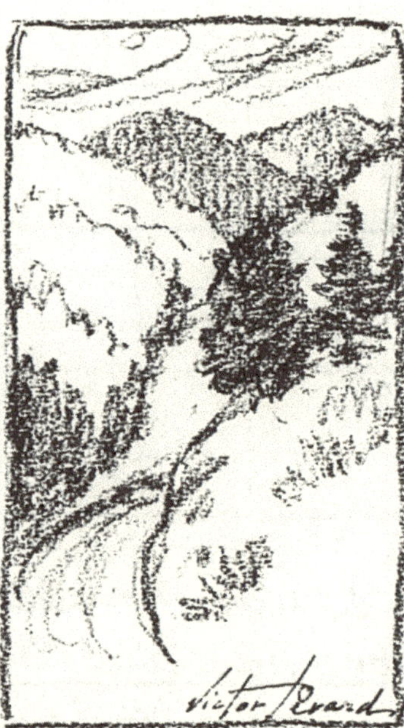

The above are examples of sketches made through the windshield of an automobile while traveling. Such sketches can be practiced to advantage in training the mind to see passing compositions as they present themselves to view.

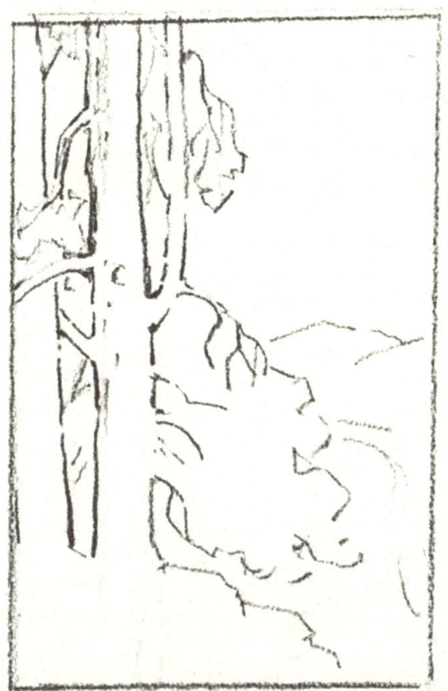
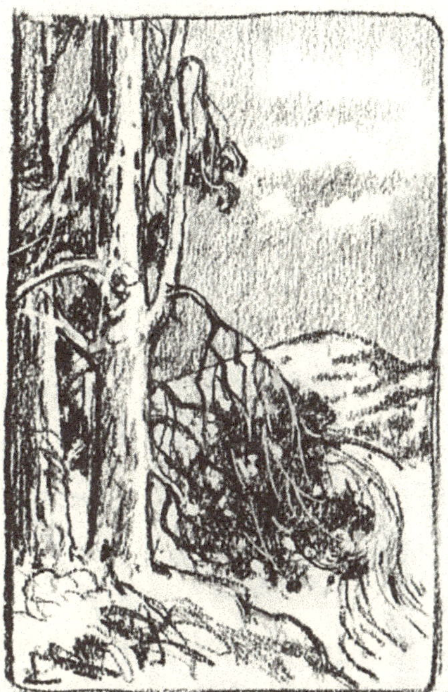
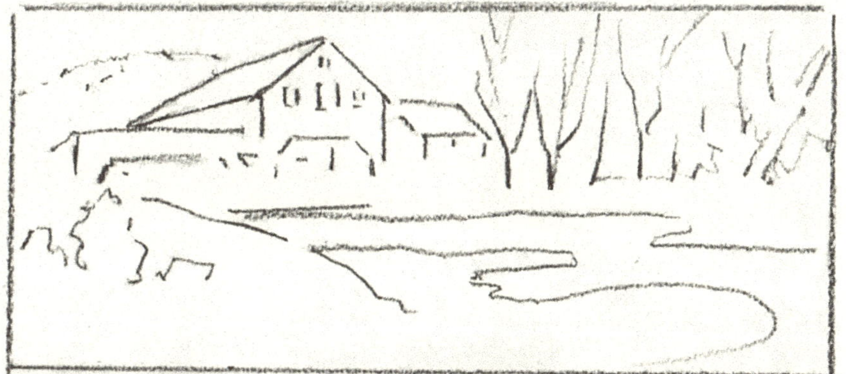
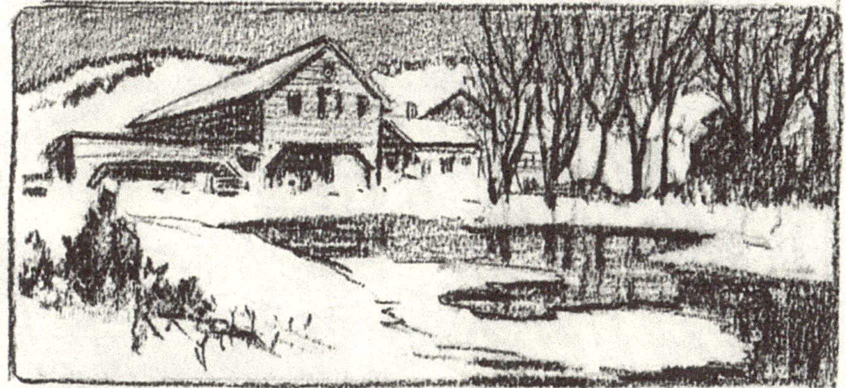
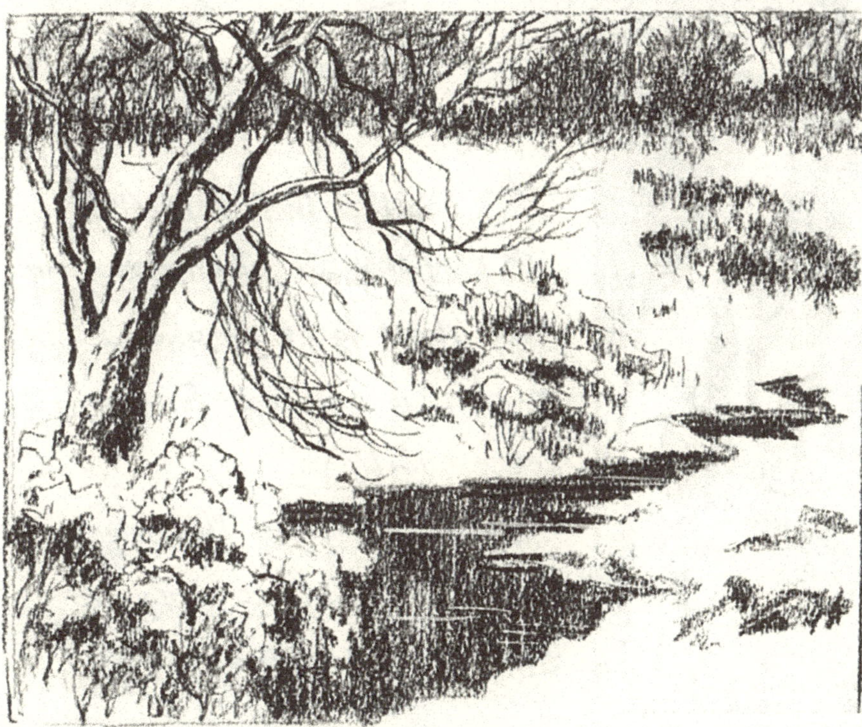
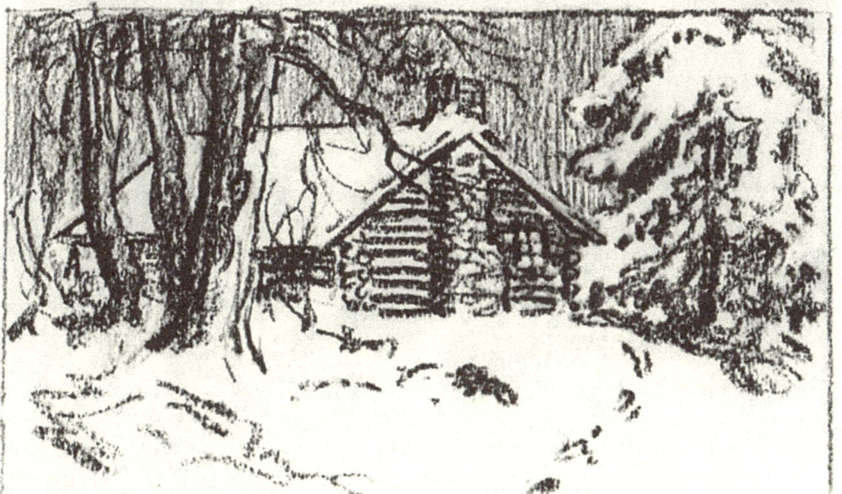

Small winter landscapes made boldly with a soft pencil prove of great value and can be quickly drawn.

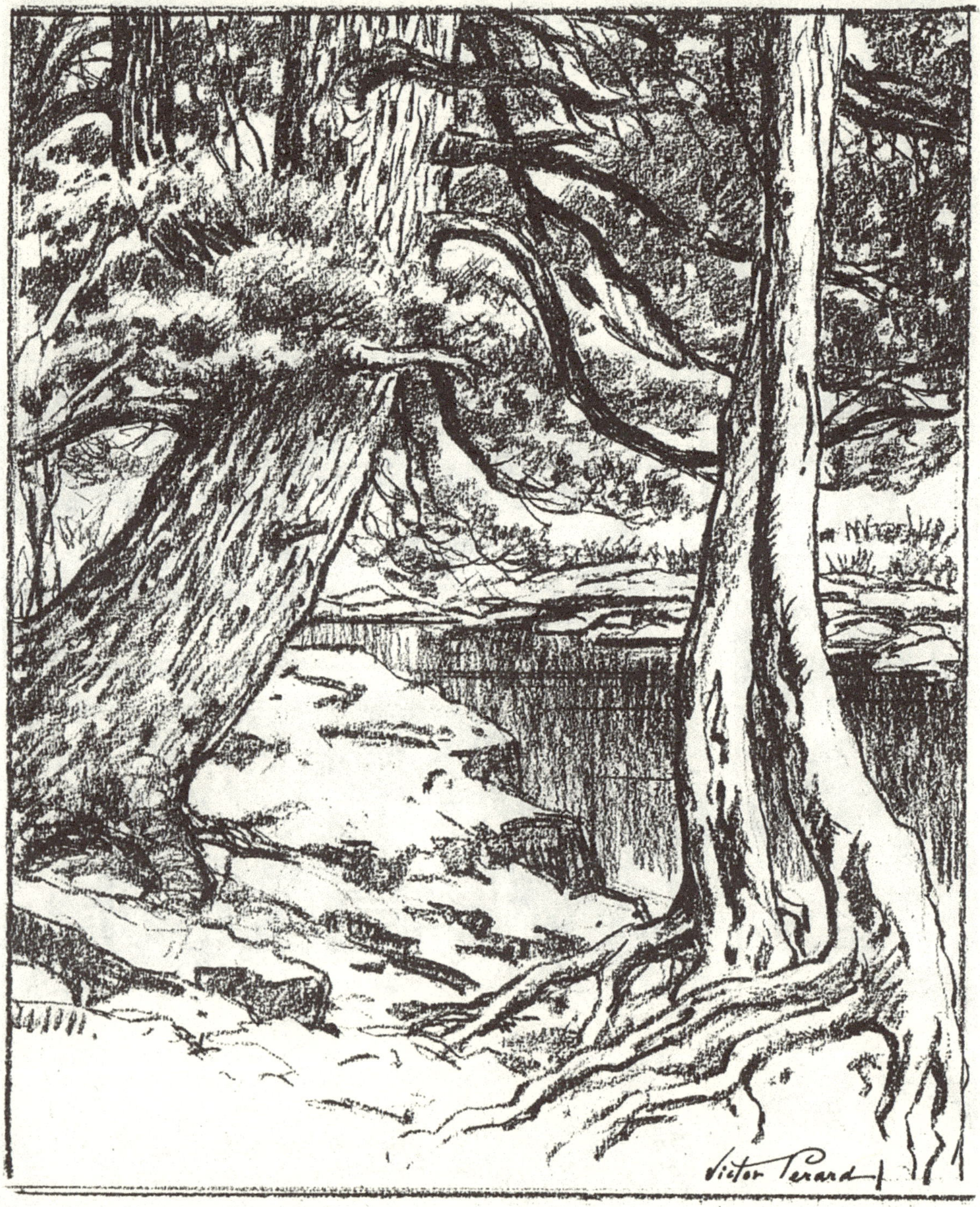

The movement suggested by the lines made by the trees was the appeal for making this sketch.

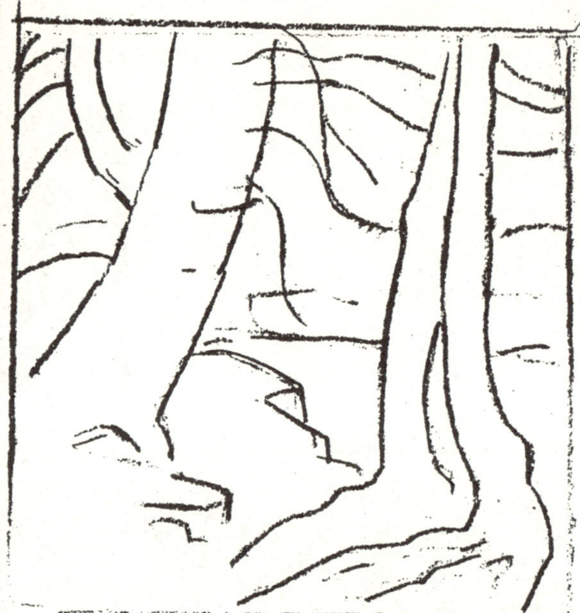

This subject in nature, with its play of sunlight and varying colors, had to be simplified, and much was omitted for a pencil representation.

Through practice this selective process can be acquired and unnecessary detail avoided.

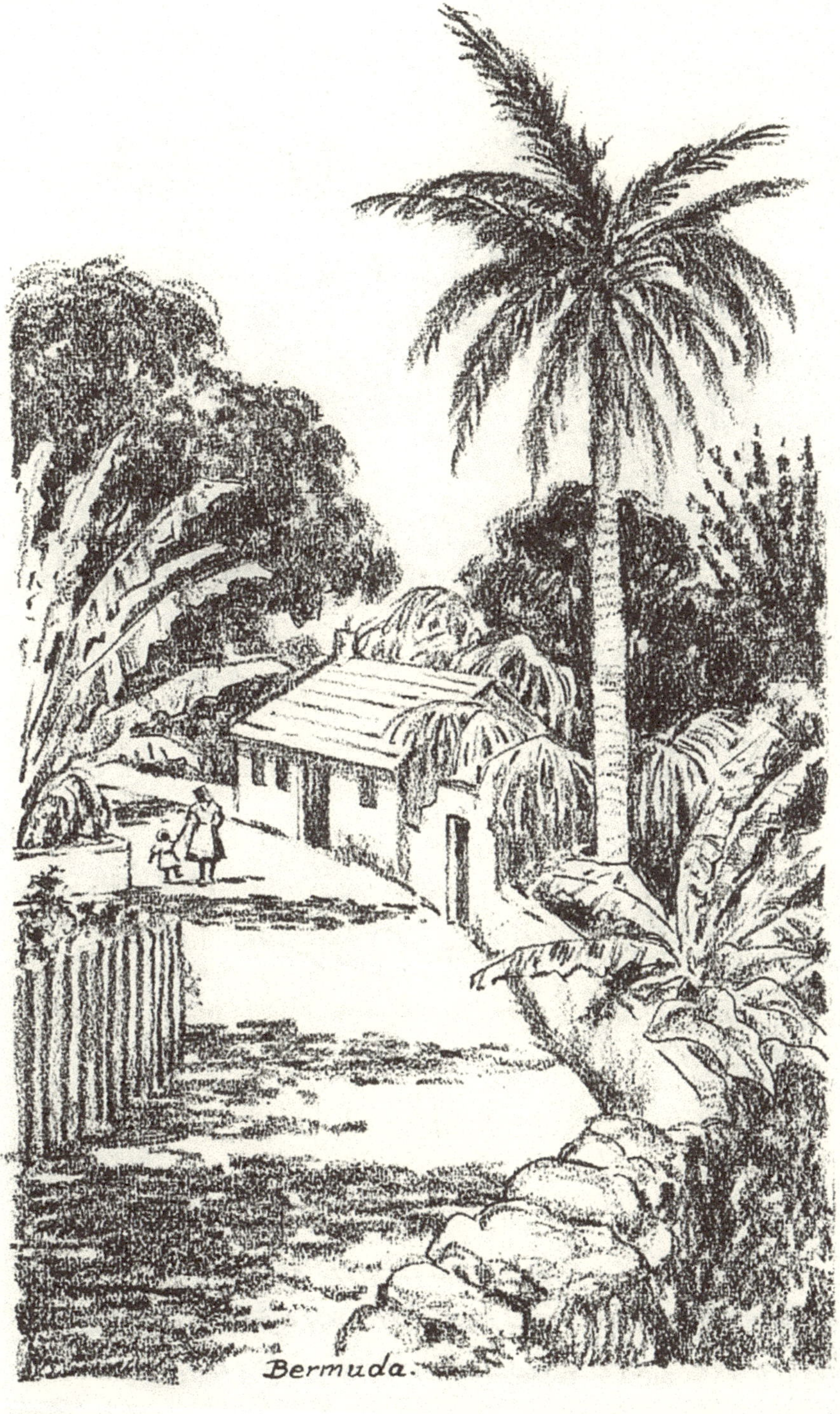

Bermuda.

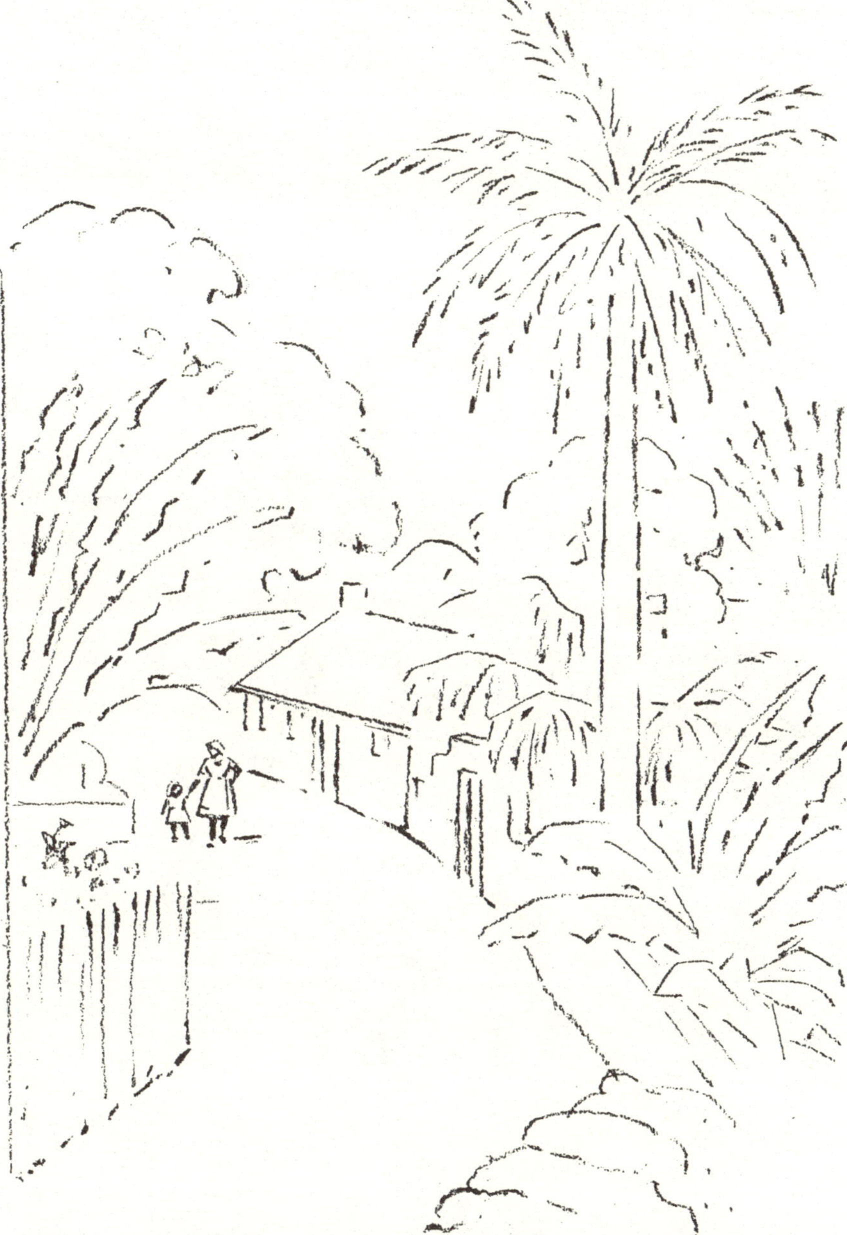

This outline should be carried to completion by using a very soft pencil to obtain richness of tone. It will prove a good study of pencil technique.

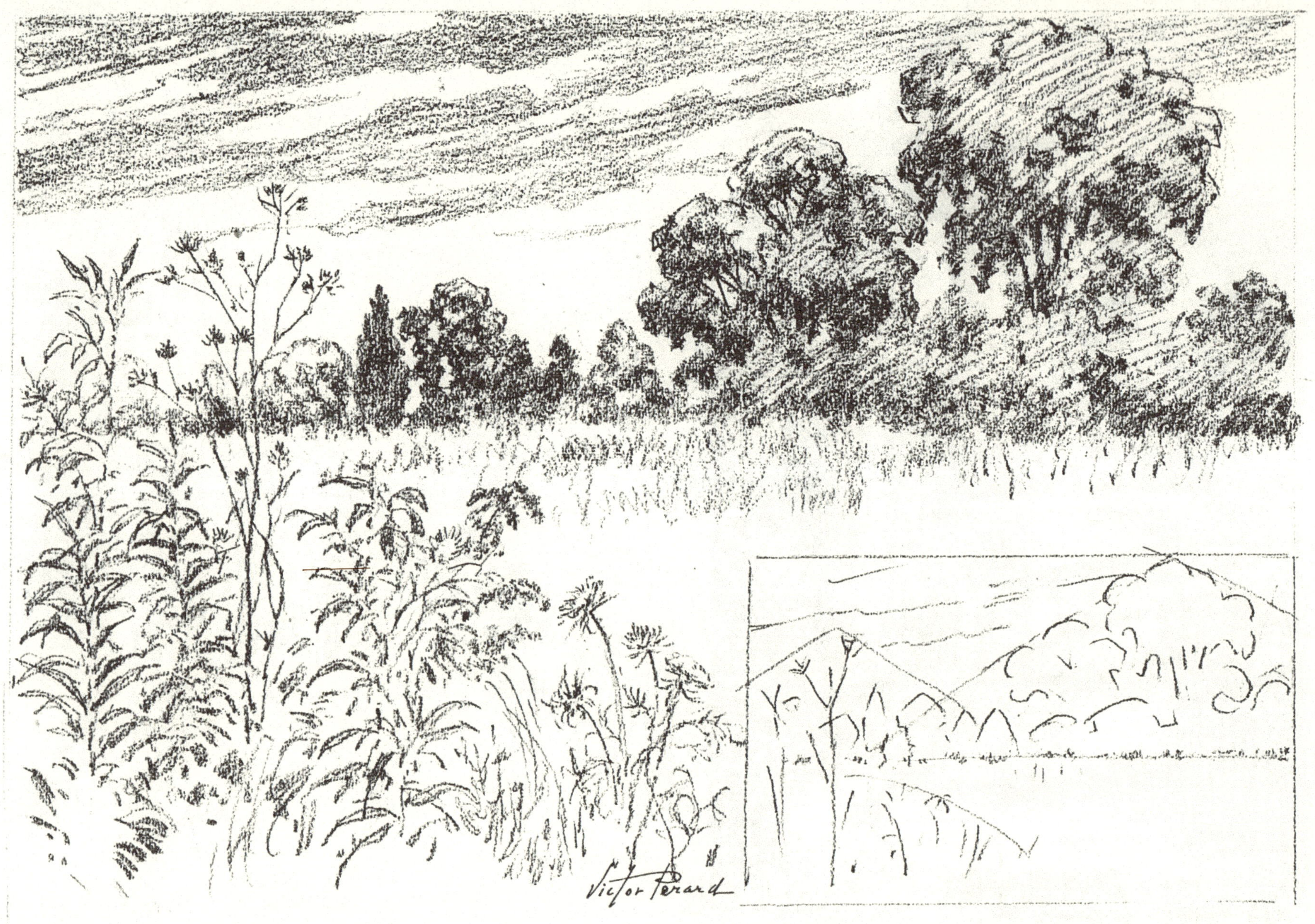

The solid masses of foliage silhouetting against the sky in this composition do not require a heavy foreground, so previous studies of plants and tall grasses served to lighten the effect. The side of a pencil worn flat was used for the deep shadows.

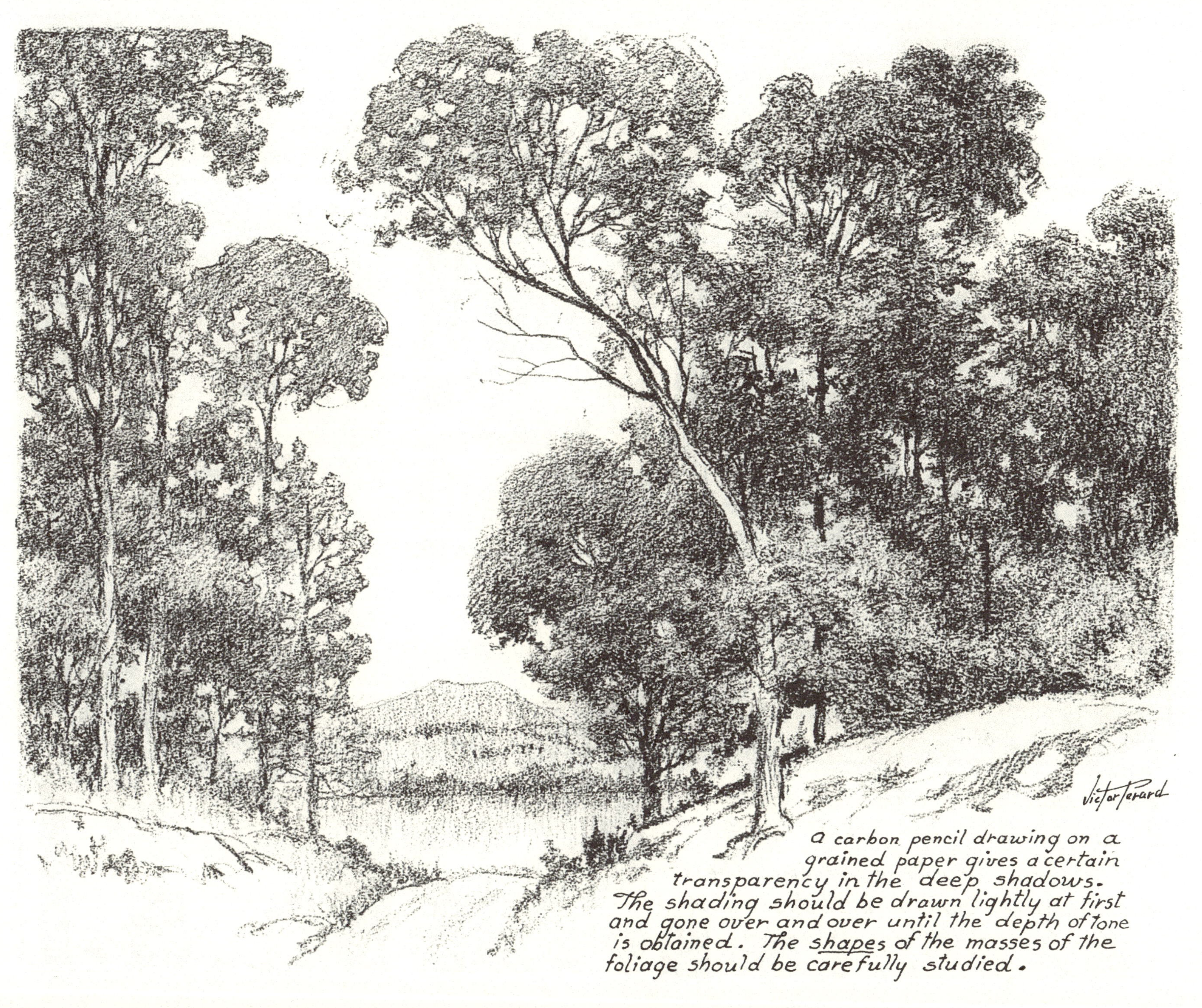

A carbon pencil drawing on a grained paper gives a certain transparency in the deep shadows. The shading should be drawn lightly at first and gone over and over until the depth of tone is obtained. The shapes of the masses of the foliage should be carefully studied.

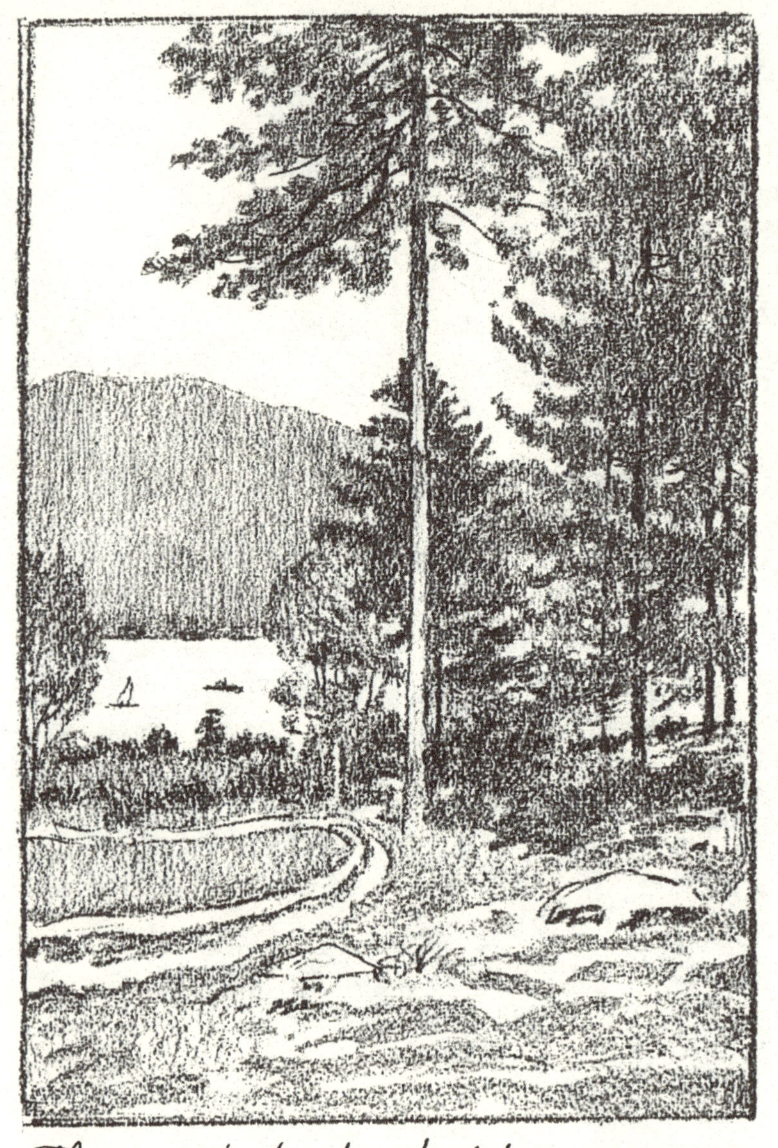

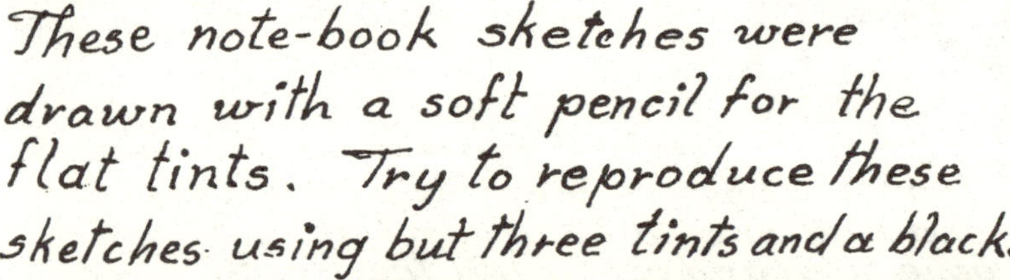

These note-book sketches were drawn with a soft pencil for the flat tints. Try to reproduce these sketches using but three tints and a black.

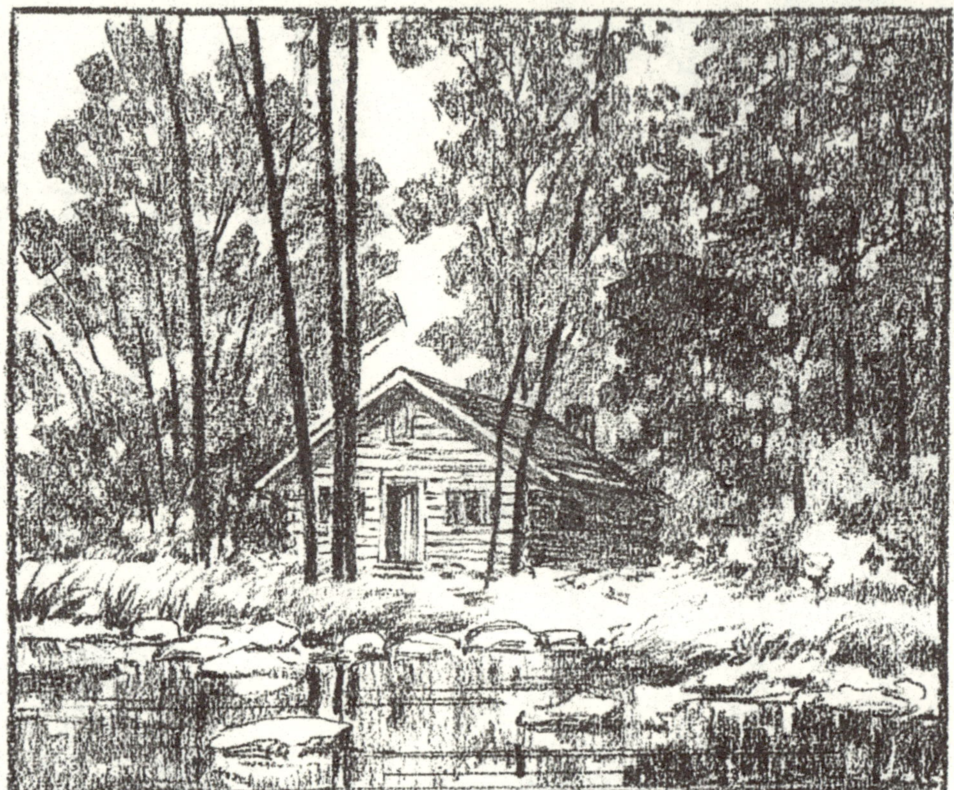

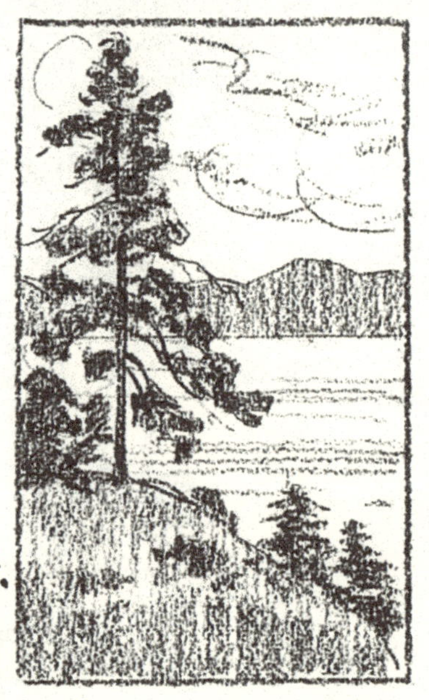

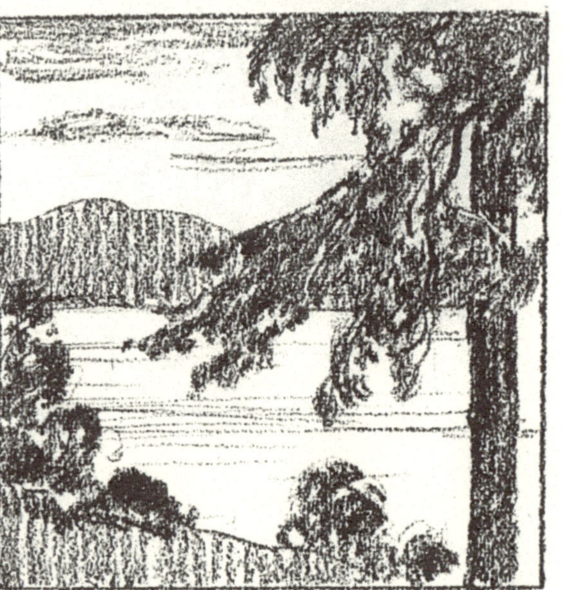

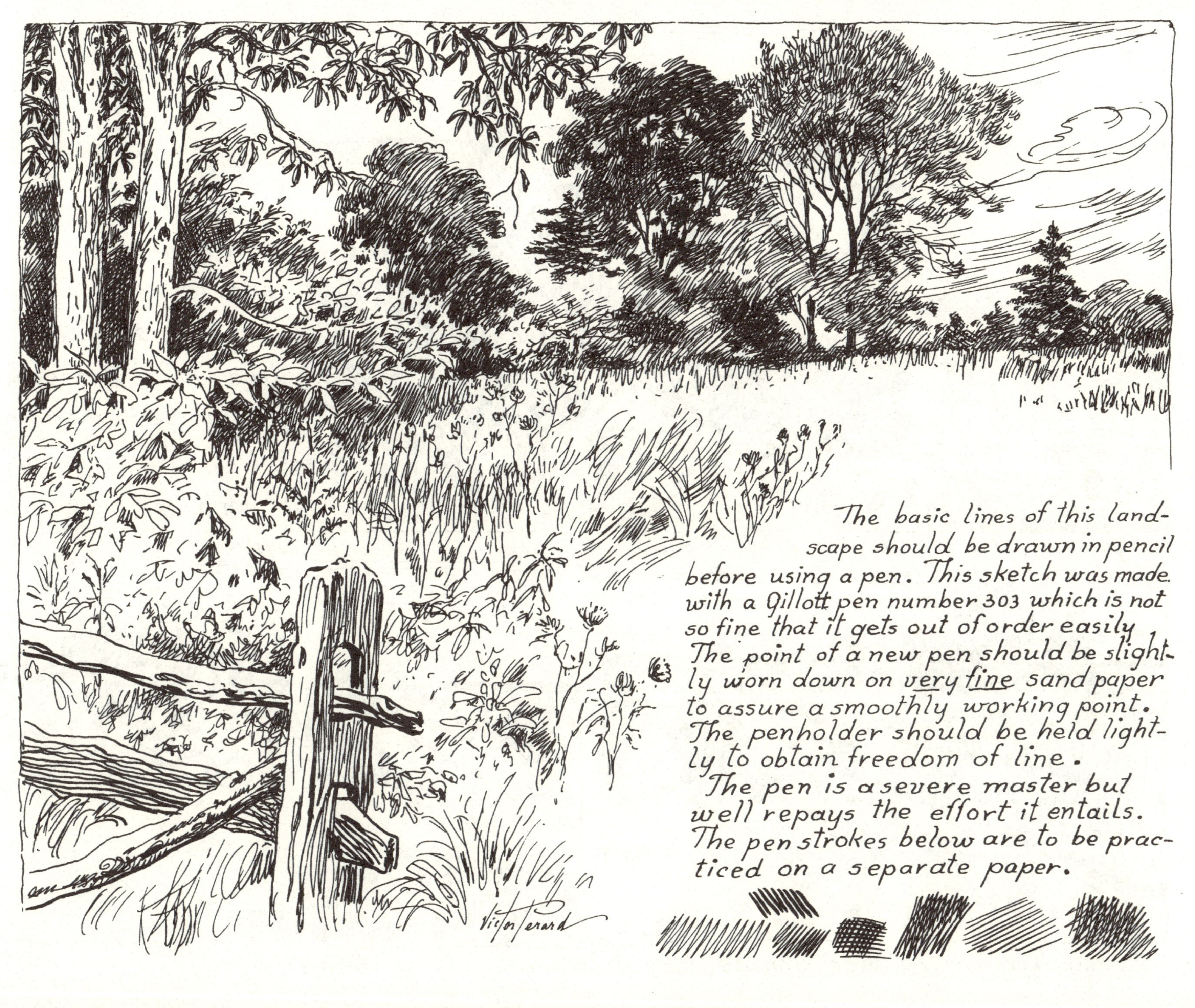
The basic lines of this land-
scape should be drawn in pencil
before using a pen. This sketch was made
with a Gillott pen number 303 which is not
so fine that it gets out of order easily.
The point of a new pen should be slight-
ly worn down on very fine sand paper
to assure a smoothly working point.
The penholder should be held lightly to obtain freedom of line.
The pen is a severe master but
well repays the effort it entails.
The pen strokes below are to be practiced on a separate paper.
Victor Perard

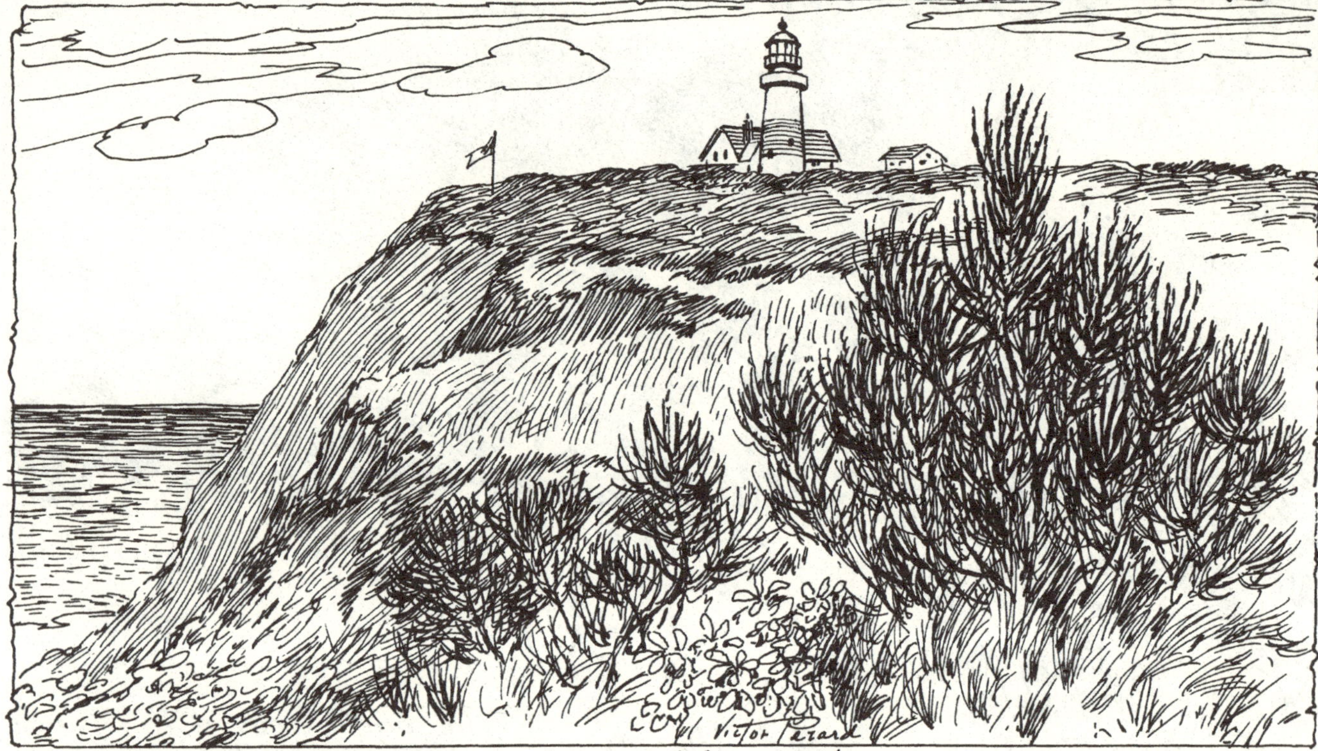

Lighthouse at Siasconset, Nantucket Island. Mass

A pen and ink drawing should not be copied line for line but the direction of the lines and their closeness should be kept to obtain the depth of tint. The usual procedure would be to make a pencil drawing and then work over it in ink.

A road through the moors on Nantucket Island

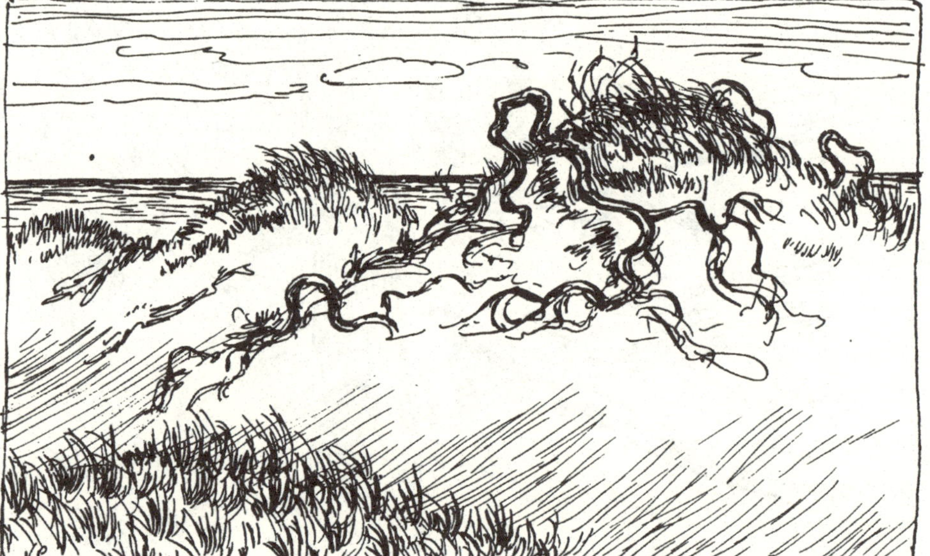

Sand dunes.

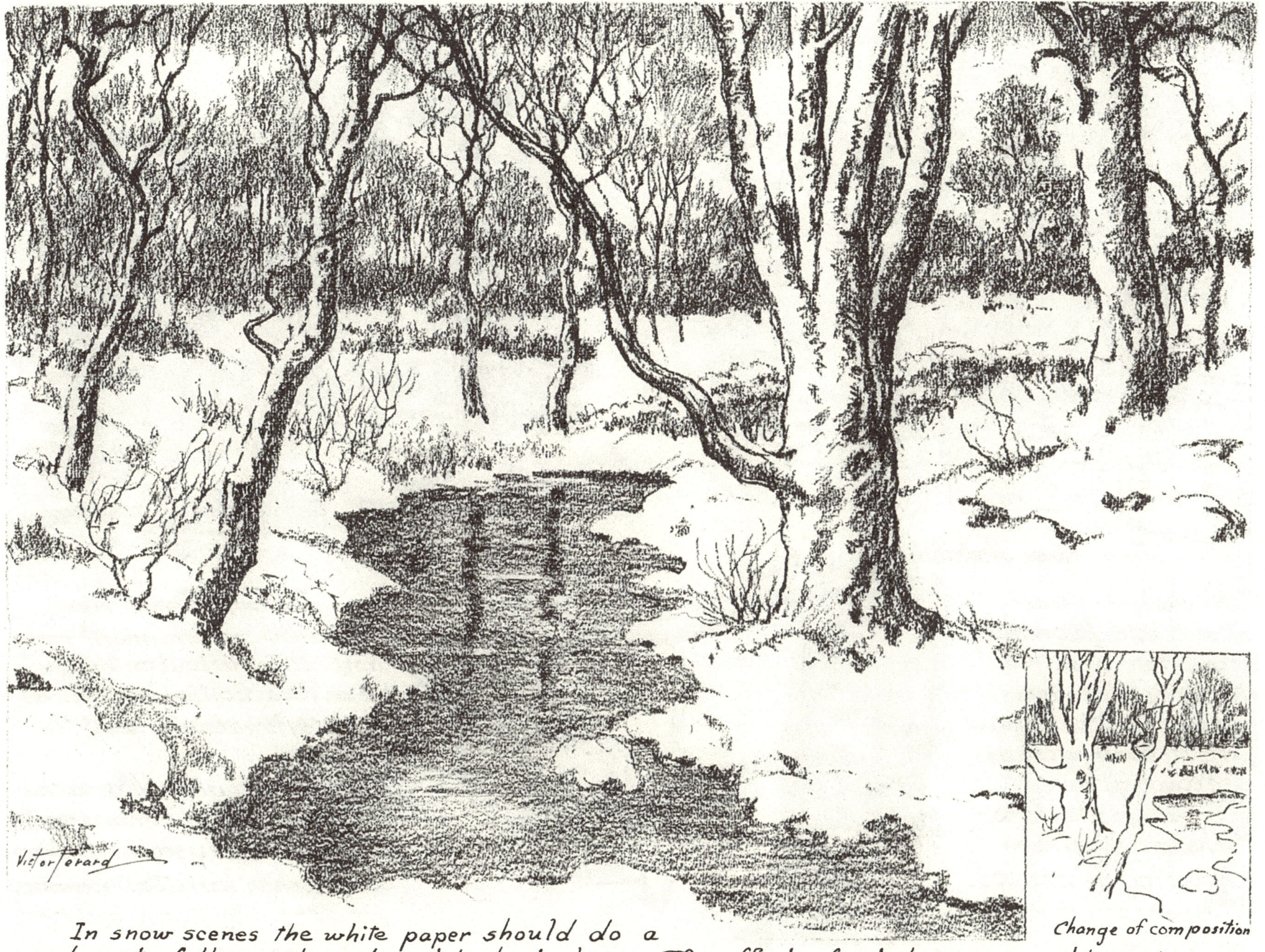

Change of composition

In snow scenes the white paper should do a good part of the work and must be kept clean. The effect of white snow is obtained by strong contrast of dark and white. A soft pencil should be used.

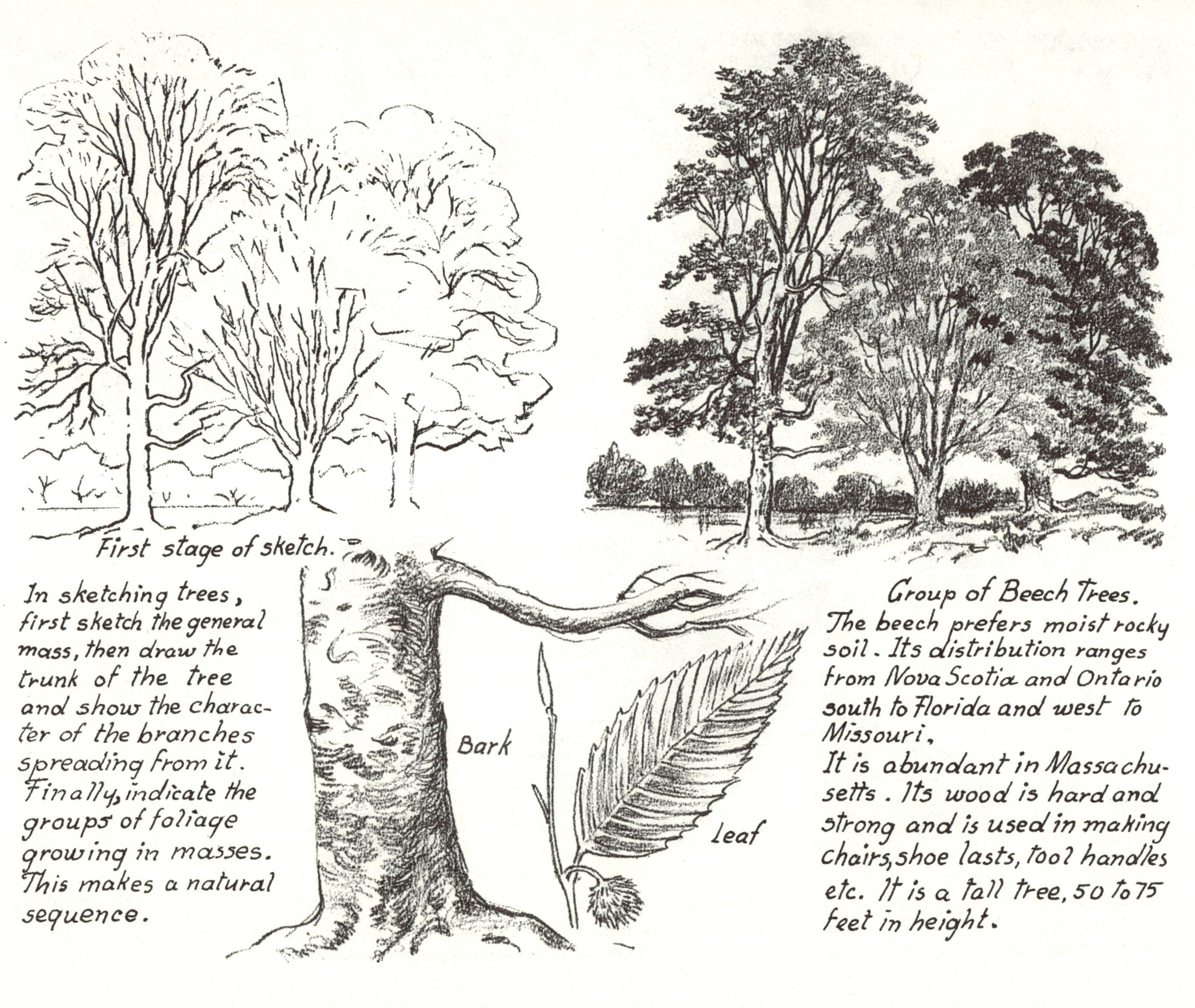
First stage of sketch.
In sketching trees, first sketch the general mass, then draw the trunk of the tree and show the character of the branches spreading from it. Finally, indicate the groups of foliage growing in masses. This makes a natural sequence.
Bark
leaf
Group of Beech Trees.
The beech prefers moist rocky soil. Its distribution ranges from Nova Scotia and Ontario south to Florida and west to Missouri.
It is abundant in Massachusetts. Its wood is hard and strong and is used in making chairs, shoe lasts, tool handles etc. It is a tall tree, 50 to 75 feet in height.

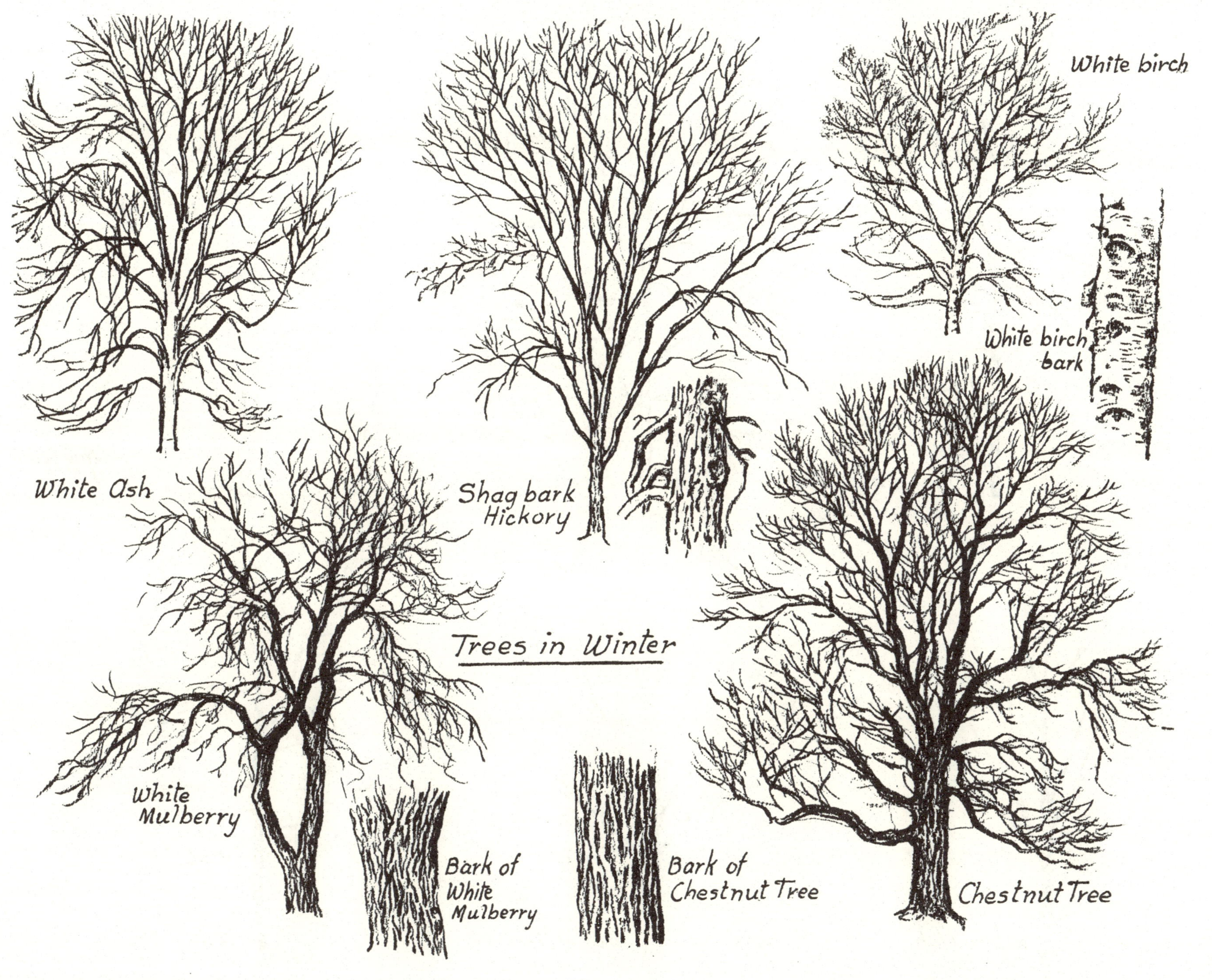
White birch
White birch bark
White Ash
Shag bark Hickory
Trees in Winter
White Mulberry
Bark of White Mulberry
Bark of Chestnut Tree
Chestnut Tree

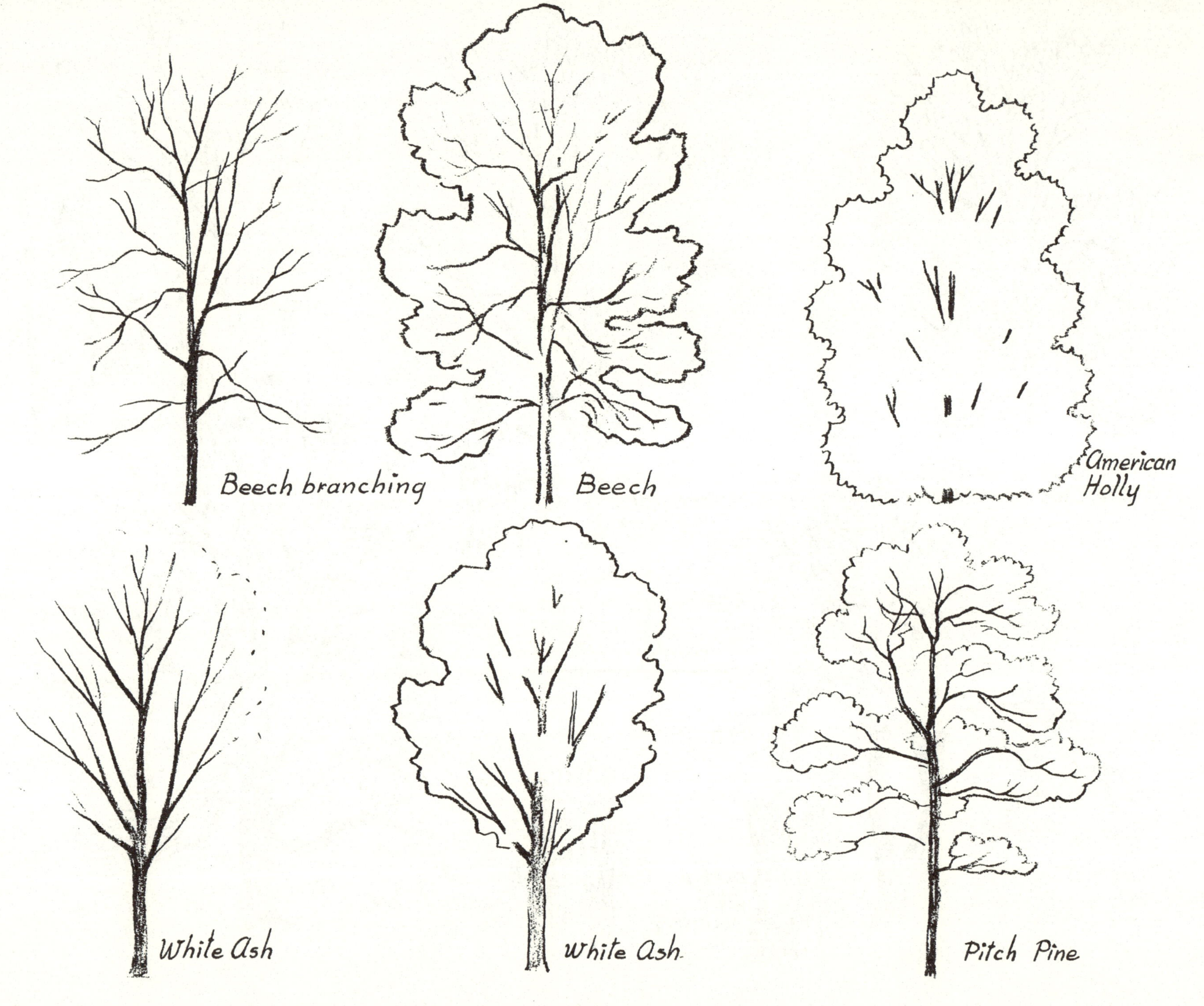
Beech branching
Beech
American Holly
White Ash
White Ash
Pitch Pine

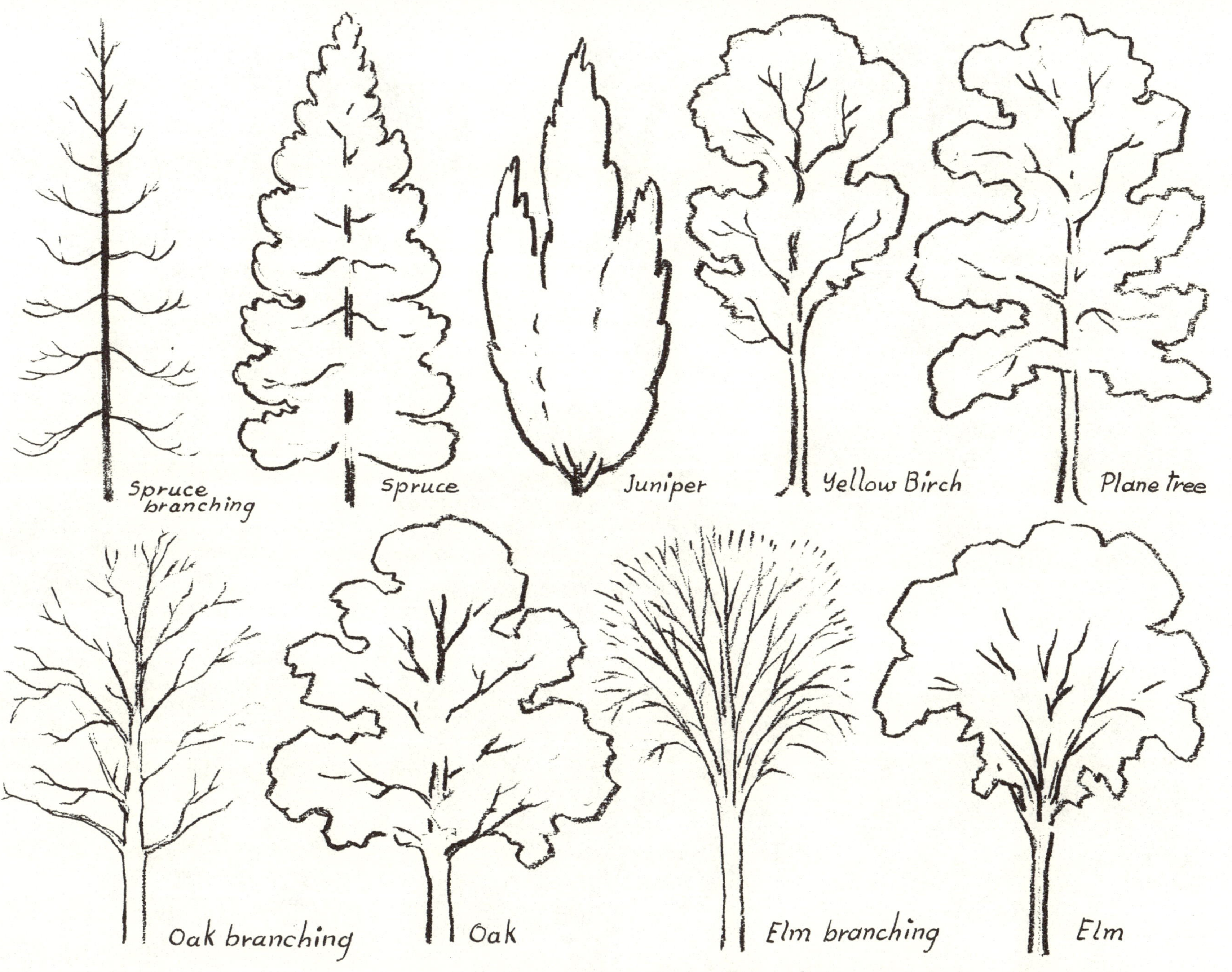

Draw simple forms of trees, to get acquainted with their characteristics. When the trees are reduced to basic lines, their individual types are more clearly brought out.

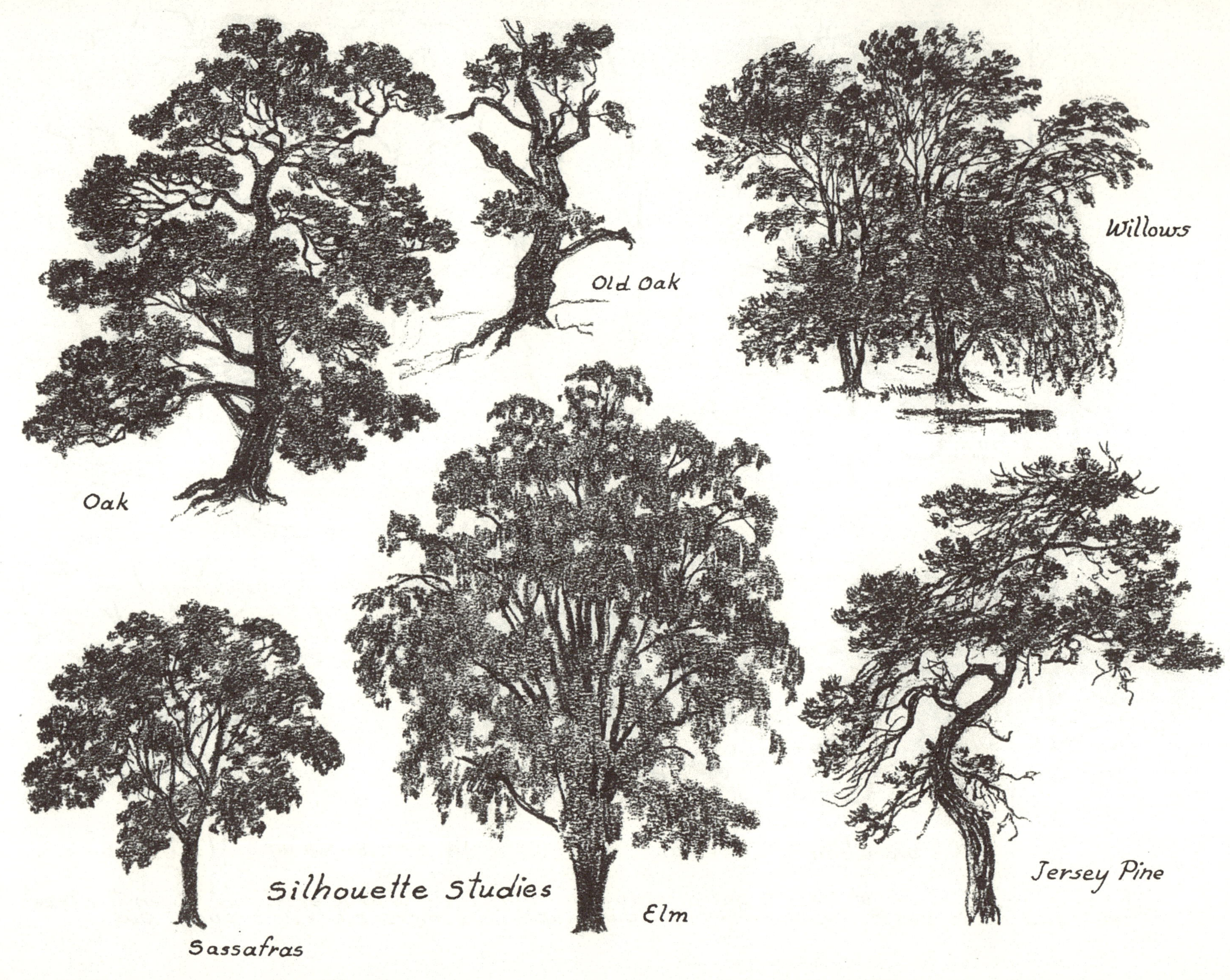

Silhouette Studies

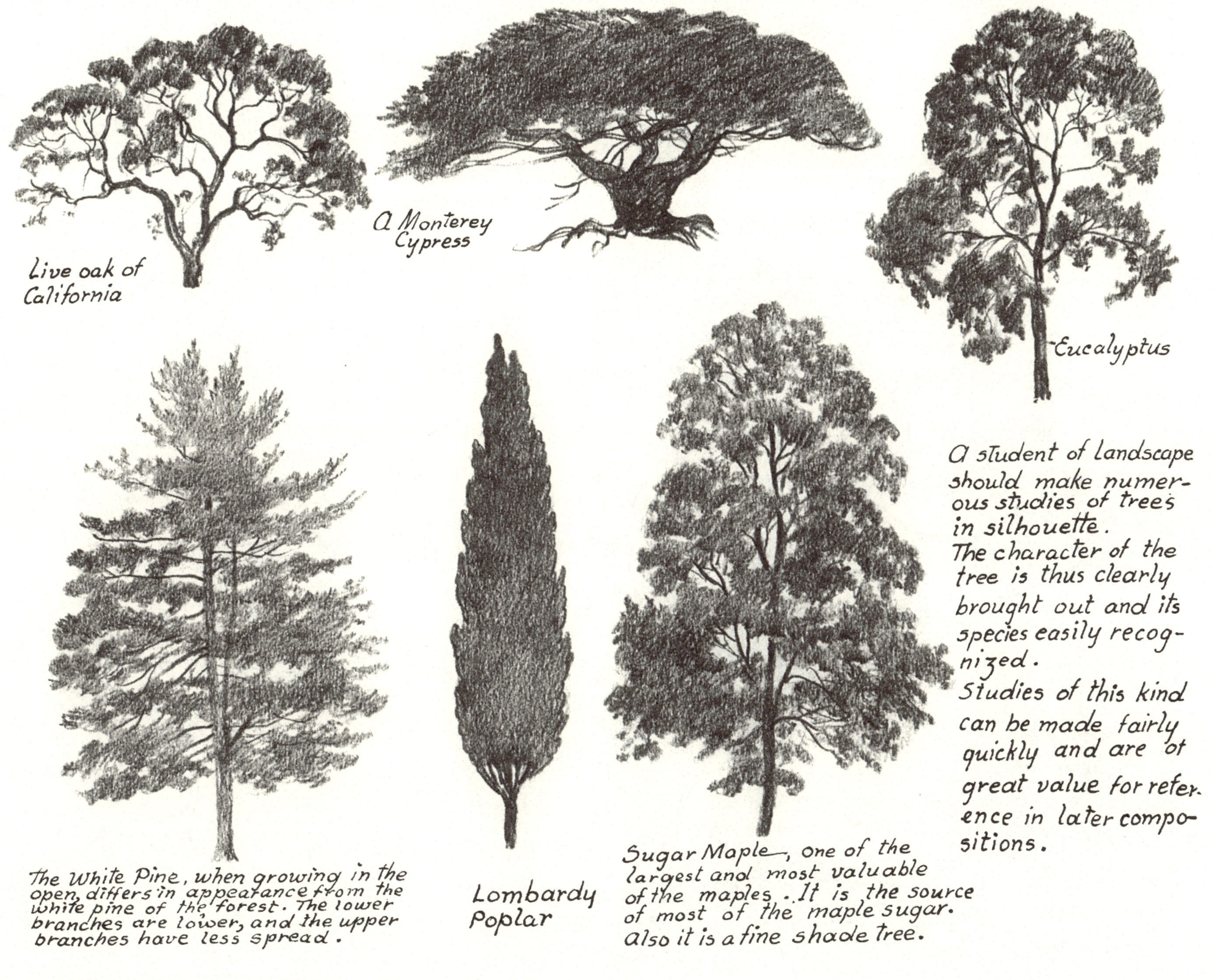
Live oak of California
A Monterey Cypress
Eucalyptus
A student of landscape should make numerous studies of trees in silhouette. The character of the tree is thus clearly brought out and its species easily recognized. Studies of this kind can be made fairly quickly and are of great value for reference in later compositions.
The White Pine, when growing in the open, differs in appearance from the white pine of the forest. The lower branches are lower, and the upper branches have less spread.
Lombardy Poplar
Sugar Maple, one of the largest and most valuable of the maples. It is the source of most of the maple sugar. Also it is a fine shade tree.

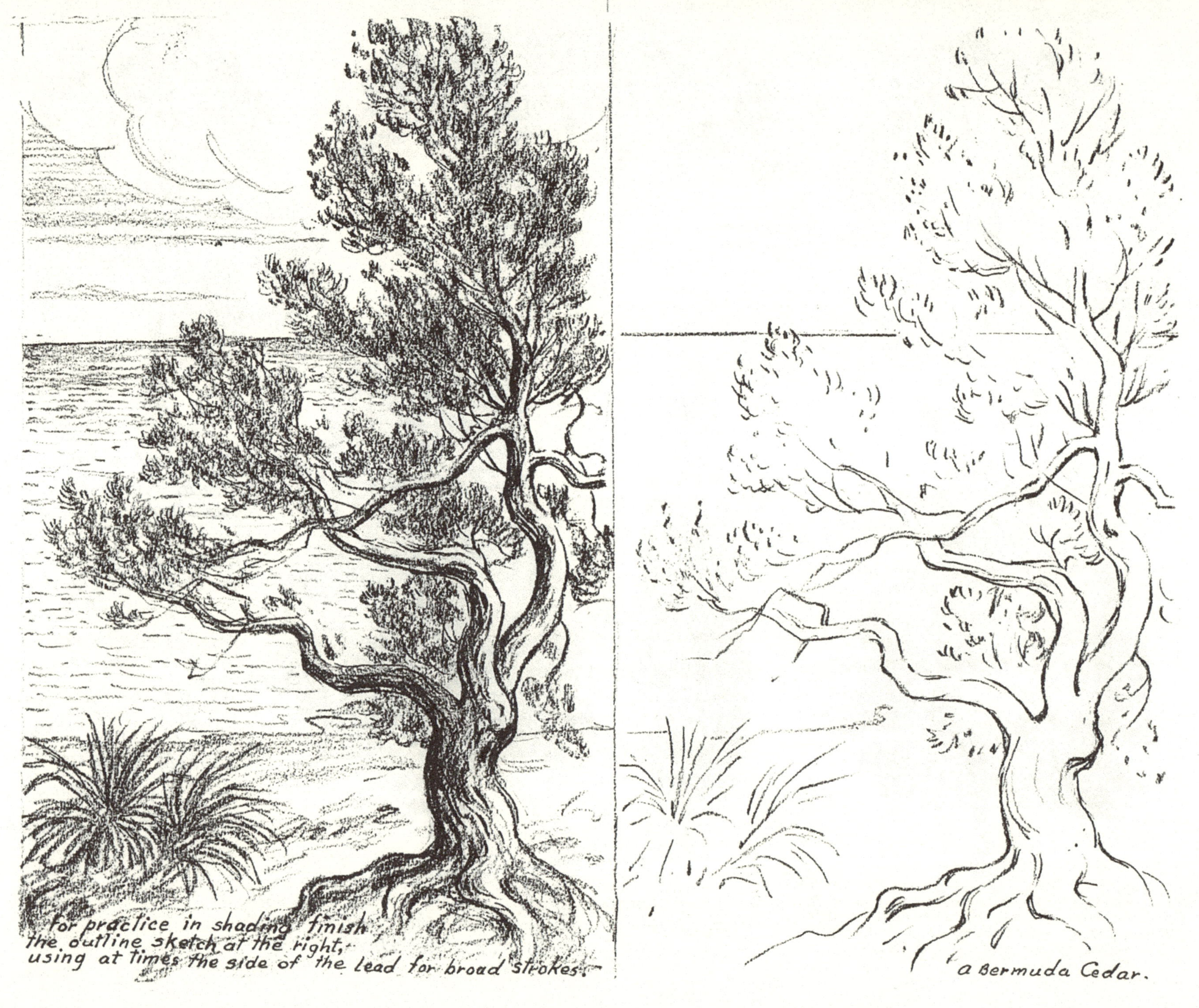
for practice in shading finish
the outline sketch at the right,
using at times the side of the lead for broad strokes.
a Bermuda Cedar.

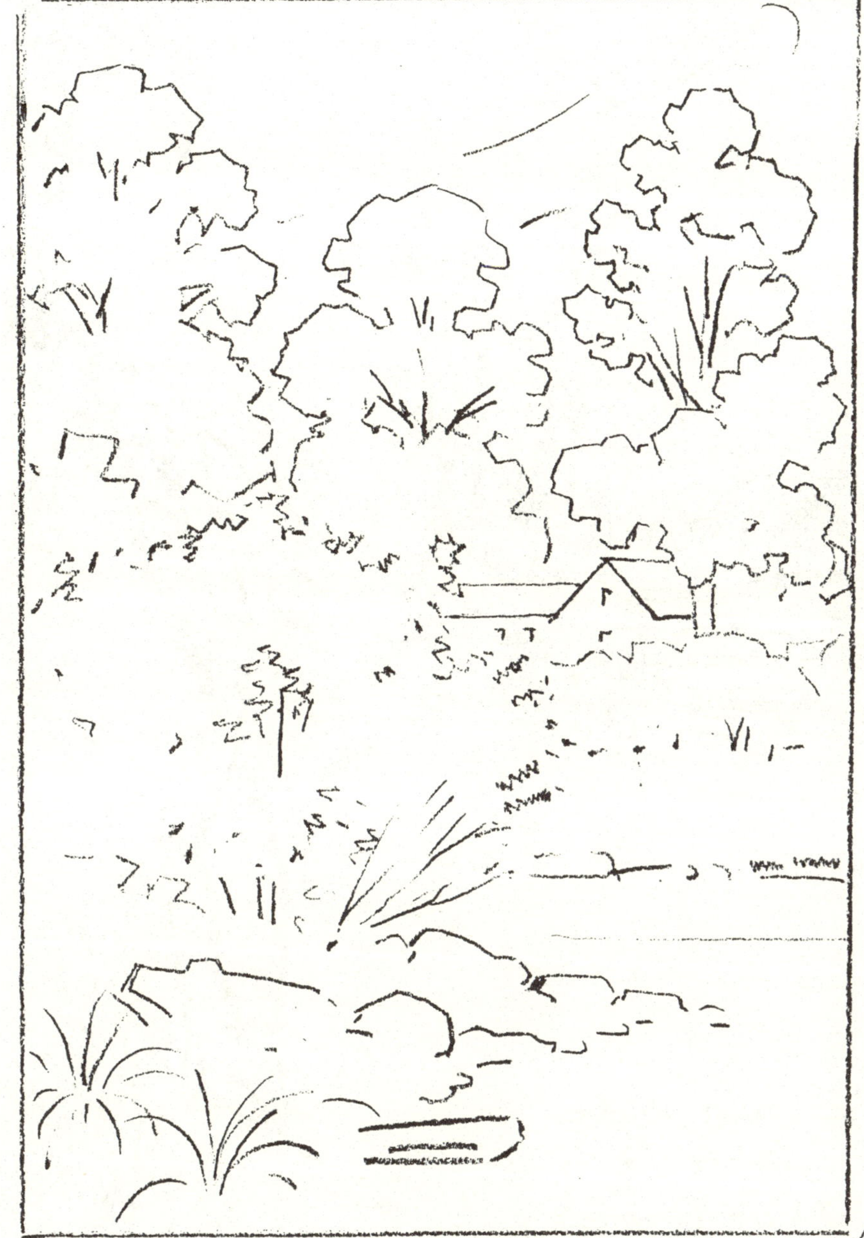

Learn to see the large forms first and details later. A beginner, unguided, might attempt to draw the leaves on a tree first. After patient toil his efforts would be wasted.

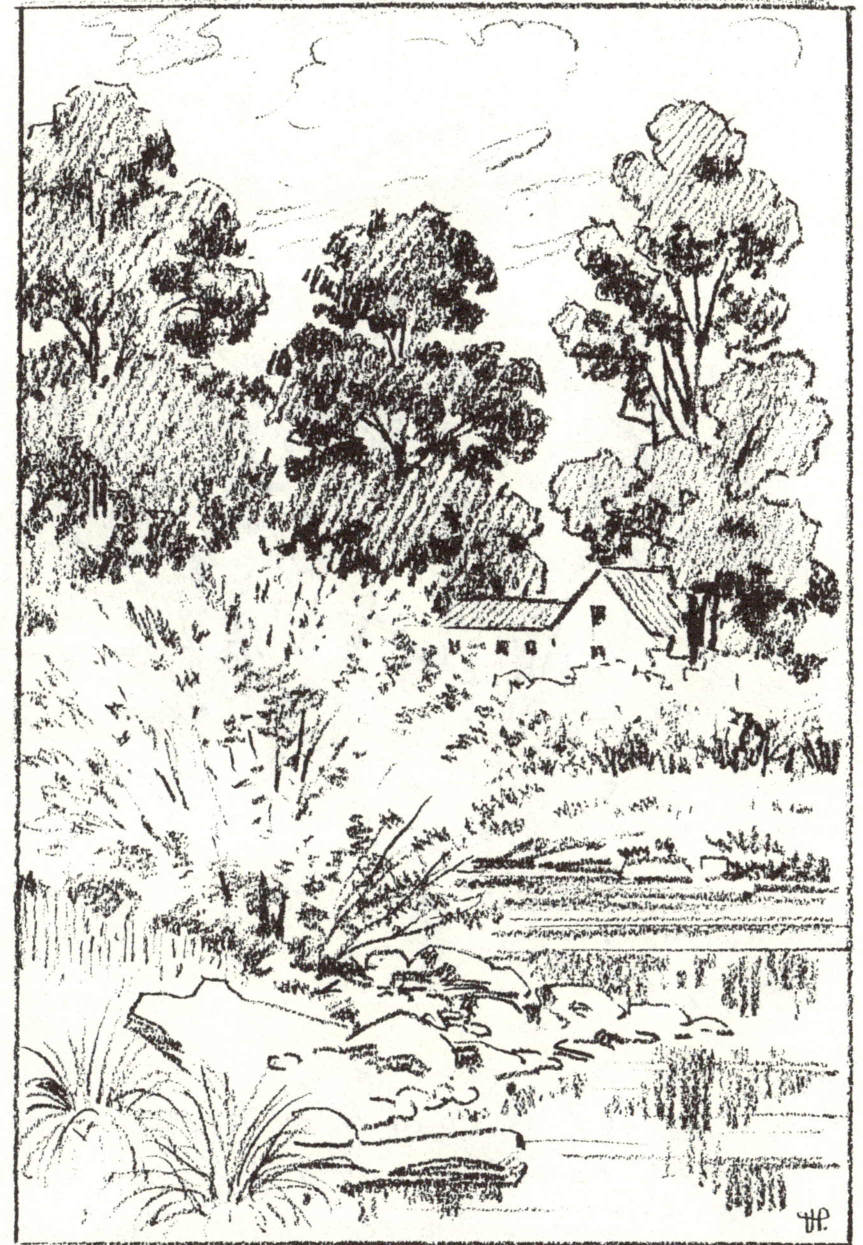

Pussy Willow ↑ Chestnut ↑ Poplar ↑

After the outline is drawn in, a few well-placed shadows will easily complete this picture.

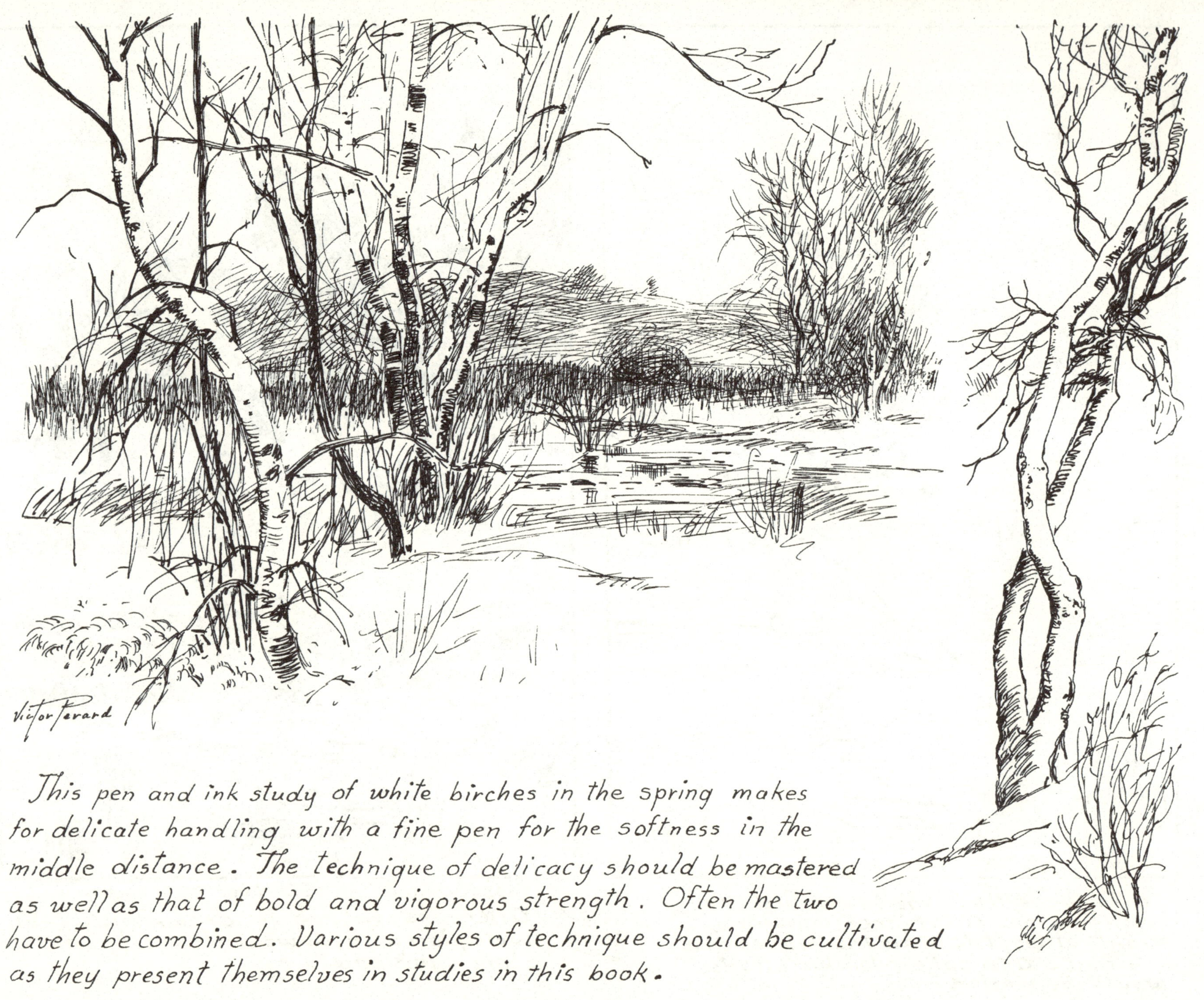

This pen and ink study of white birches in the spring makes for delicate handling with a fine pen for the softness in the middle distance. The technique of delicacy should be mastered as well as that of bold and vigorous strength. Often the two have to be combined. Various styles of technique should be cultivated as they present themselves in studies in this book.

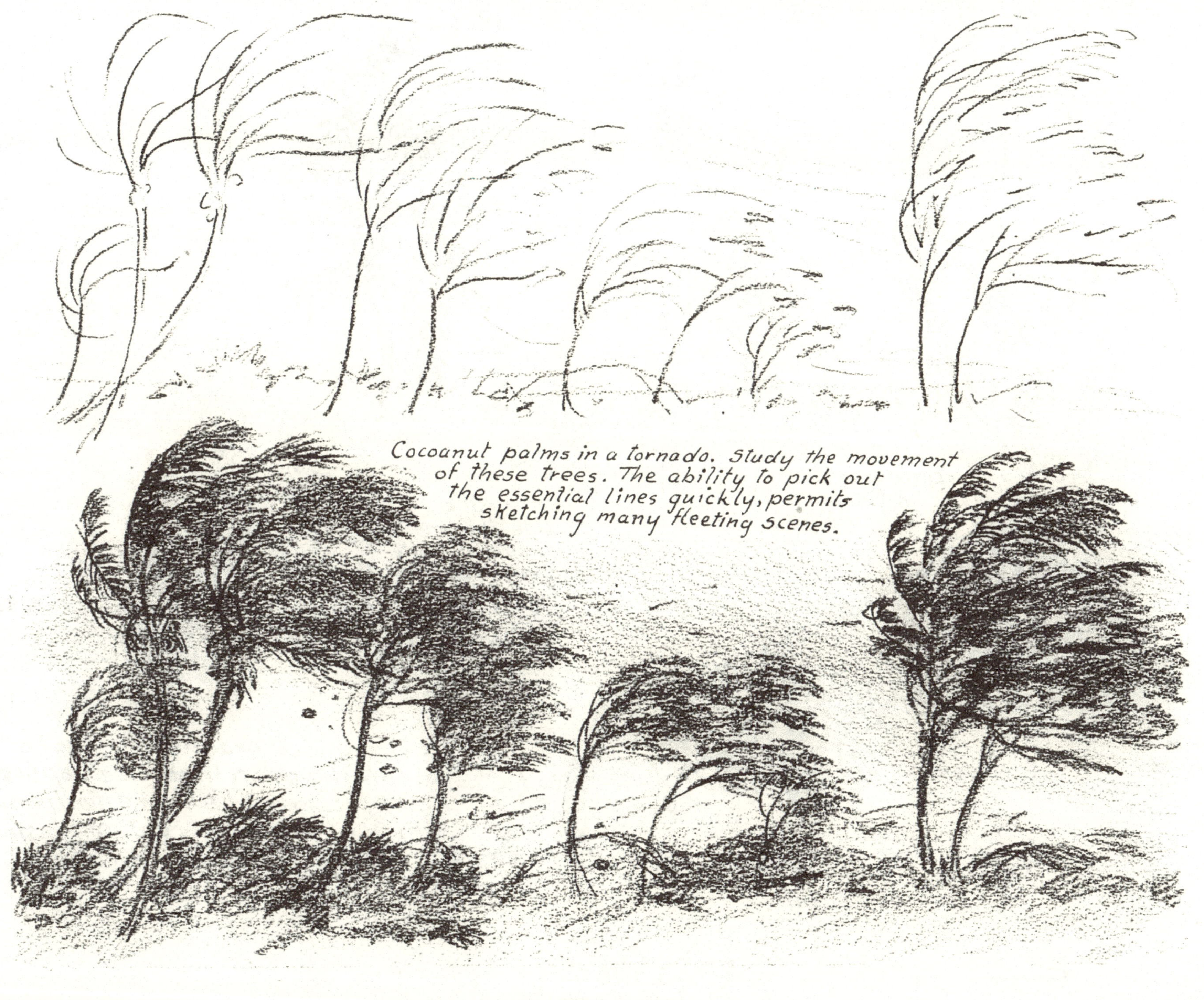

Cocoanut palms in a tornado. Study the movement of these trees. The ability to pick out the essential lines quickly, permits sketching many fleeting scenes.

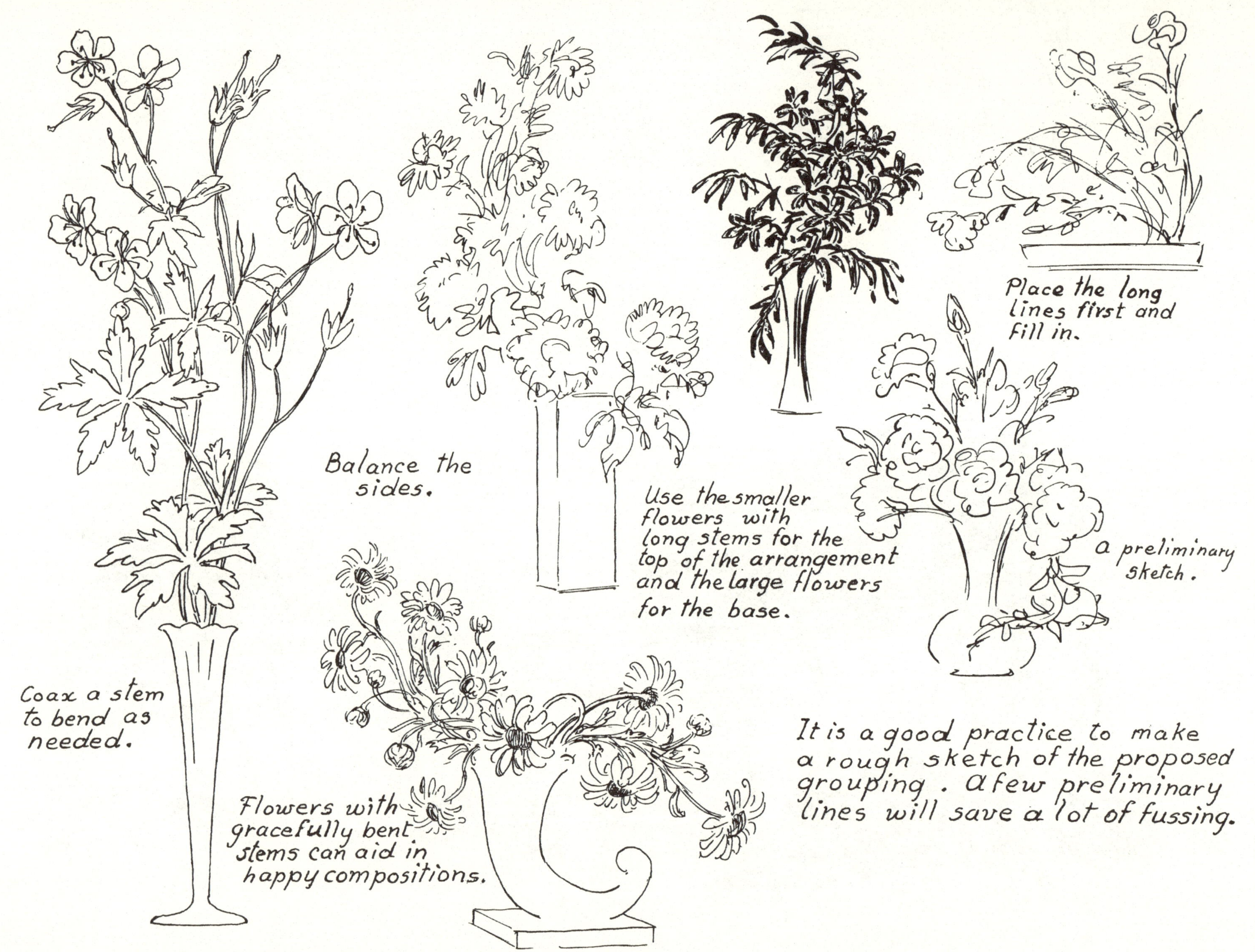
Balance the sides.
Place the long lines first and fill in.
Use the smaller flowers with long stems for the top of the arrangement and the large flowers for the base.
a preliminary sketch.
Coax a stem to bend as needed.
Flowers with gracefully bent stems can aid in happy compositions.
It is a good practice to make a rough sketch of the proposed grouping. A few preliminary lines will save a lot of fussing.

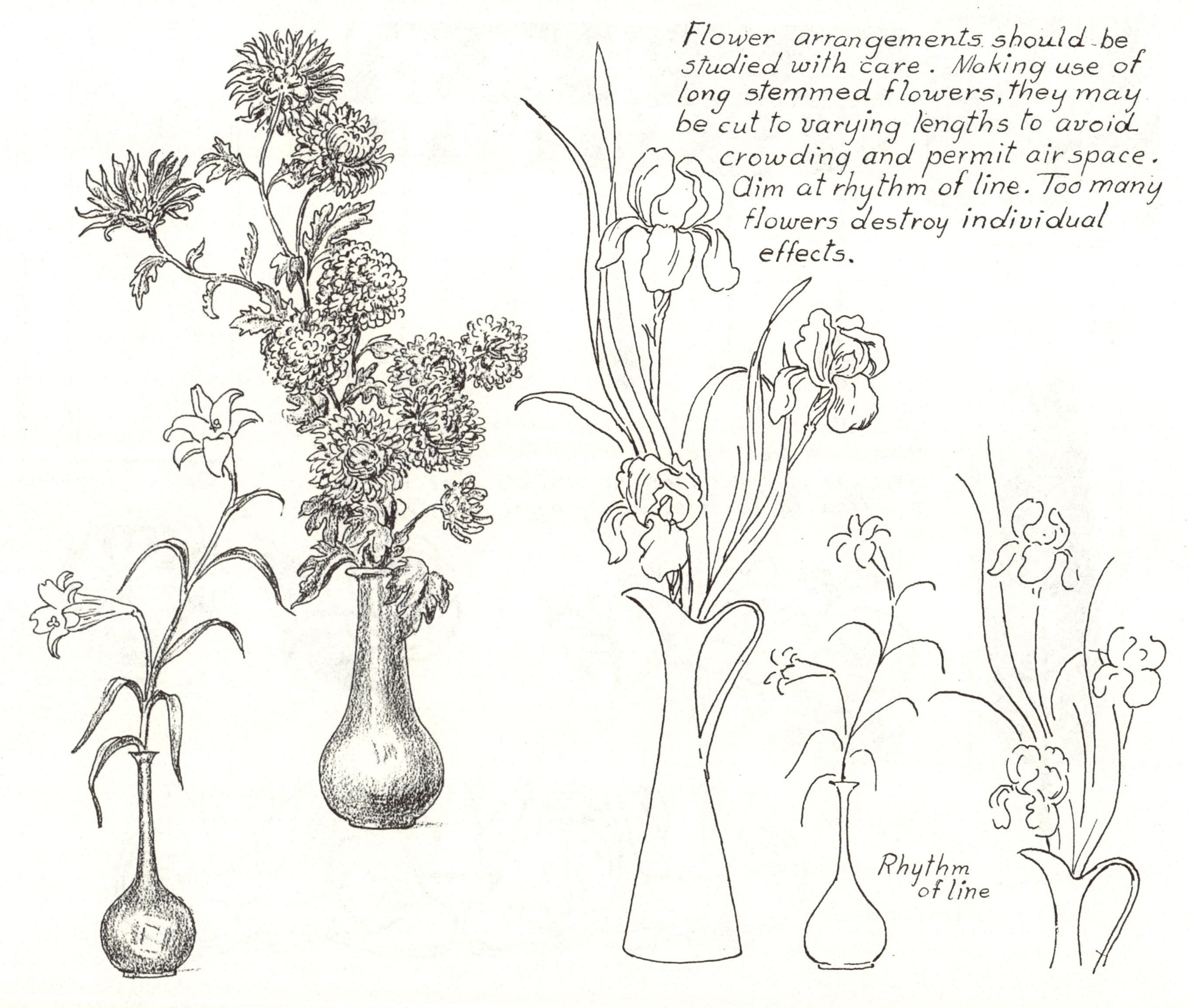
Flower arrangements should be studied with care. Making use of long stemmed flowers, they may be cut to varying lengths to avoid crowding and permit air space. Aim at rhythm of line. Too many flowers destroy individual effects.
Rhythm of line

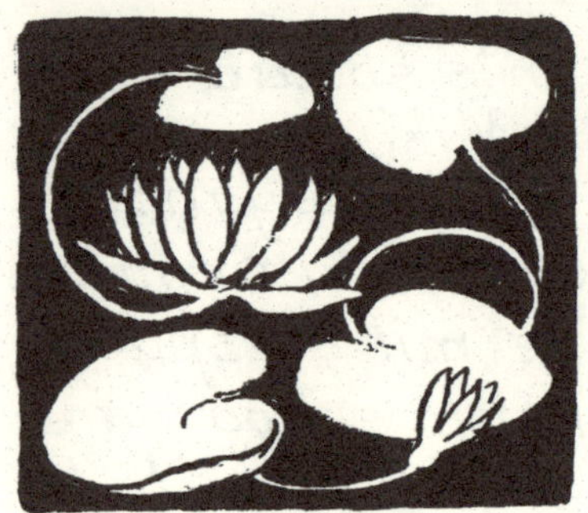

Water lily

Daffodil design

Conventionalized flower studies. While copying these motives, keep in mind the idea of creating designs of your own invention that could be applied to textile, wall-paper or other practical uses.

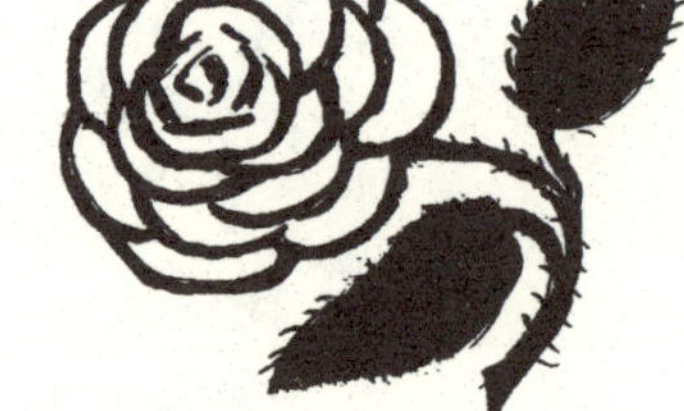

Rose

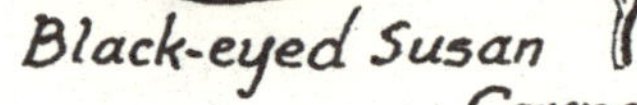

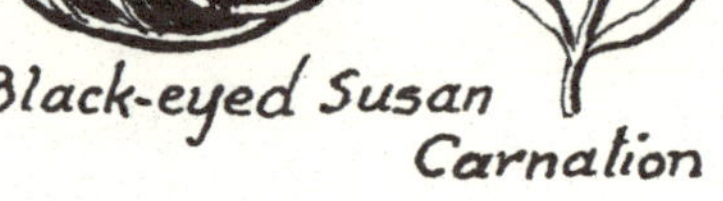

Black-eyed Susan

Carnation

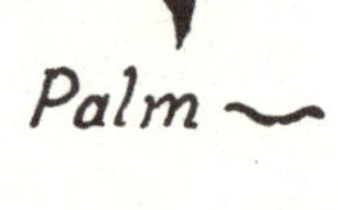

Palm ~

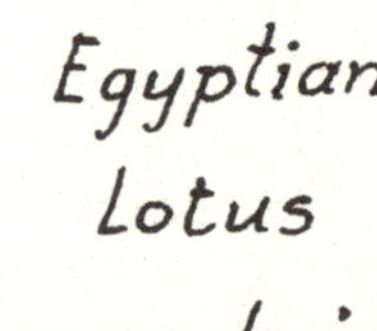

Egyptian Lotus flower design

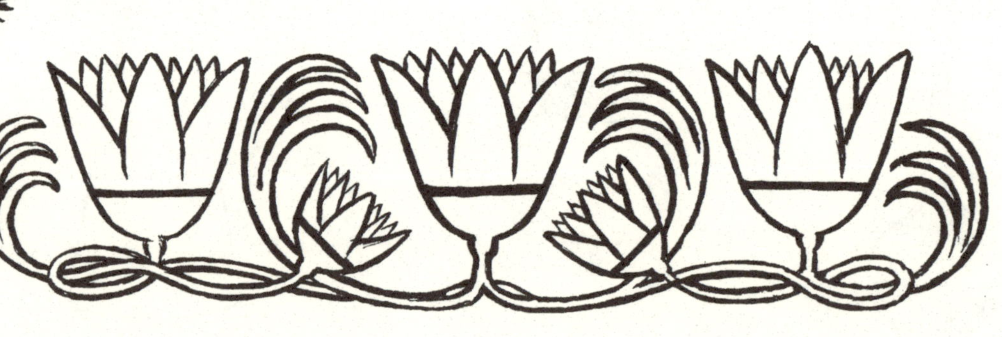

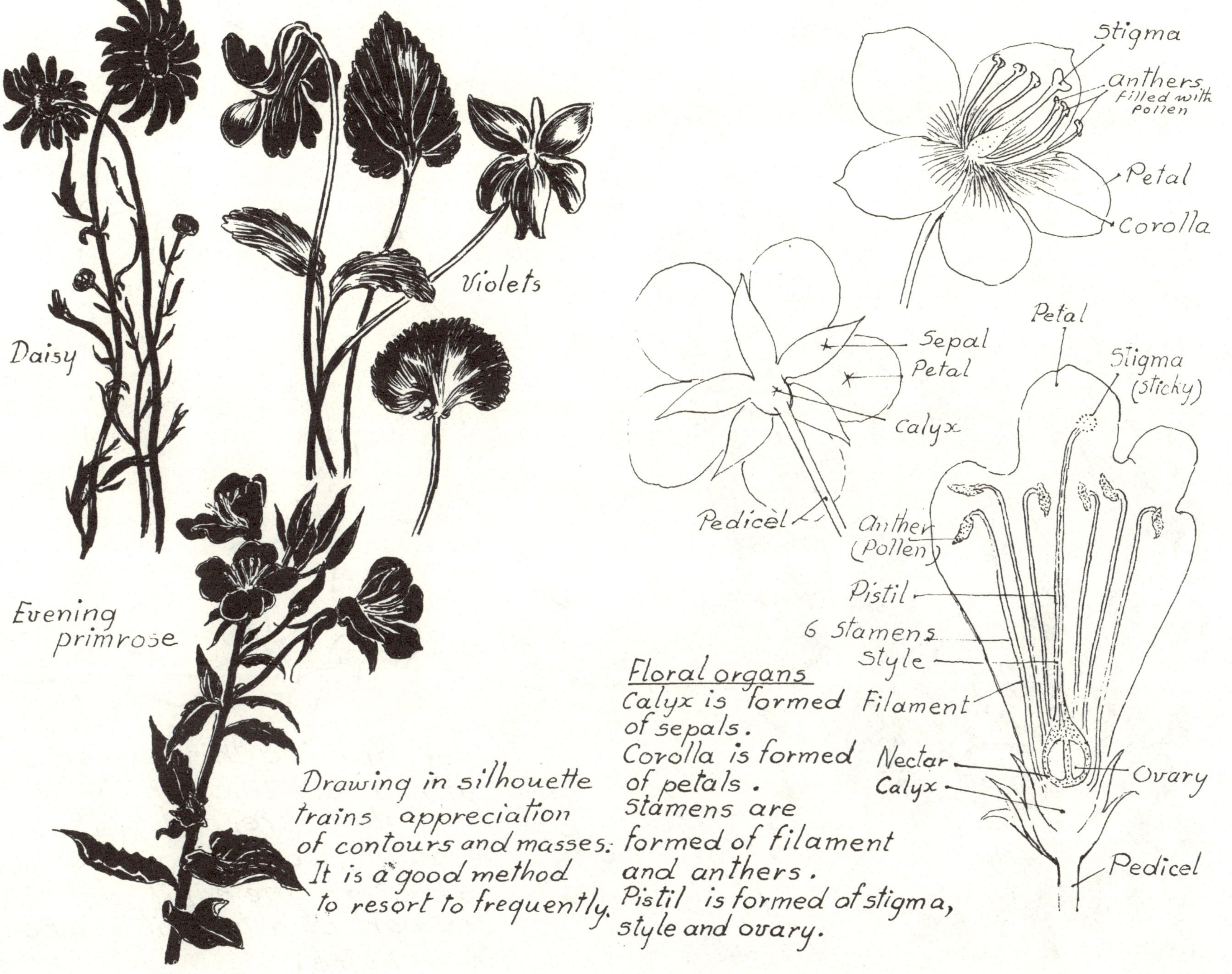
Names of parts of flowers
Stigma
anthers filled with pollen
Petal
Corolla
Violets
Daisy
Sepal
Petal
Calyx
Pedicel
Petal
Stigma (sticky)
Anther (Pollen)
Pistil
6 Stamens
Style
Filament
Nectar
Calyx
Ovary
Pedicel
Evening primrose
Drawing in silhouette trains appreciation of contours and masses. It is a good method to resort to frequently.
Floral organs
Calyx is formed of sepals.
Corolla is formed of petals.
Stamens are formed of filament and anthers.
Pistil is formed of stigma, style and ovary.

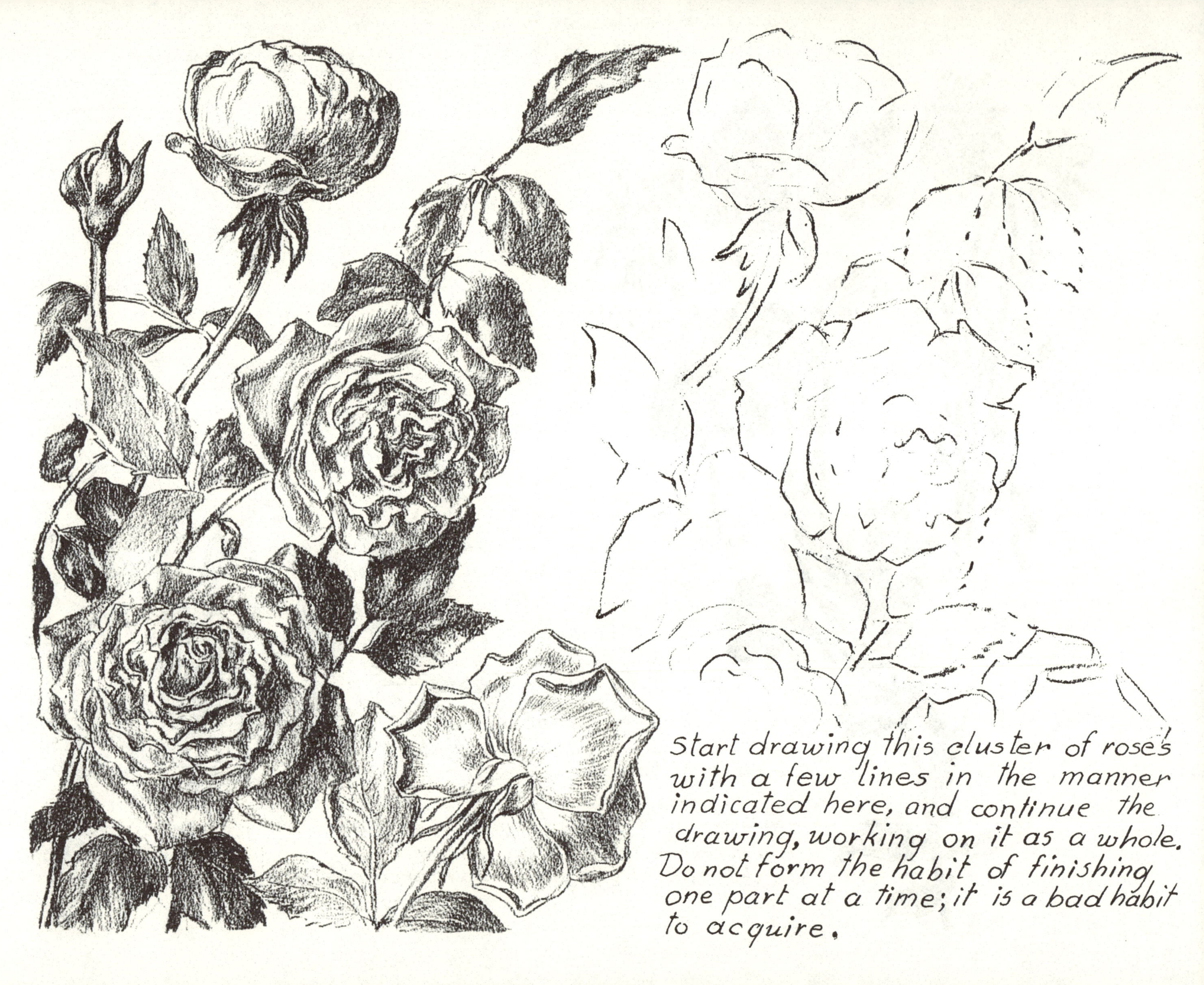

Start drawing this cluster of roses with a few lines in the manner indicated here, and continue the drawing, working on it as a whole. Do not form the habit of finishing one part at a time; it is a bad habit to acquire.

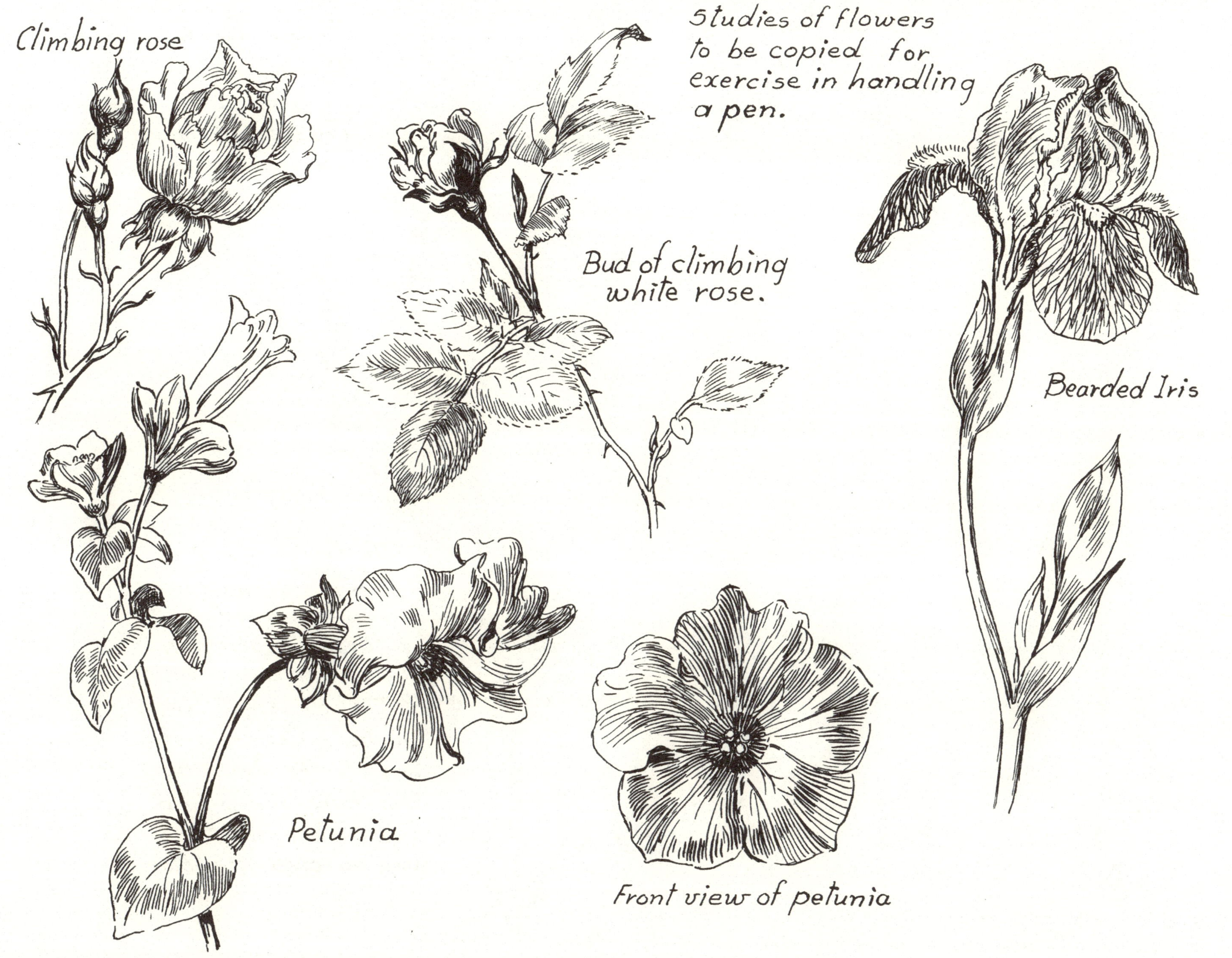
Climbing rose
Studies of flowers
to be copied for
exercise in handling
a pen.
Bud of climbing
white rose.
Bearded Iris
Petunia
Front view of petunia

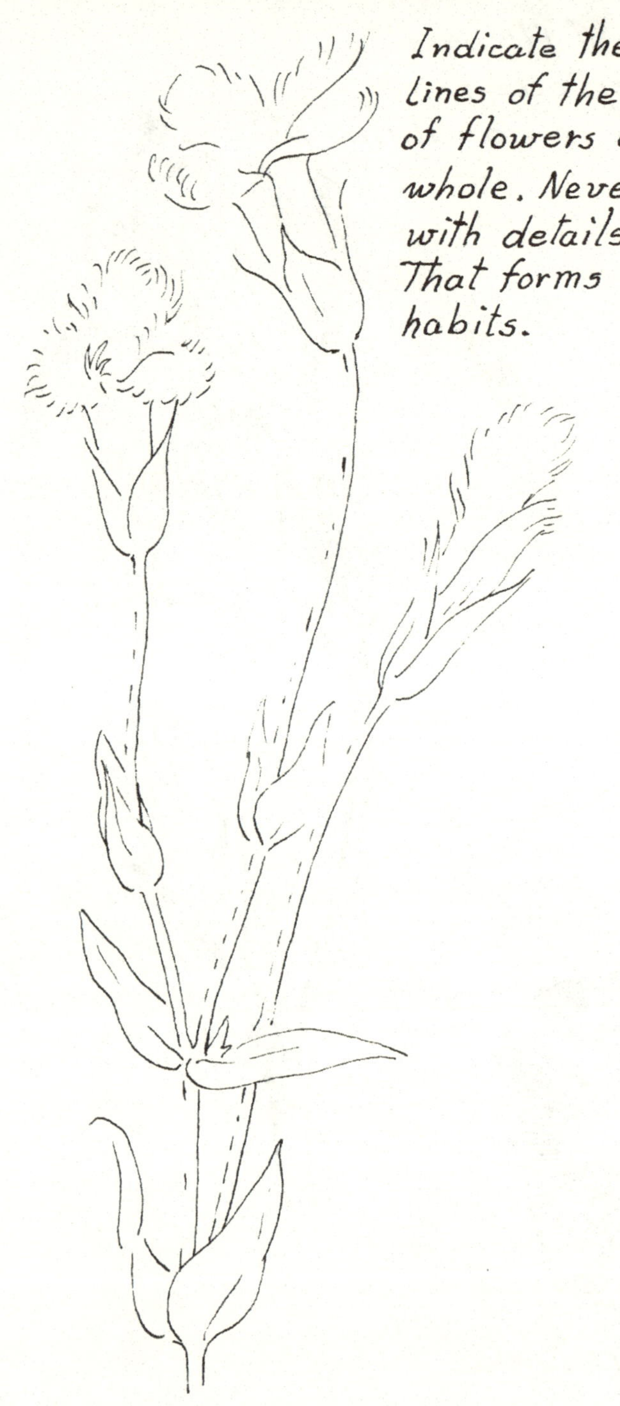

Indicate the basic lines of the group of flowers as a whole. Never start with details. That forms bad habits.

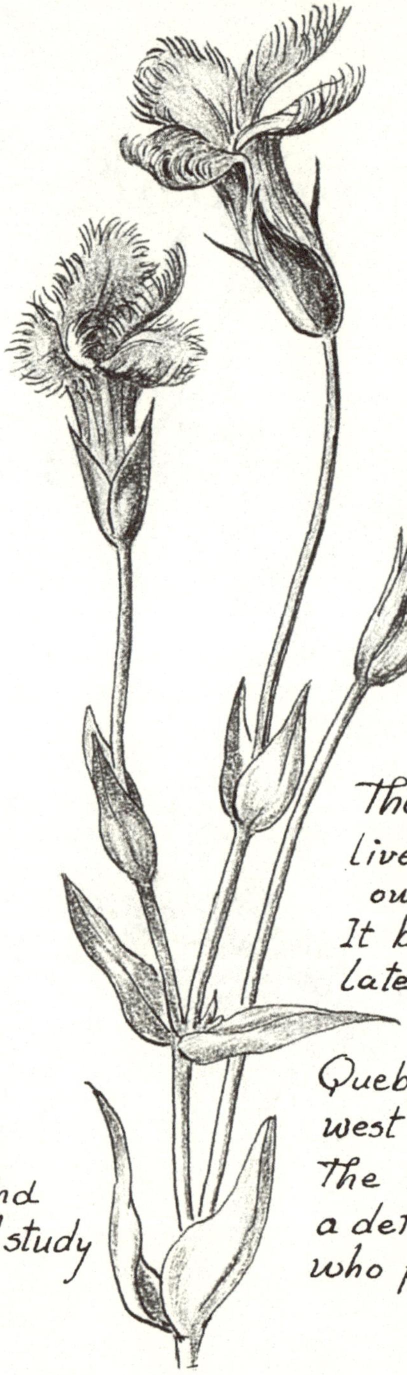

Fringed Gentian. The flower is an intense blue. The stem and leaves a warm green.

The Fringed Gentian lives in low, moist meadows and woods. It begins to bloom in late summer

One meets it from Quebec to Georgia and west to the Mississippi. The fringe has proved a defense against ants who pilfered the nectar.

Pen and pencil study

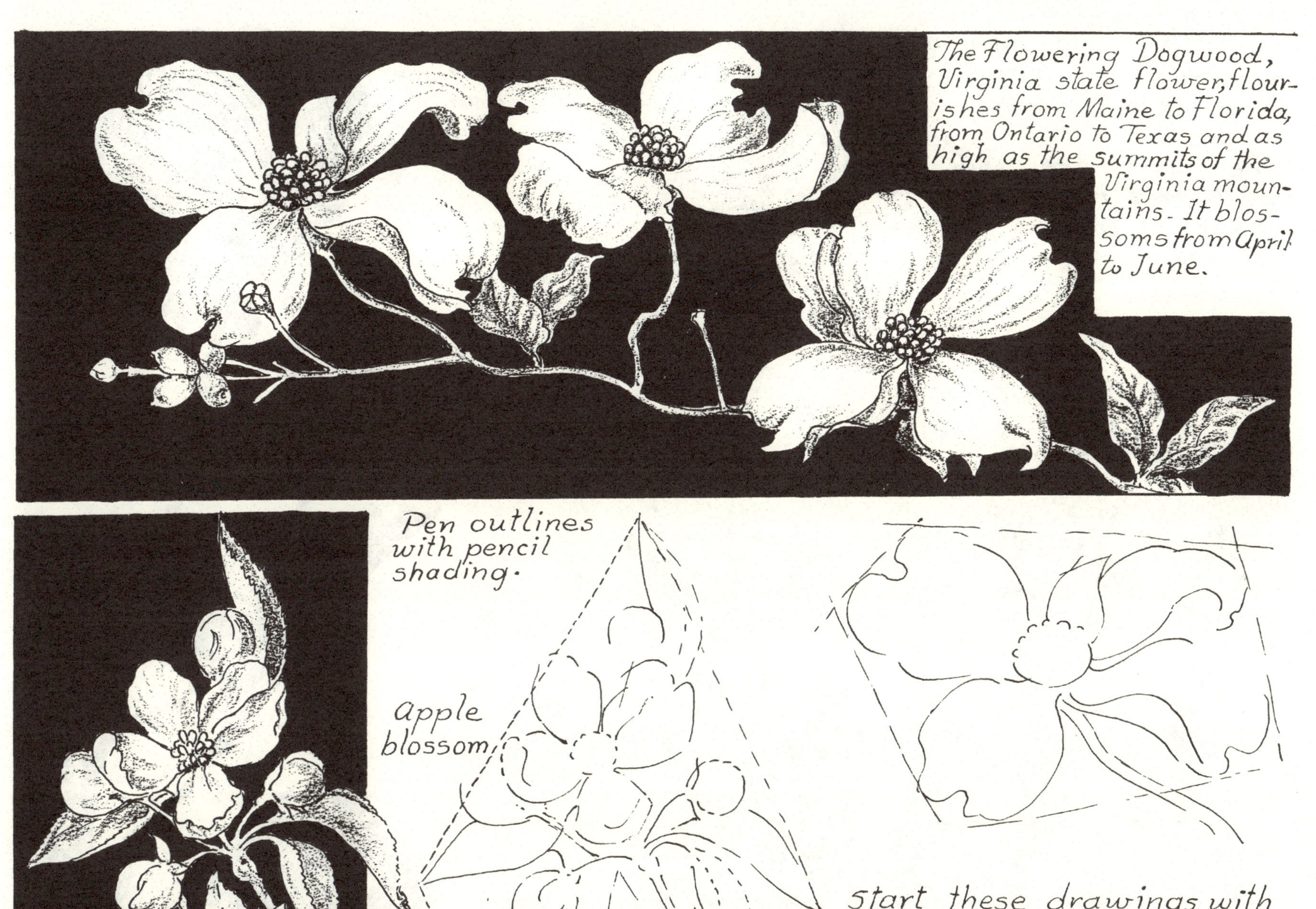

Start these drawings with the outer space lines to obtain the size required, then sketch in correctly the flower leaves and buds.

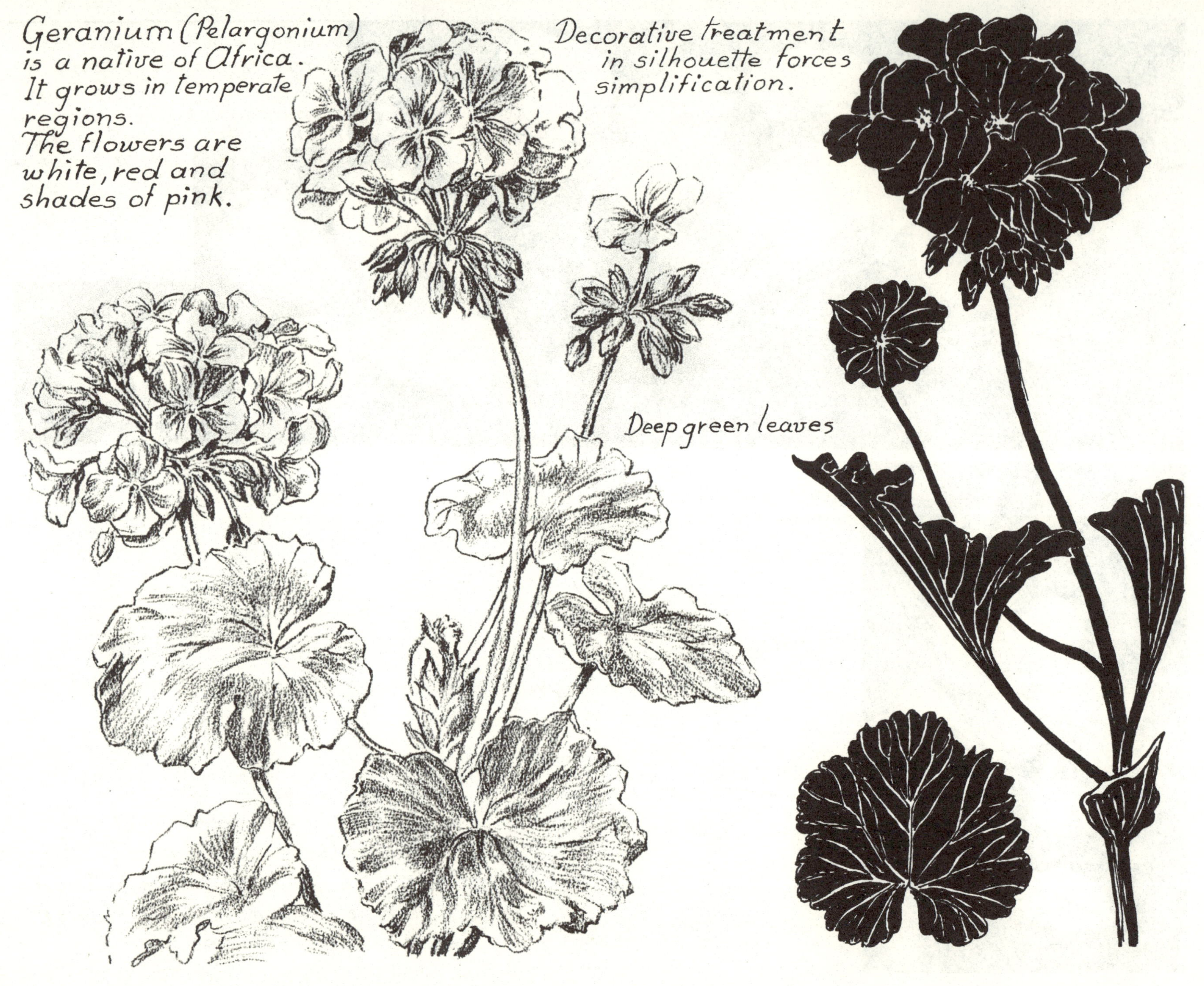
Geranium (Pelargonium)
is a native of Africa.
It grows in temperate
regions.
The flowers are
white, red and
shades of pink.
Decorative treatment
in silhouette forces
simplification.
Deep green leaves

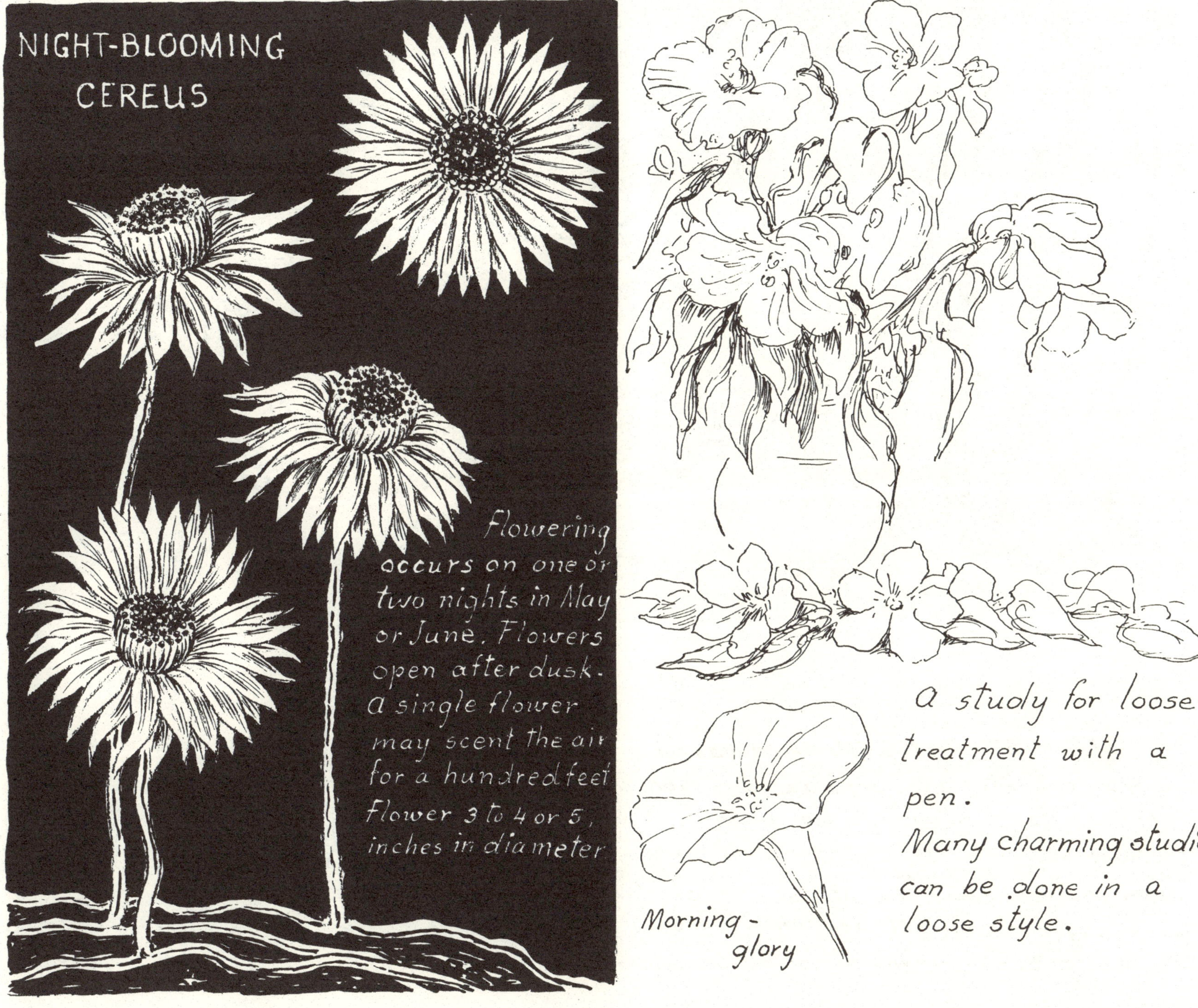
NIGHT-BLOOMING
CEREUS
Flowering
occurs on one or
two nights in May
or June. Flowers
open after dusk.
A single flower
may scent the air
for a hundred feet
Flower 3 to 4 or 5,
inches in diameter
Morning-
glory
A study for loose
treatment with a
pen.
Many charming studies
can be done in a
loose style.

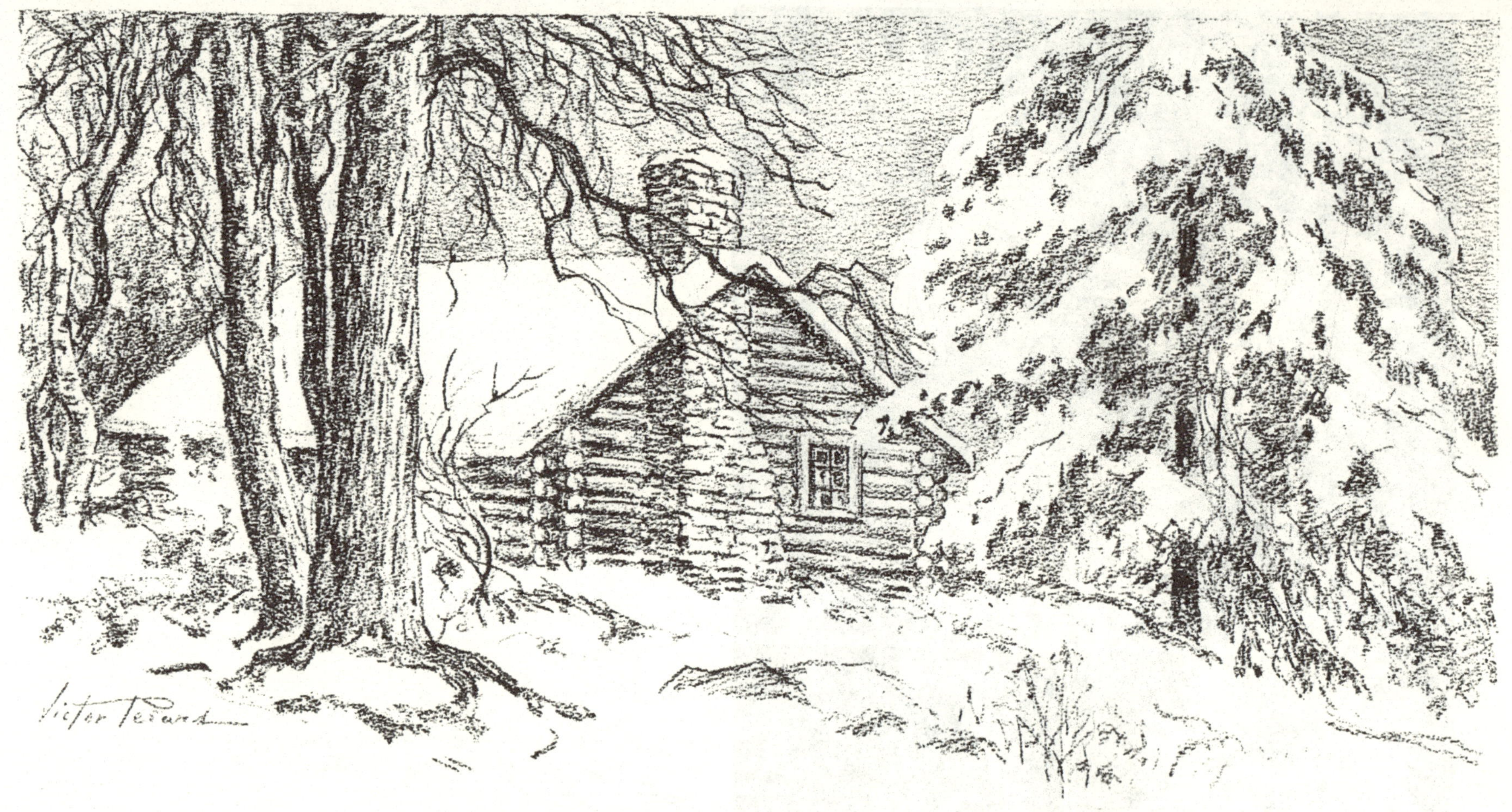

This log cabin in the Maine woods, with large fireplace and snugly built walls, provides a refuge from city living and permits a return to the primitive way of life of our forefathers.

This picturesque effect of snow is obtained by using a dark sky for contrast and showing very little detail on the white paper representing the snow.

Basic lines

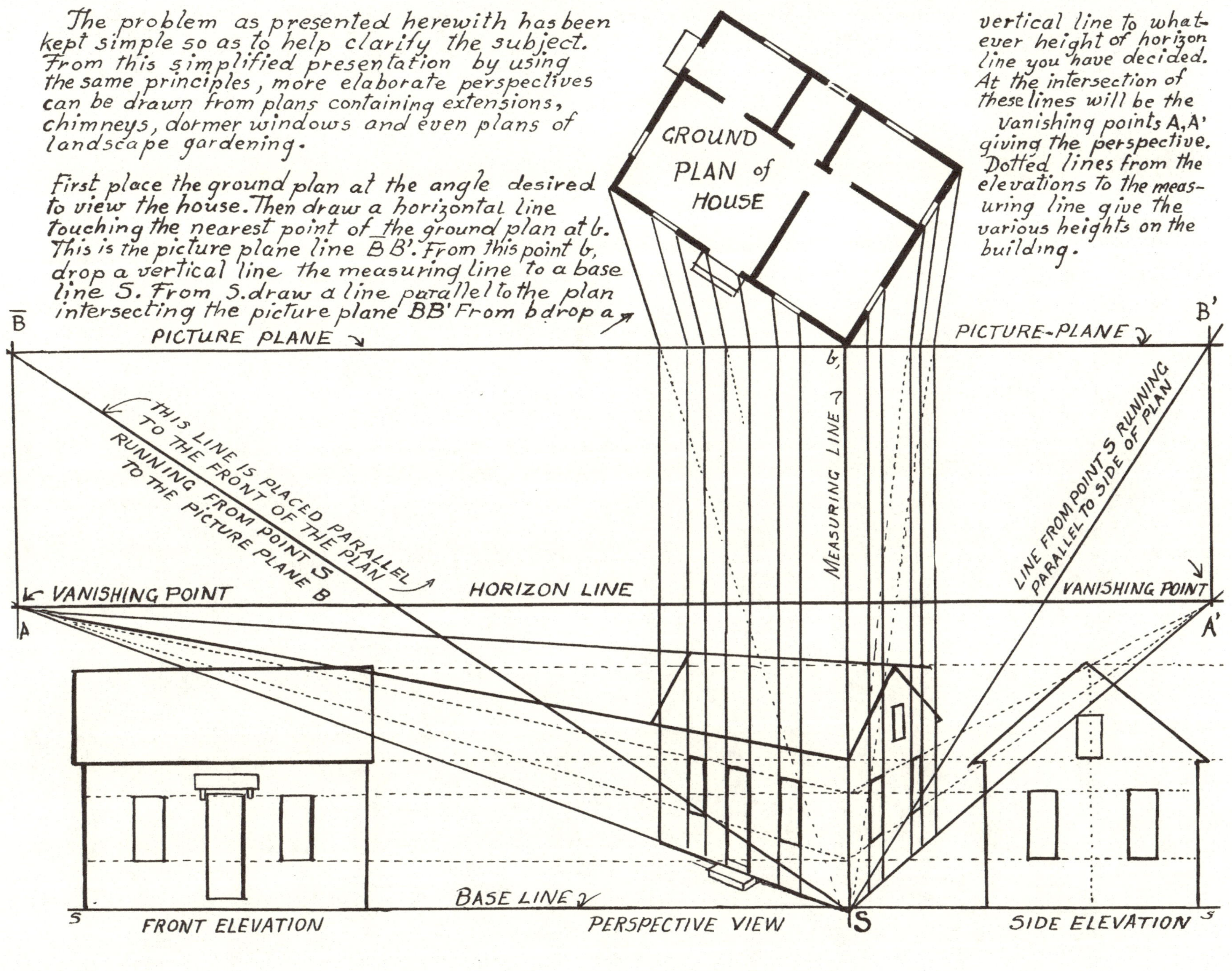
The problem as presented herewith has been kept simple so as to help clarify the subject. From this simplified presentation by using the same principles, more elaborate perspectives can be drawn from plans containing extensions, chimneys, dormer windows and even plans of landscape gardening.
First place the ground plan at the angle desired to view the house. Then draw a horizontal line touching the nearest point of the ground plan at b. This is the picture plane line BB'. From this point b, drop a vertical line the measuring line to a base line S. From S draw a line parallel to the plan intersecting the picture plane BB' From b drop a
vertical line to whatever height of horizon line you have decided. At the intersection of these lines will be the vanishing points A, A' giving the perspective. Dotted lines from the elevations to the measuring line give the various heights on the building.
GROUND PLAN of HOUSE
B
B'
PICTURE PLANE
PICTURE-PLANE
b,
MEASURING LINE
THIS LINE IS PLACED PARALLEL TO THE FRONT OF THE PLAN RUNNING FROM POINT S TO THE PICTURE PLANE B
LINE FROM POINT S RUNNING PARALLEL TO SIDE OF PLAN
VANISHING POINT
HORIZON LINE
VANISHING POINT
A
A'
BASE LINE
S
S
S
FRONT ELEVATION
PERSPECTIVE VIEW
SIDE ELEVATION

Typical of a group of apartment houses are those of the Parkchester apartments in the Bronx, New York City. These consist of fifty-one elevator apartment buildings comprising 12200 apartments covering an area of 35½ acres out of the 129 acres of landscaped park surrounding the development. Parkways and playgrounds afford sunlight and air and give healthful and pleasurable living.

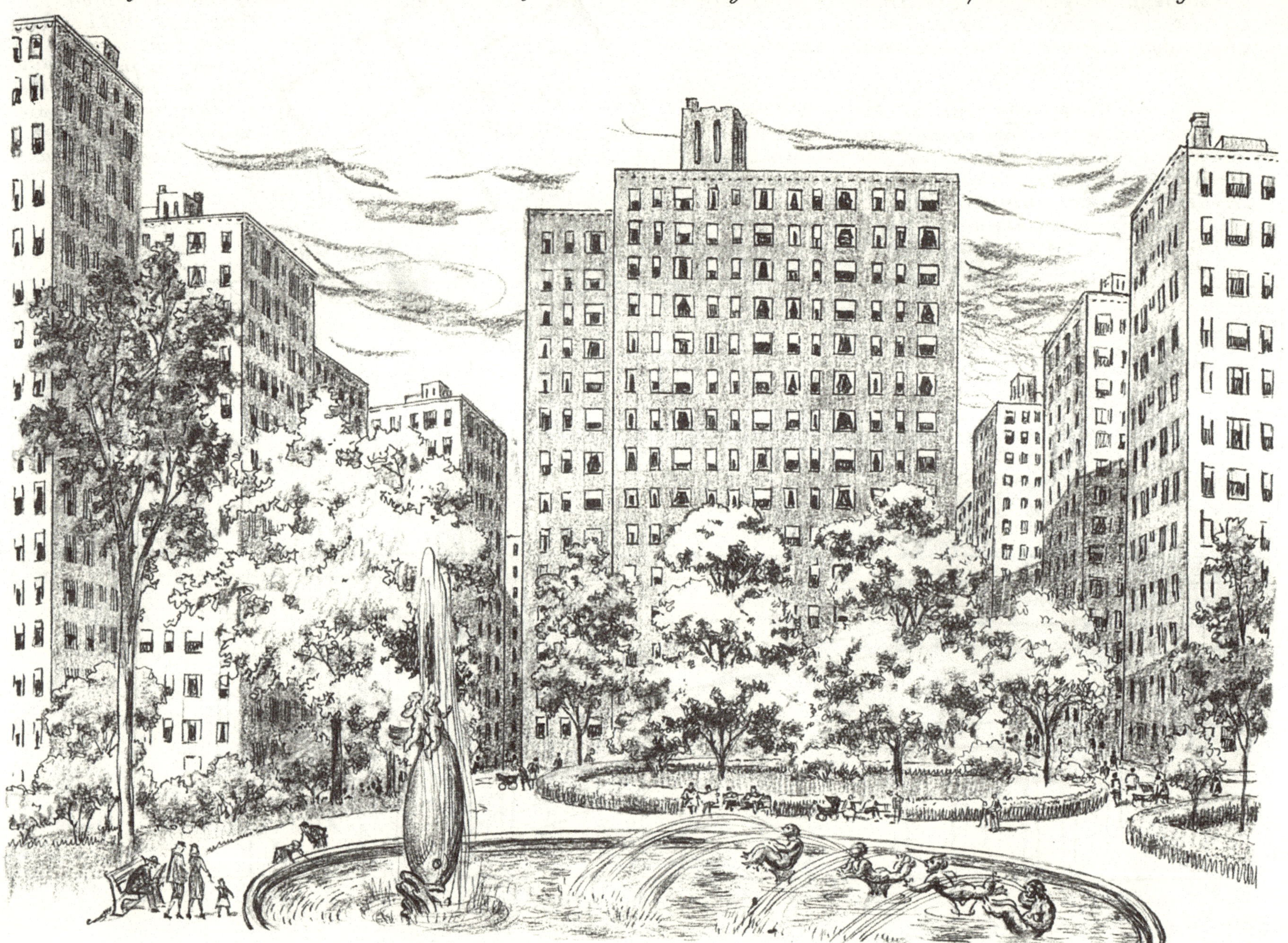

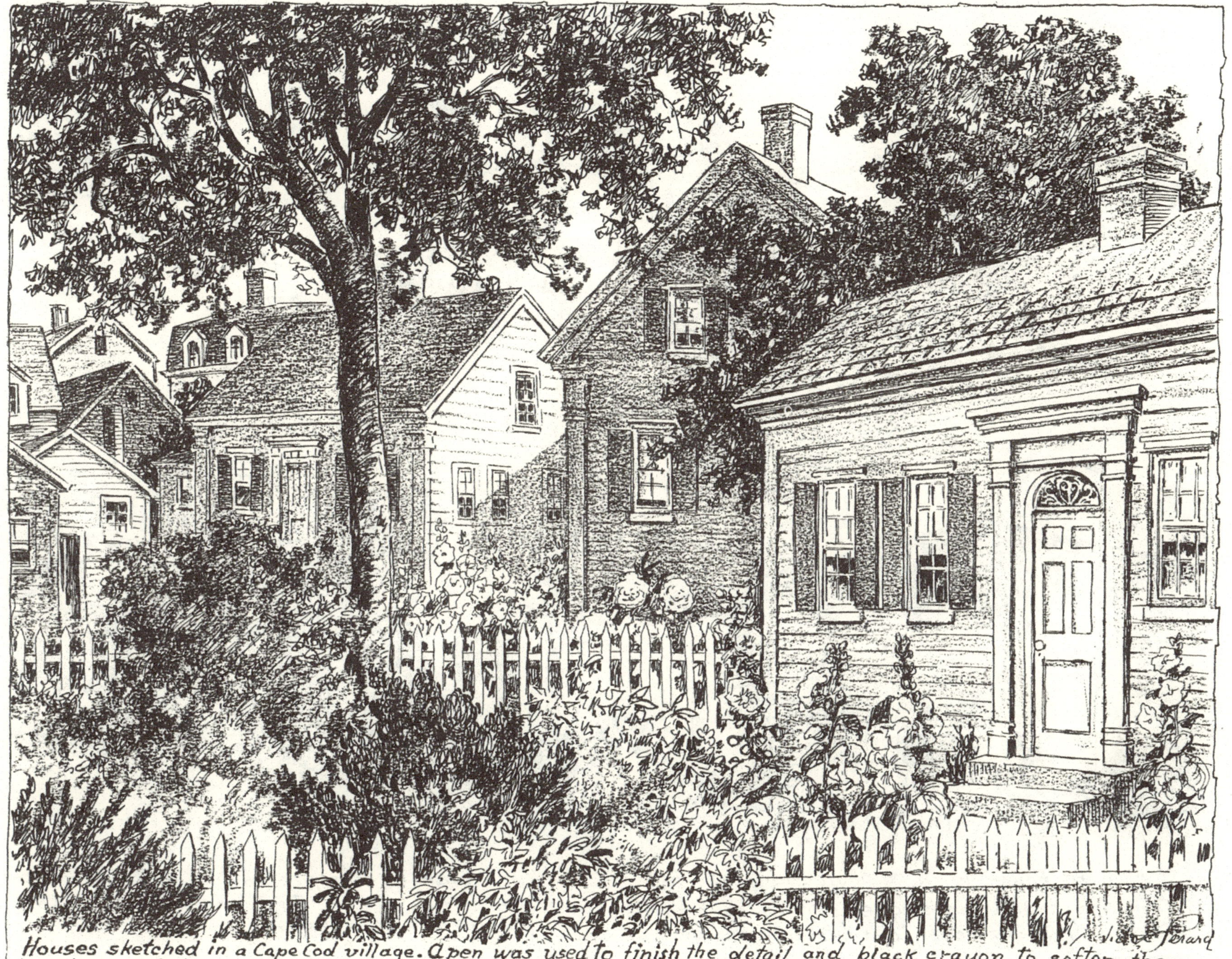

Houses sketched in a Cape Cod village. A pen was used to finish the detail and black crayon to soften the hardness of the pen lines.

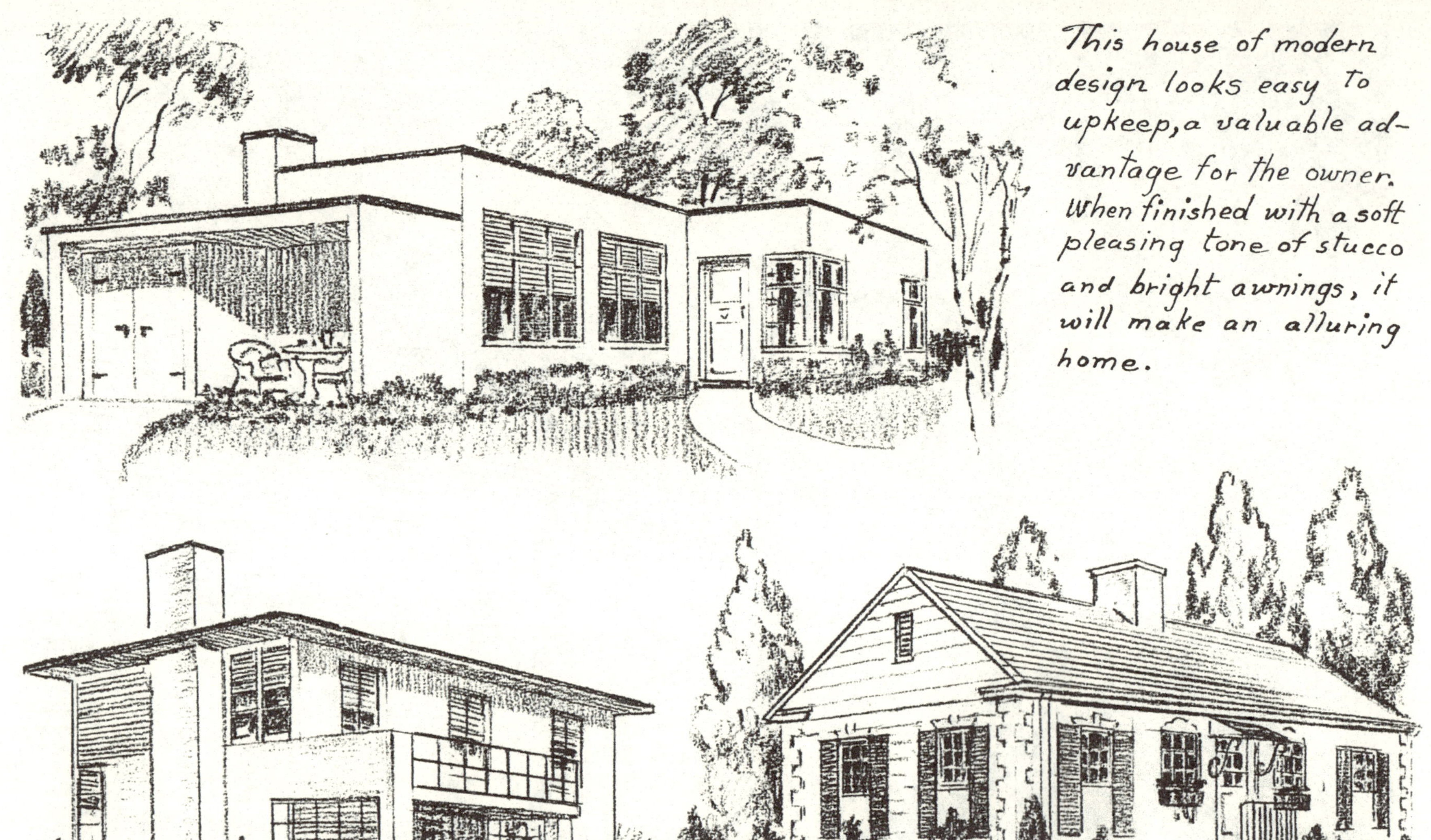

This house of modern design looks easy to upkeep, a valuable advantage for the owner. When finished with a soft pleasing tone of stucco and bright awnings, it will make an alluring home.

A modern house with a projecting roof has interesting angles and suggests practical comforts within. It throws over traditional design but compensates for this by agreeable shadows and coloring.

The plan of this prefabricated house is a close imitation of the Cape Cod cottage, and was put up in a few days.

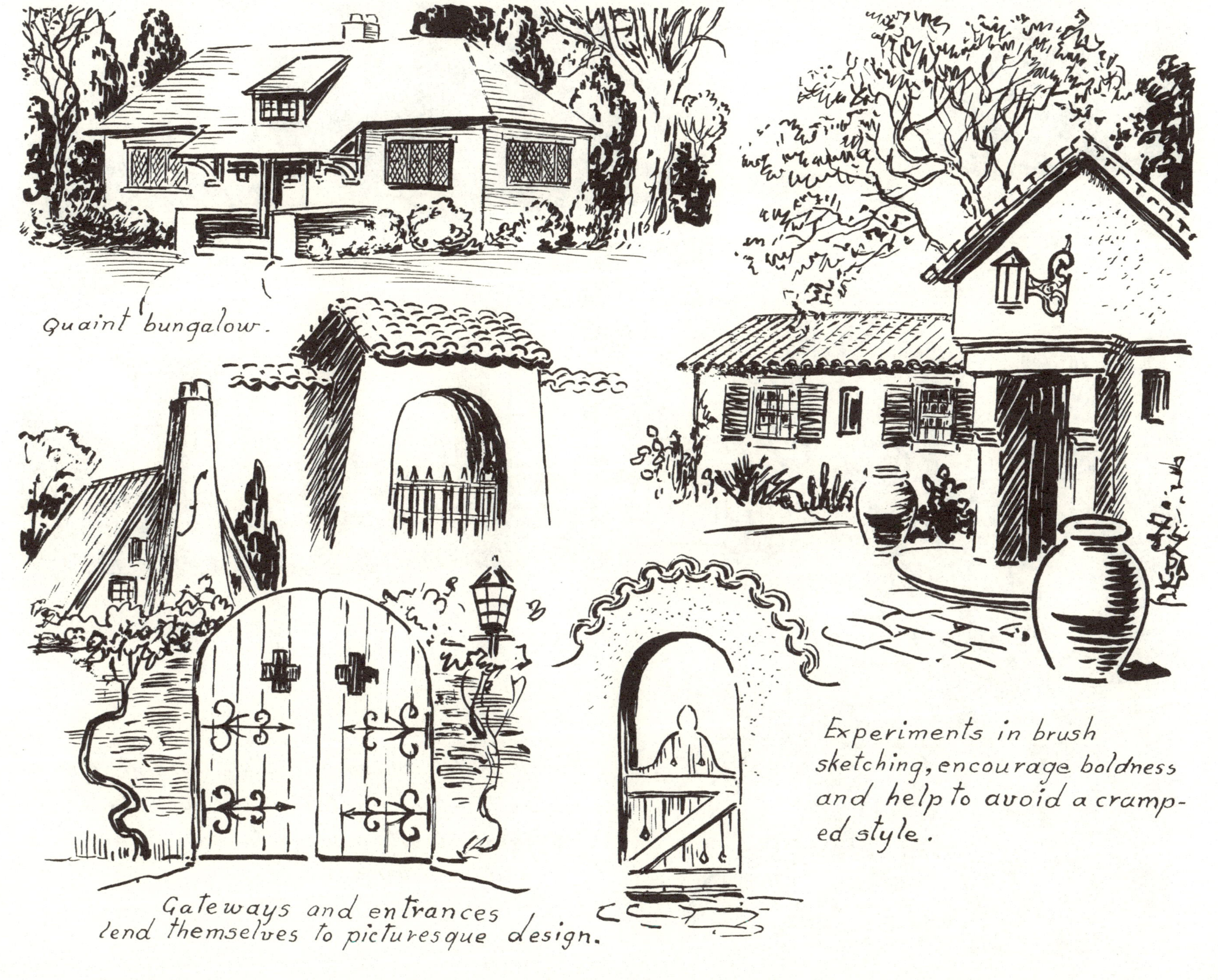

Quaint bungalow.

Gateways and entrances lend themselves to picturesque design.

Experiments in brush sketching, encourage boldness and help to avoid a cramped style.

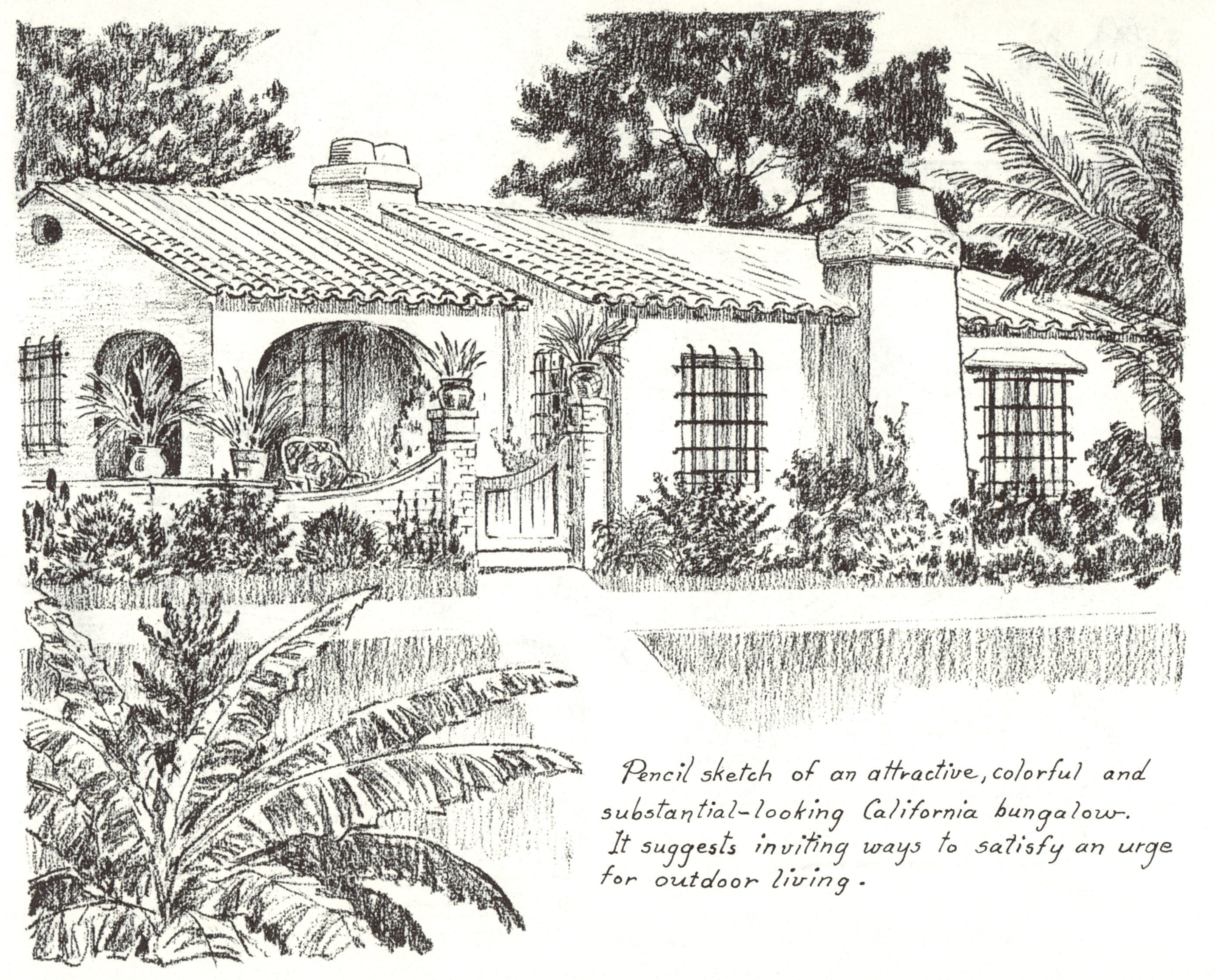

Pencil sketch of an attractive, colorful and substantial-looking California bungalow. It suggests inviting ways to satisfy an urge for outdoor living.

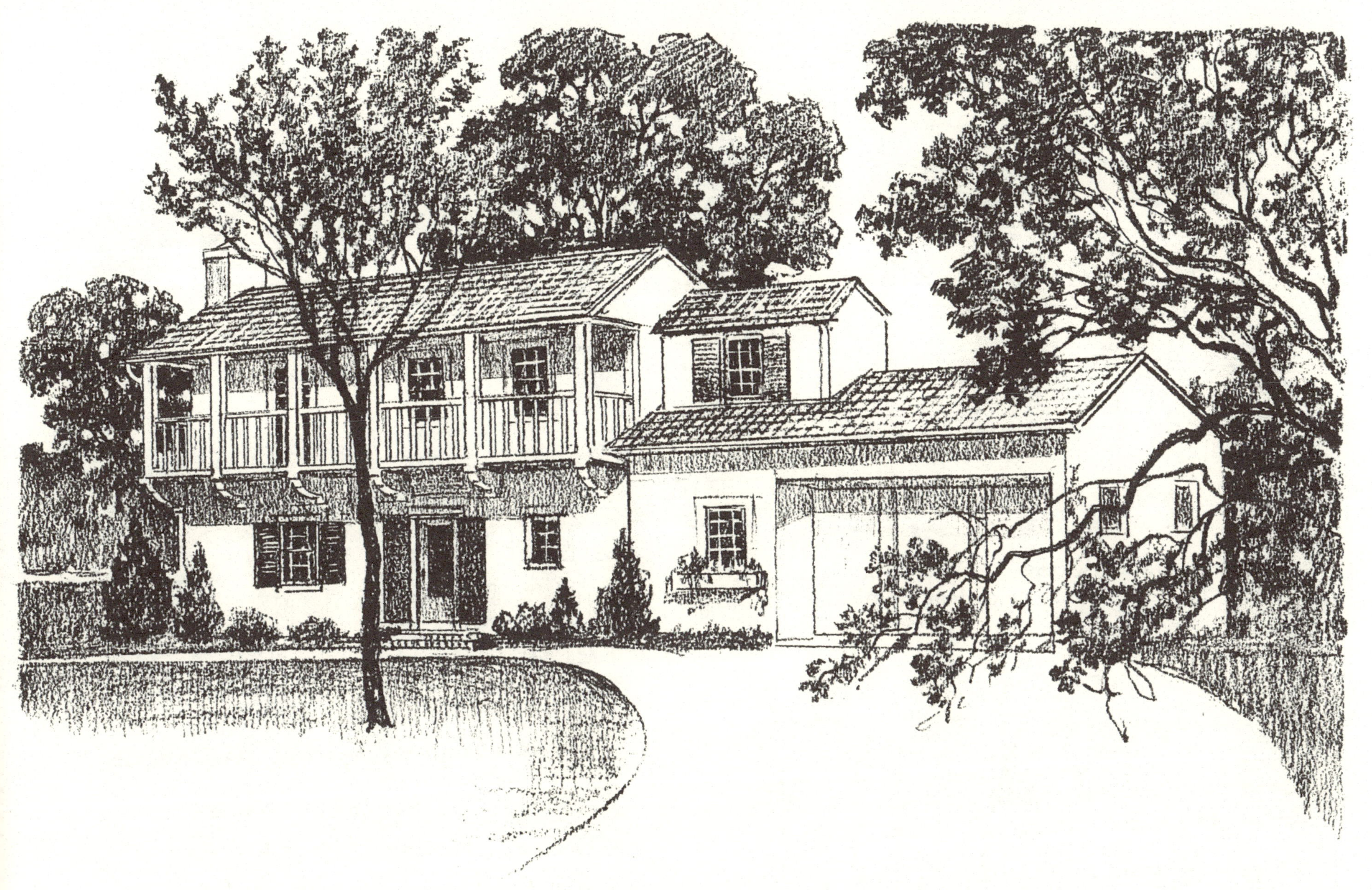

A southern home in Louisiana, modern, but built in the tradition of the past, reminds one of the time of the Spanish and later the French occupation. It has a decorative pattern of trees drawn in flat tones.

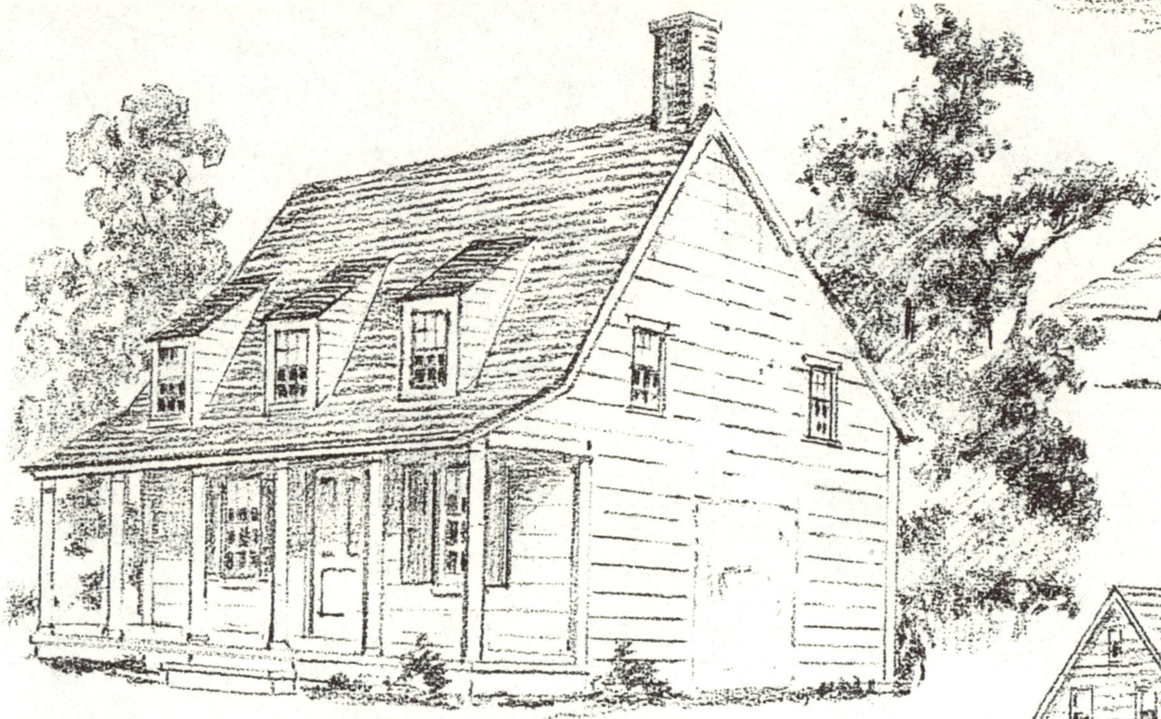

Schenck-Cooke House 63rd st., Brooklyn, N.Y.
Built in 1656. One of the oldest homes in the City.

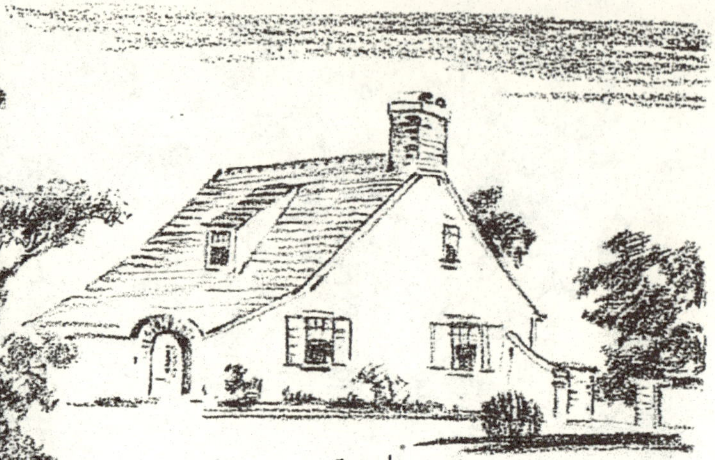

Gardener's cottage at entrance of an estate.

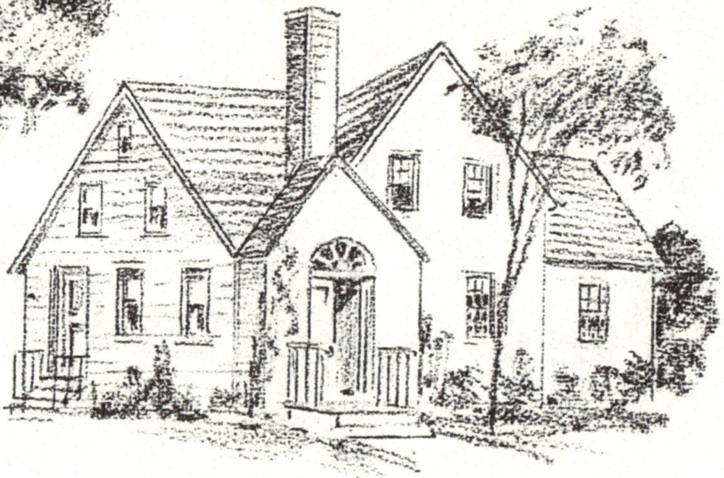

New England type of parish house.

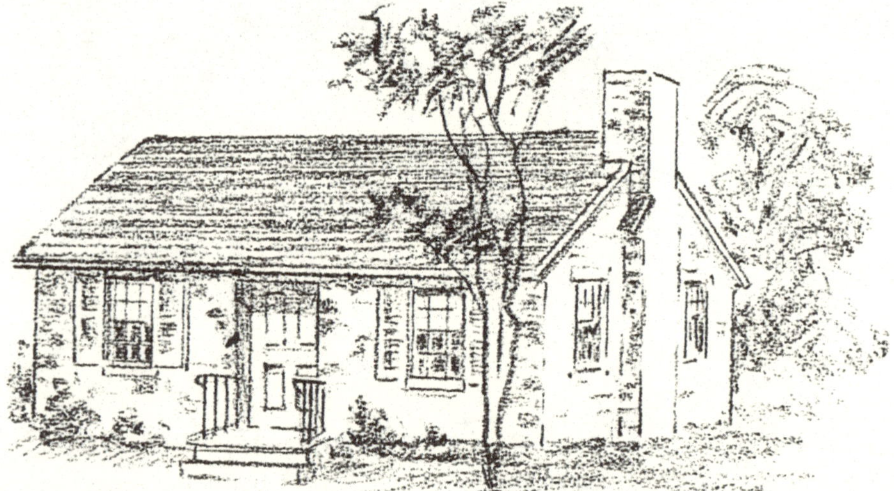

A typical old stone house, built in 1785.

These old houses have varied influences, brought about by the conditions of the locality and materials obtainable.

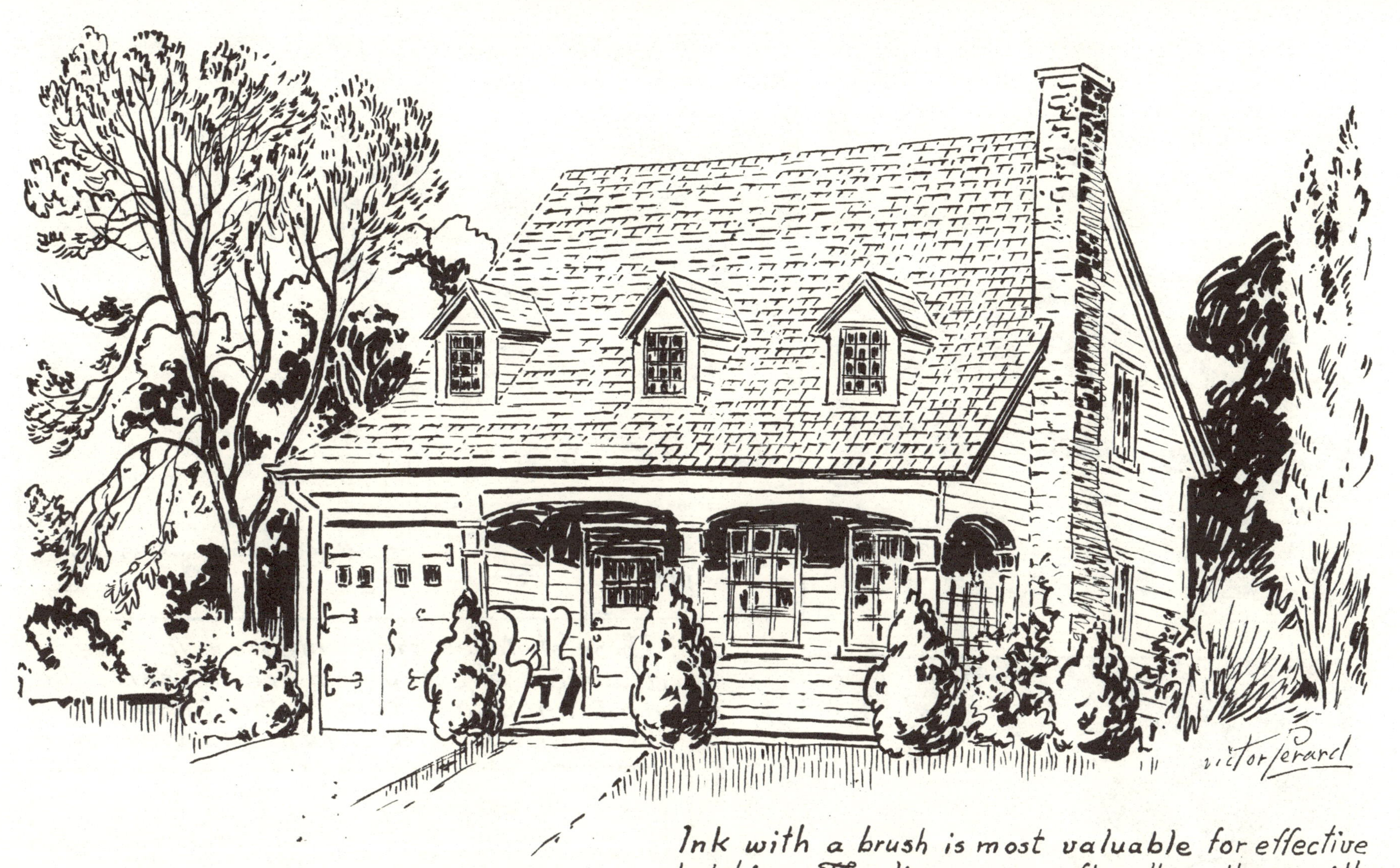

Ink with a brush is most valuable for effective sketching. The lines are softer than those with a pen and solid blacks bring out the sunny effects.

Drawing with a brush will be a help for future work in water-colors and oils. Paintings are started by this method.

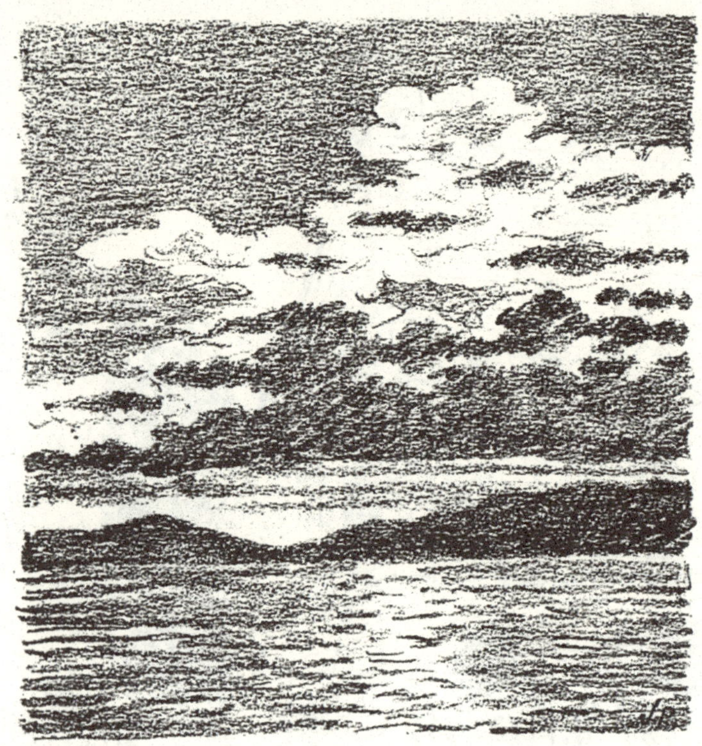

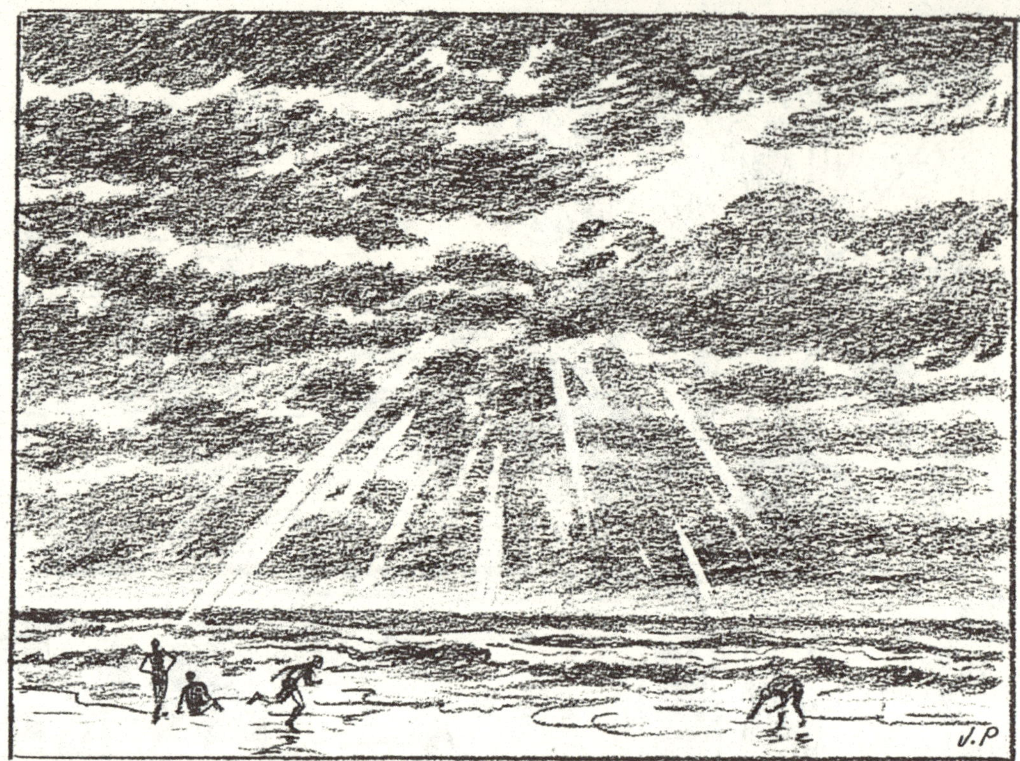

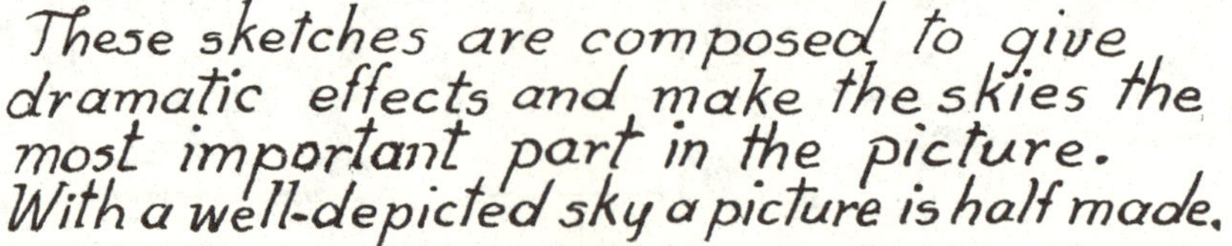

These sketches are composed to give dramatic effects and make the skies the most important part in the picture. With a well-depicted sky a picture is half made.

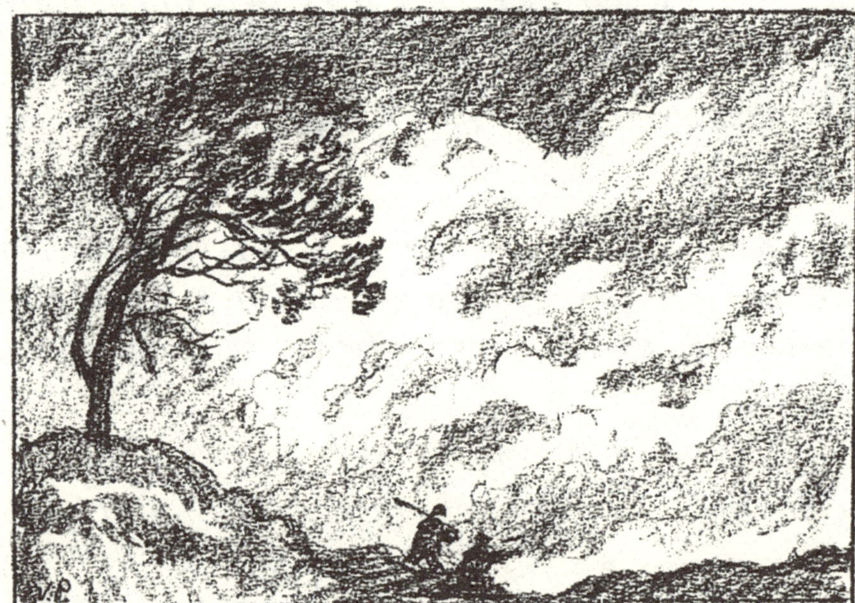

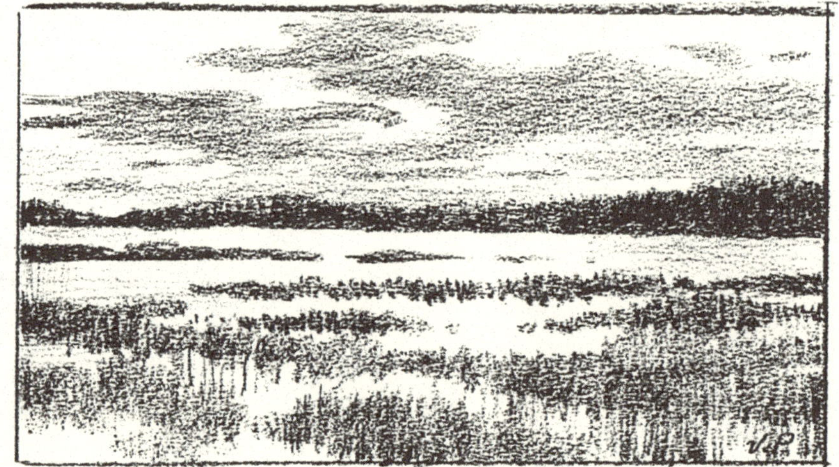

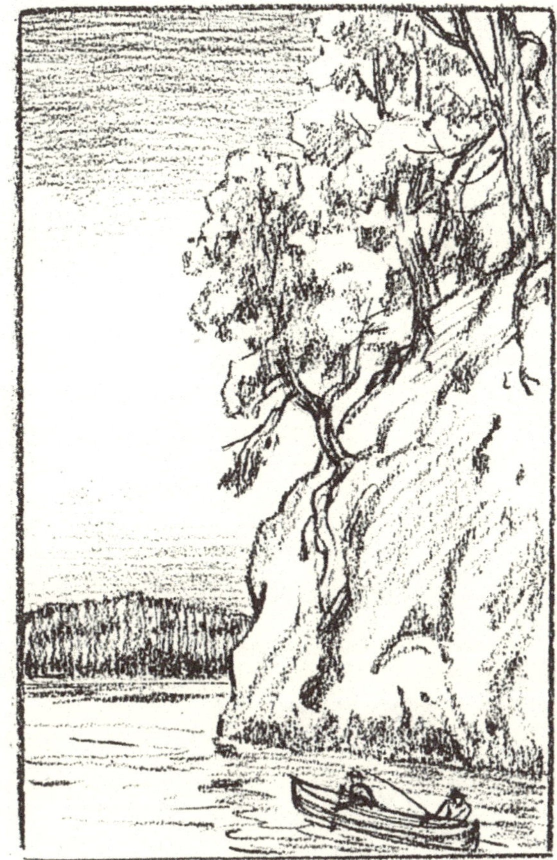

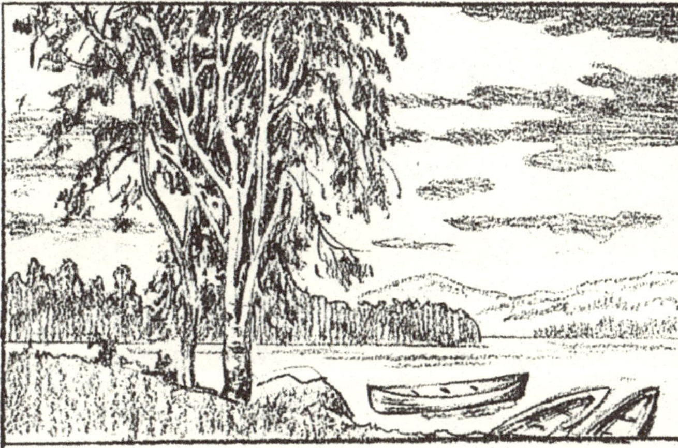

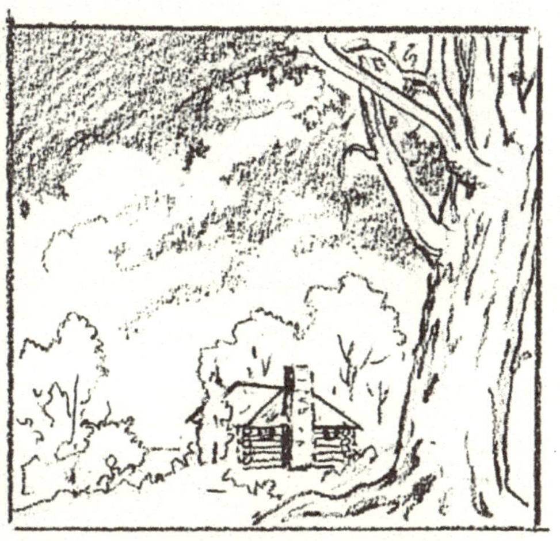

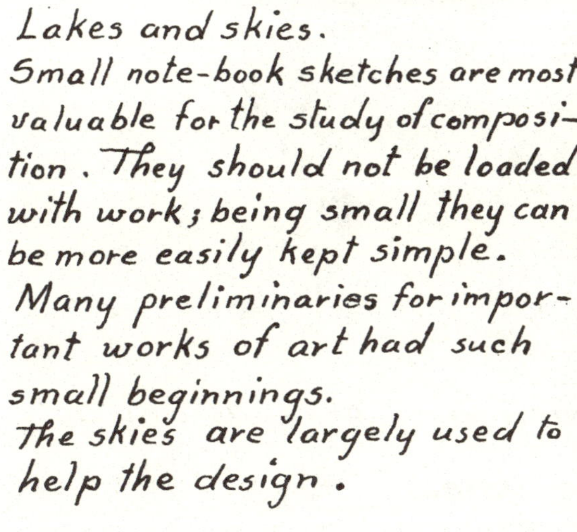

Lakes and skies.

Small note-book sketches are most valuable for the study of composition. They should not be loaded with work; being small they can be more easily kept simple.

Many preliminaries for important works of art had such small beginnings.

The skies are largely used to help the design.

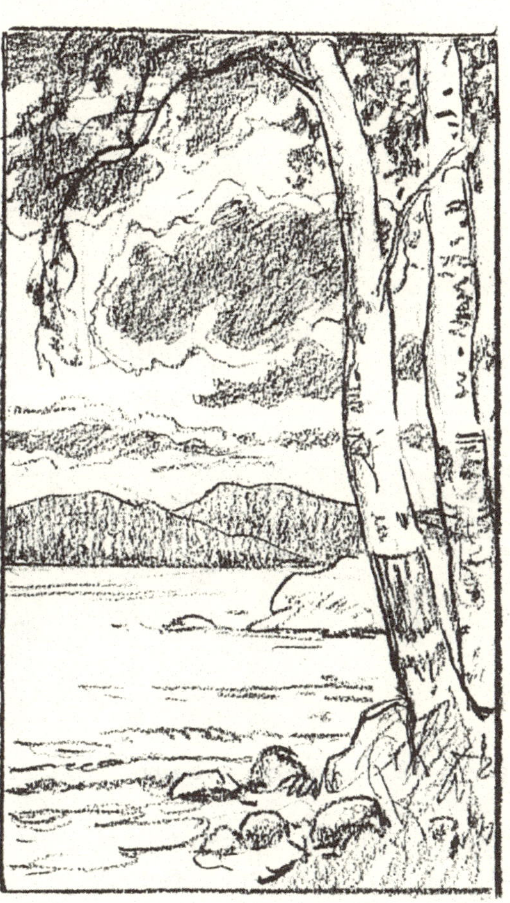

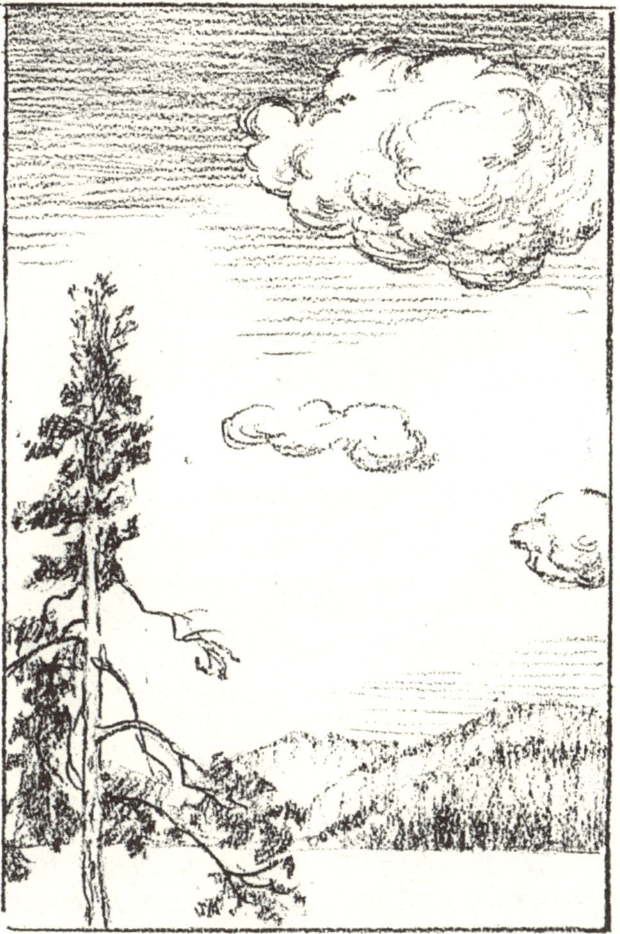

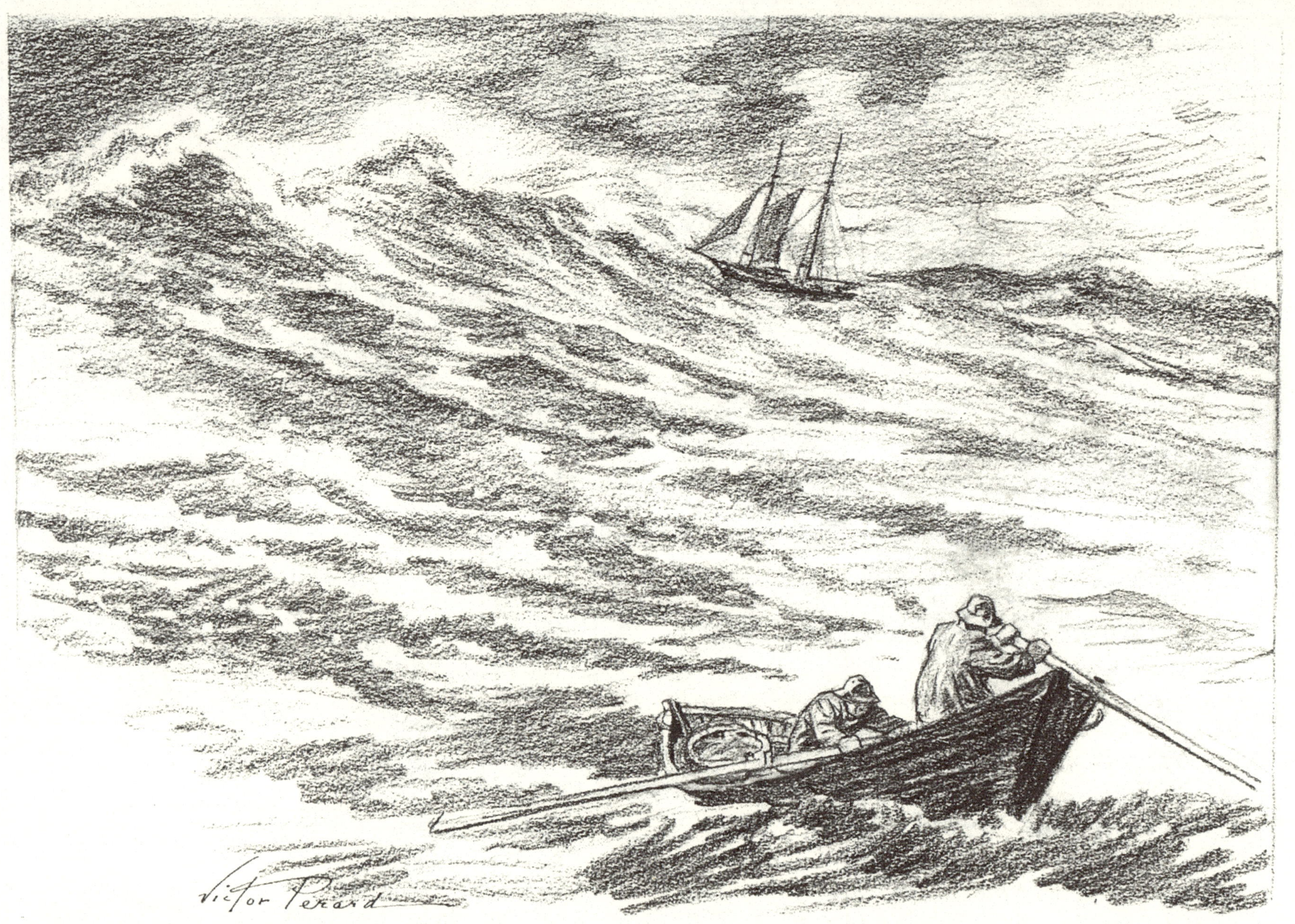

Trawlers regaining their schooner after being blown off their fishing grounds and battling with high waves.
This subject should first be drawn with care, then emboldened to suggest the movement of the water and the spirit of an angry sea.

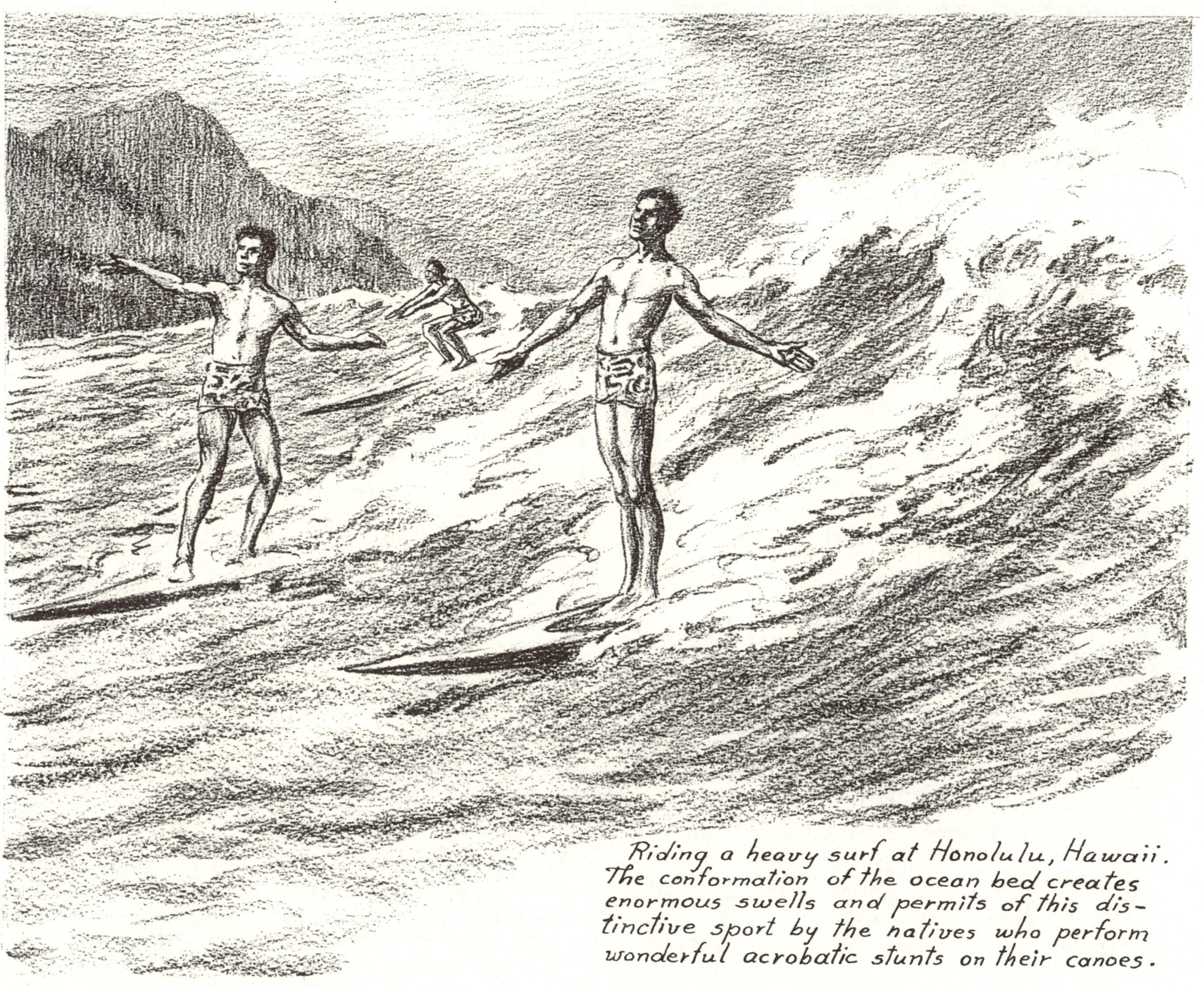

Riding a heavy surf at Honolulu, Hawaii. The conformation of the ocean bed creates enormous swells and permits of this distinctive sport by the natives who perform wonderful acrobatic stunts on their canoes.

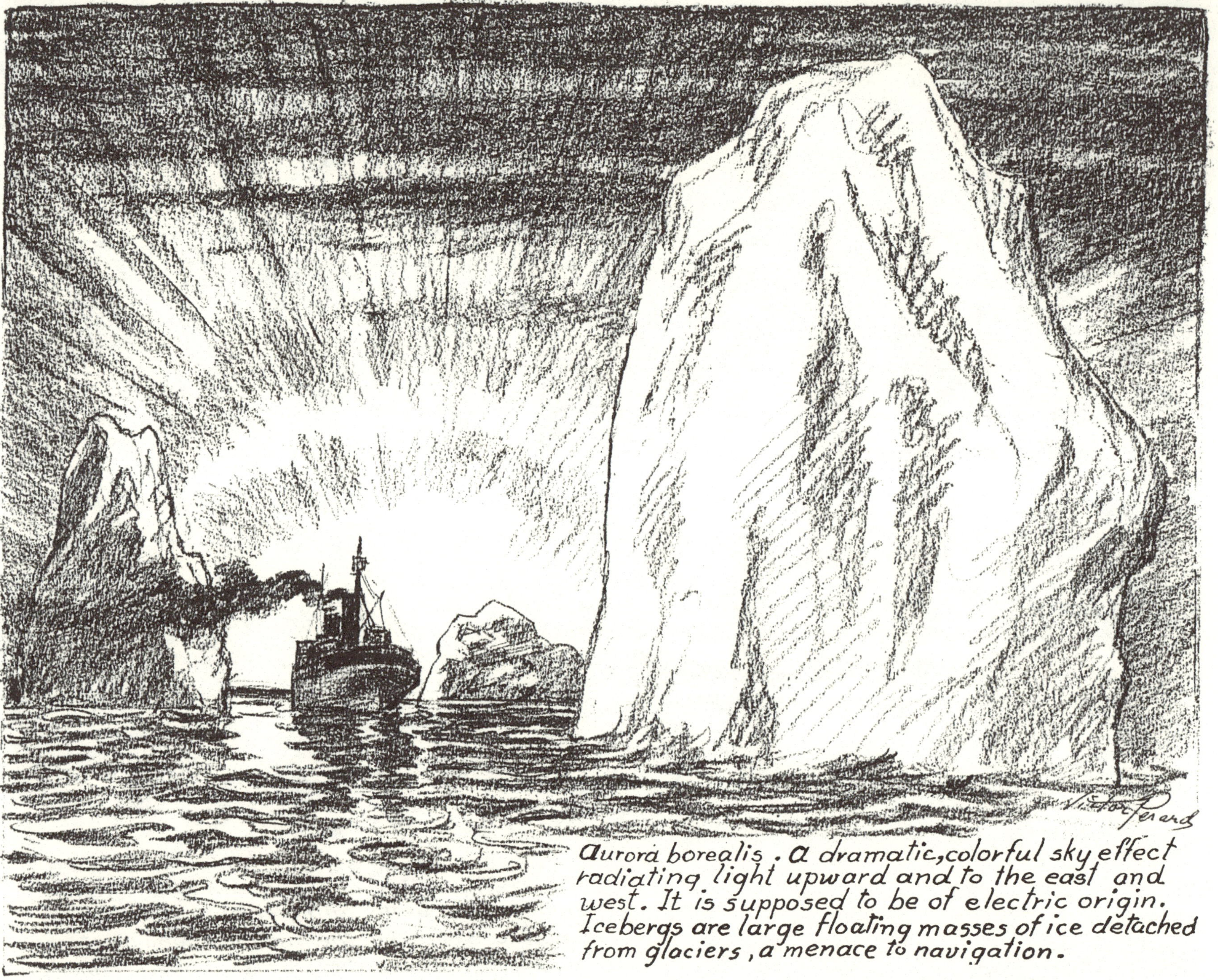

Aurora borealis. A dramatic, colorful sky effect radiating light upward and to the east and west. It is supposed to be of electric origin. Icebergs are large floating masses of ice detached from glaciers, a menace to navigation.

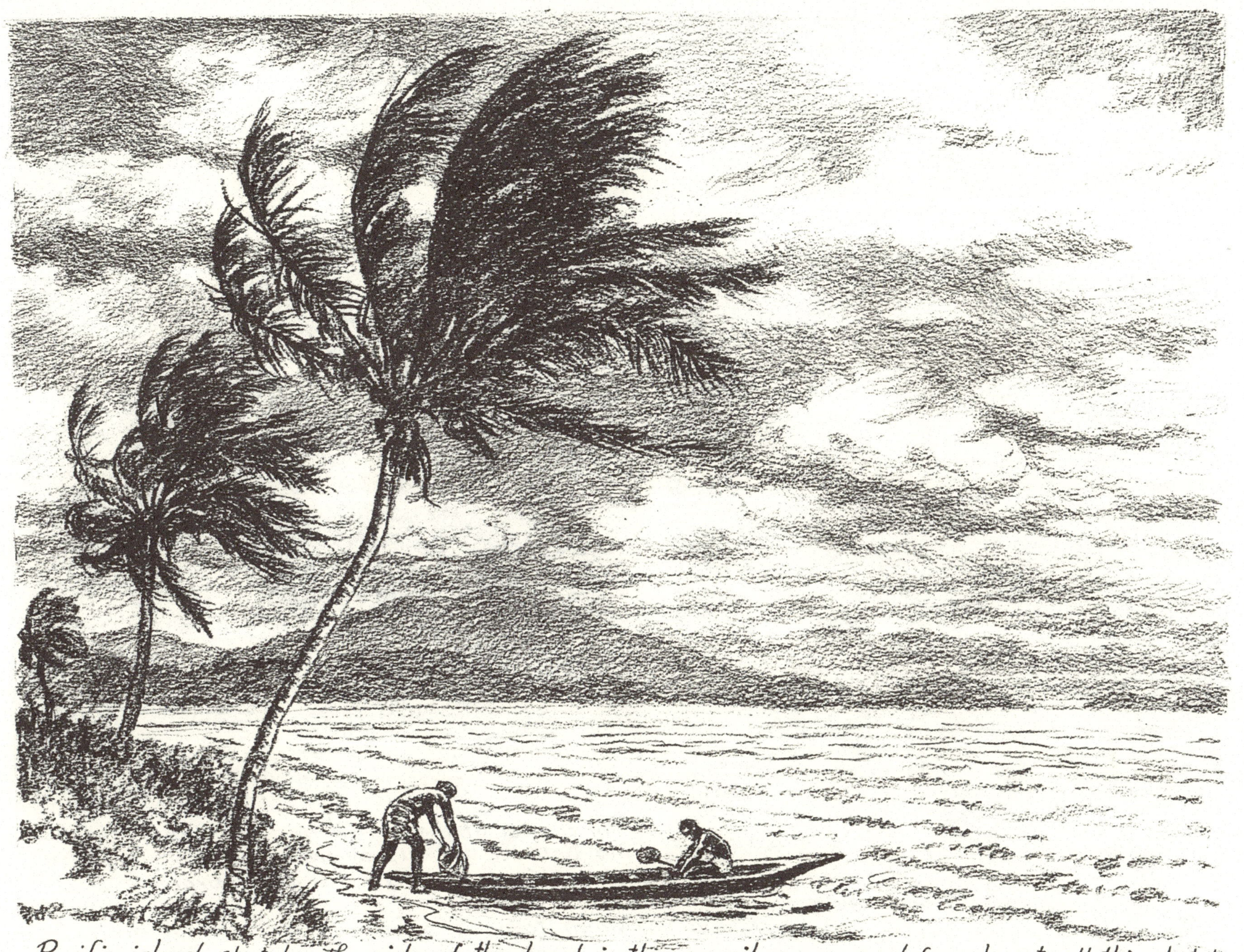

Pacific island sketch - the side of the lead in the pencil was used for almost all this sketch. The sharp point was thus kept to bring out the details in the foreground trees and figures.

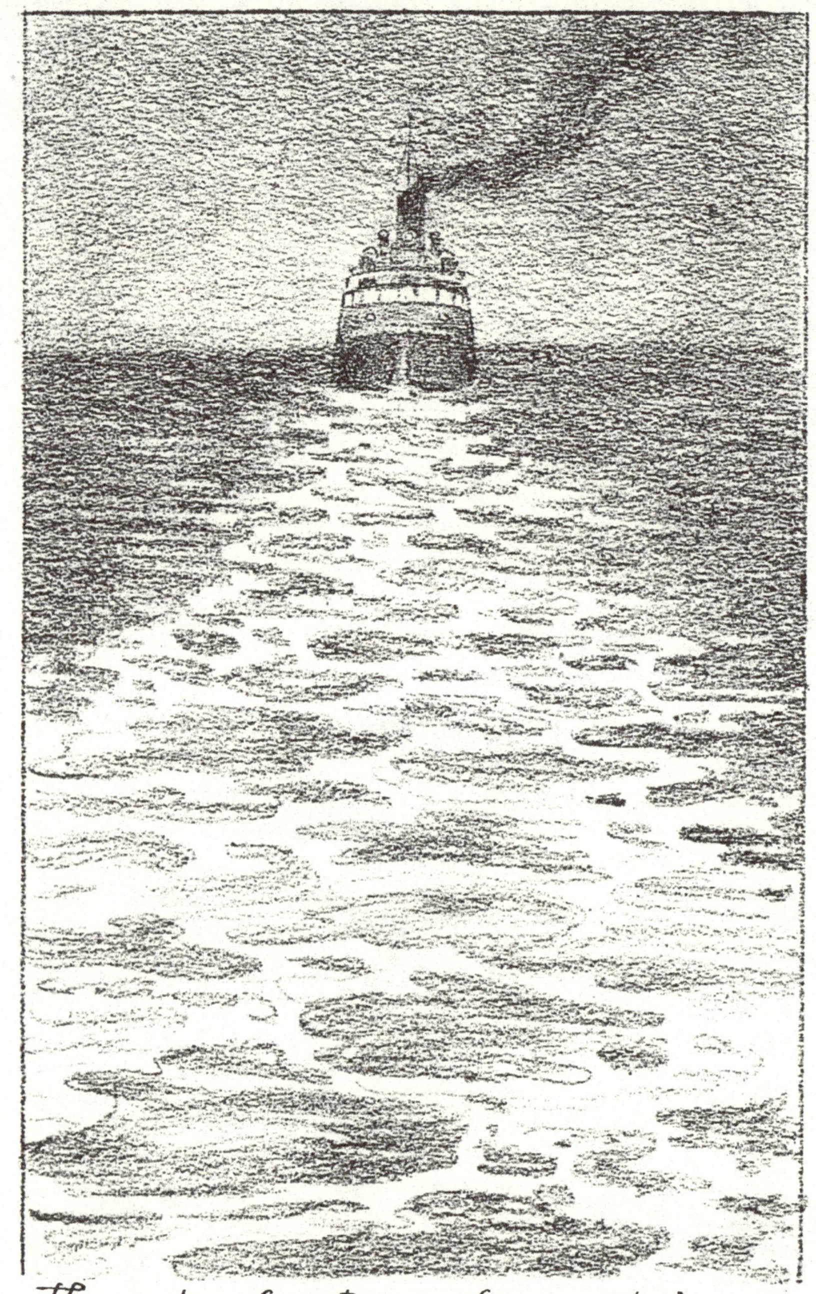

The wake of a steamer forms a design of interesting pattern. In drawing tints with a pencil lay in the light tones first.

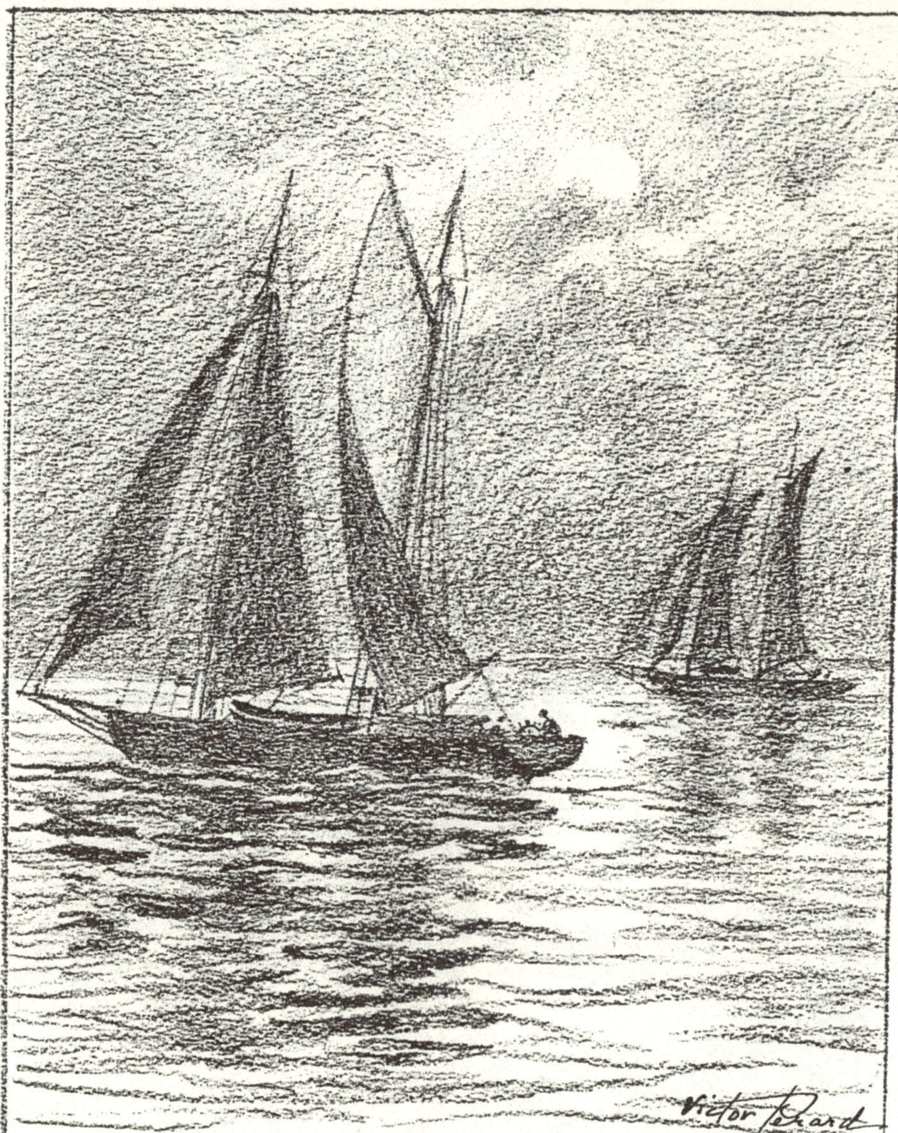

For control of the pencil and the practice of drawing tints of various degrees of intensity, these two subjects will afford good practice.

Many famous paintings have been made from pencil studies made from nature with color notes jotted down and memorized for later use.

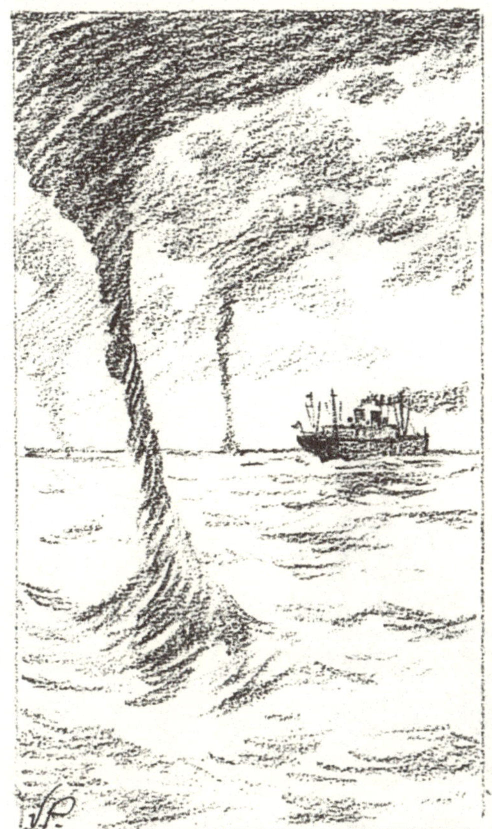

Waterspouts in mid-Atlantic

In these sea effects a certain amount of bold pencil drawing is desirable to give vitality to the work and to bring out the dramatic feeling of the scene. If the drawings are too smoothly made they become too photographic and lack life. Before undertaking to copy these subjects, it would be well to practice a few tints on the side.

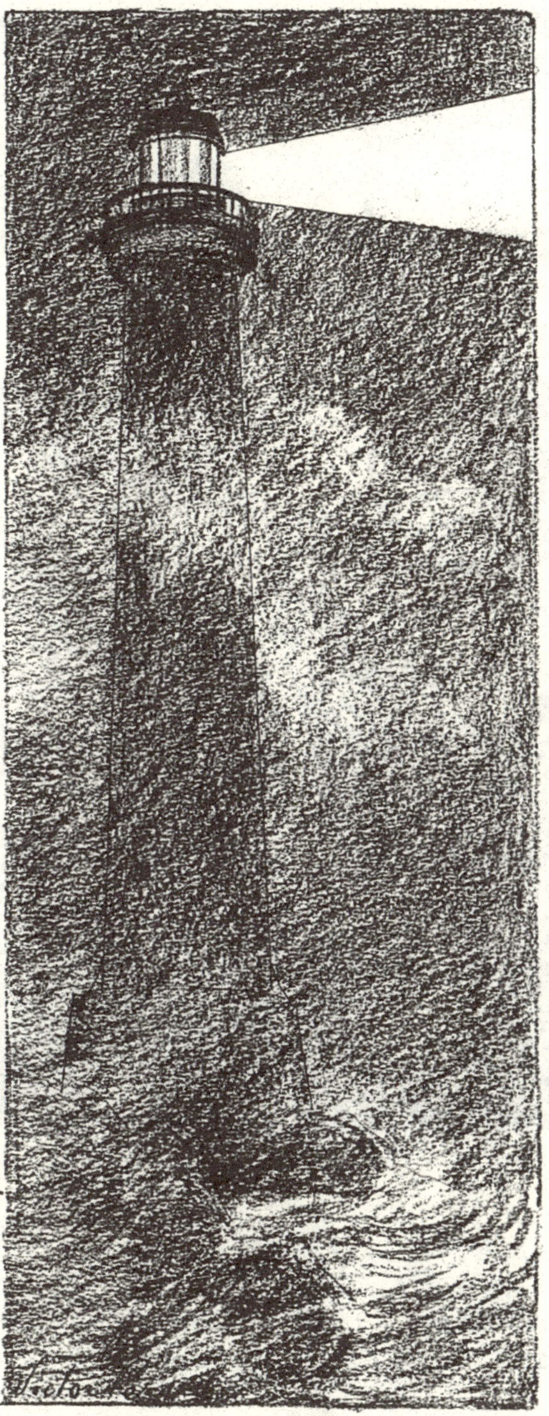

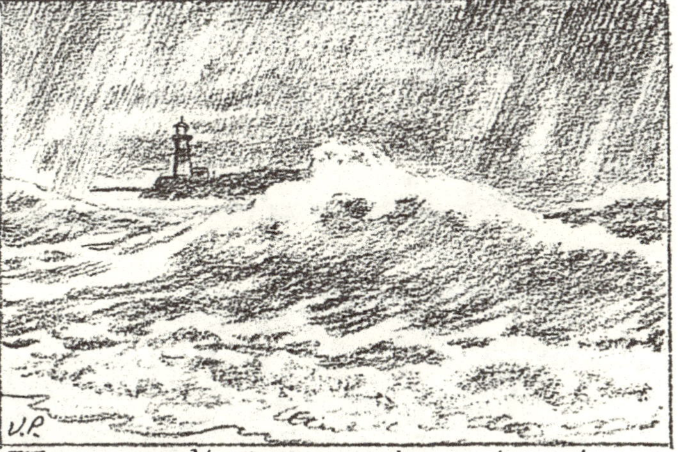

The squall. To be enlarged and drawn in one hour.

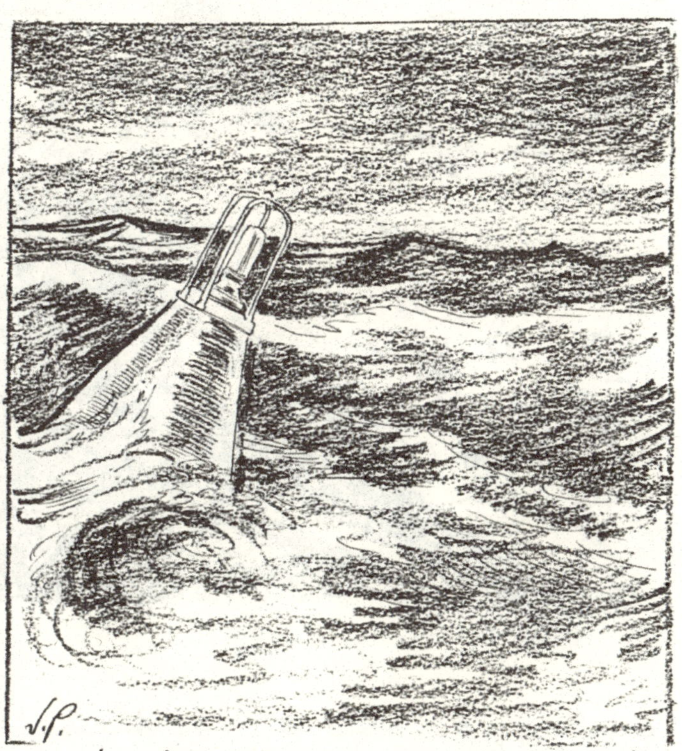

A whistling buoy anchored in shallow water. Enlarging this sketch and timing the work would be good practice.

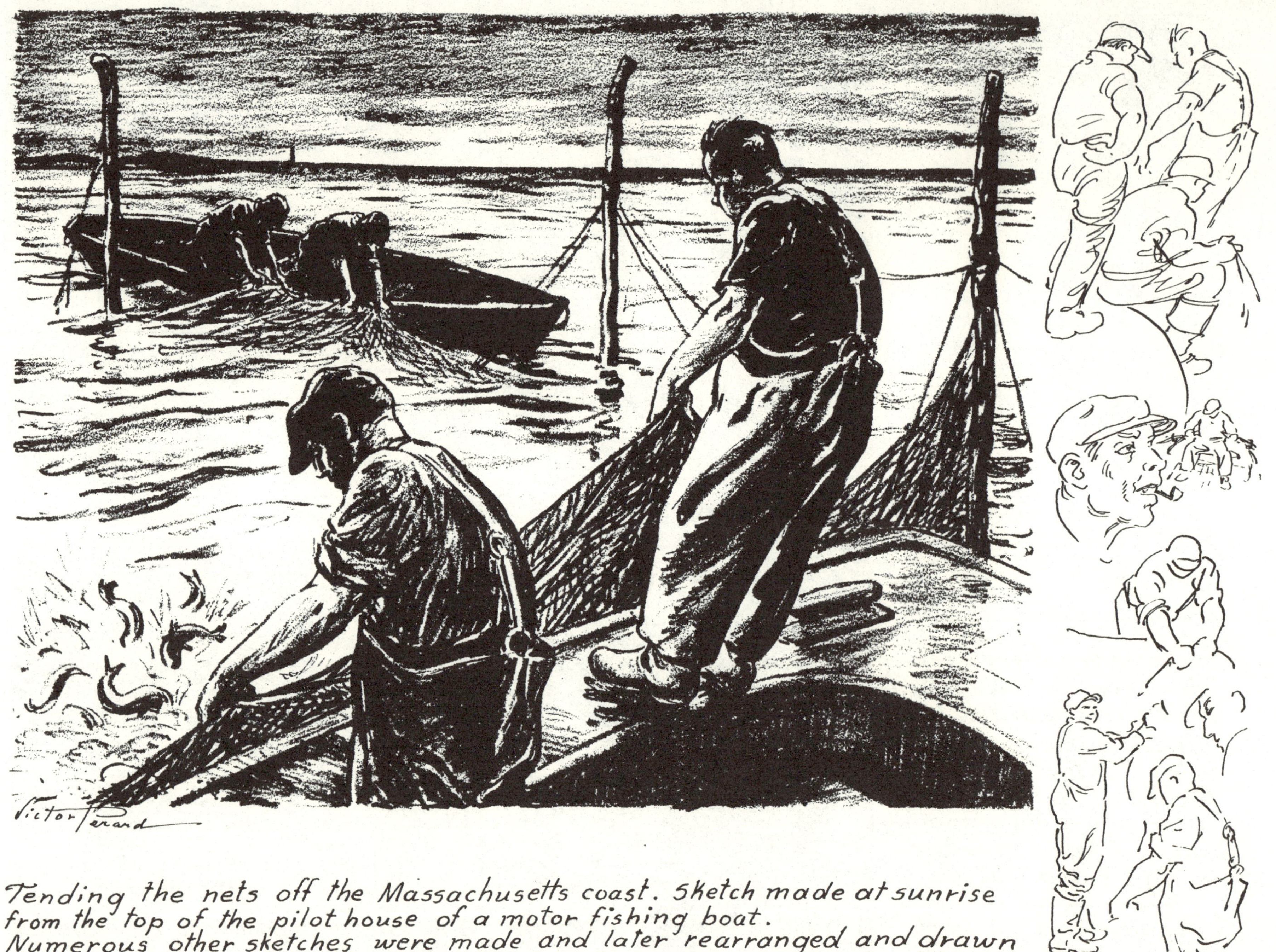

Tending the nets off the Massachusetts coast. Sketch made at sunrise from the top of the pilot house of a motor fishing boat.
Numerous other sketches were made and later rearranged and drawn on lithographic zinc with a grease crayon for reproduction by the lithographic process.

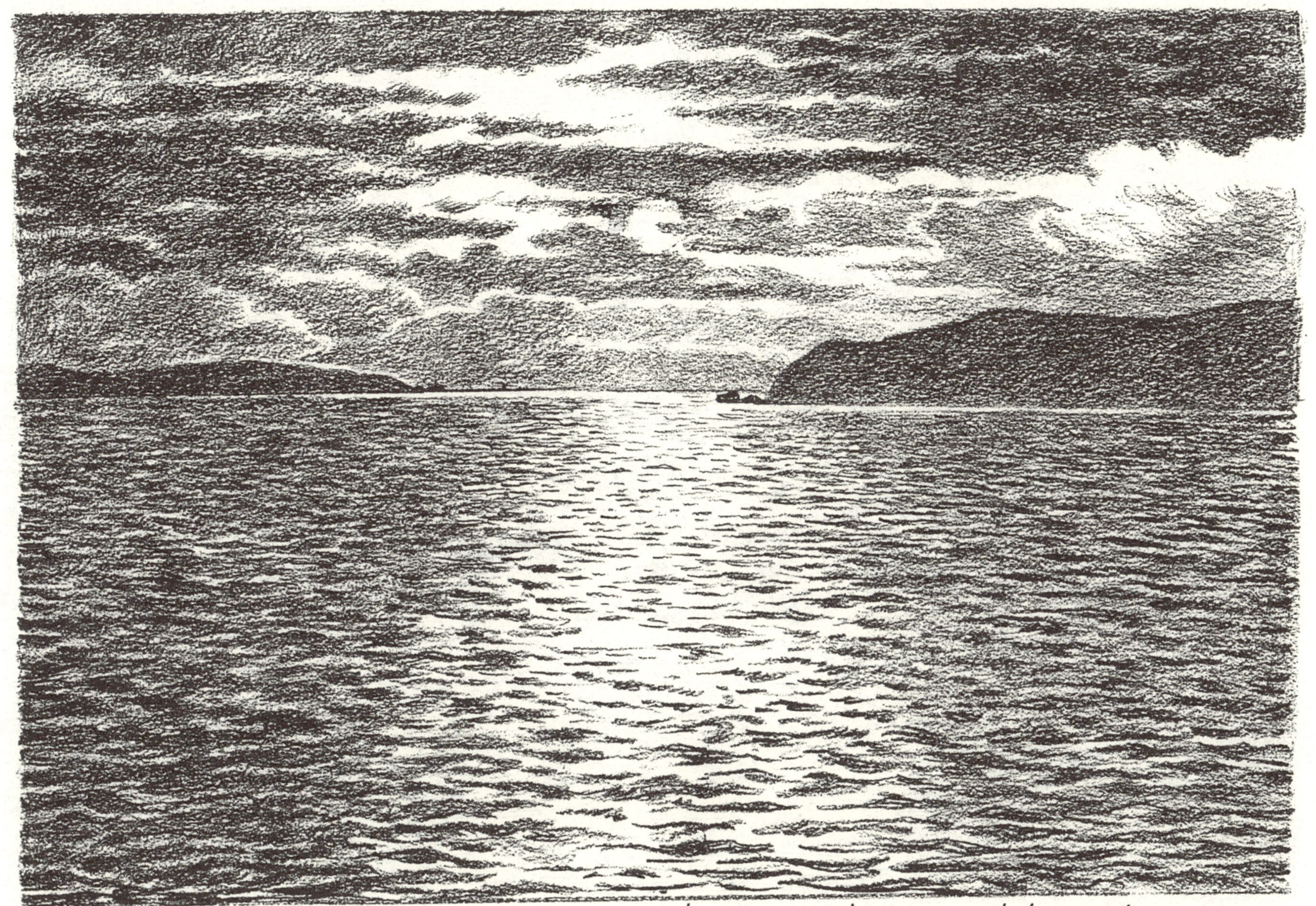

The Golden Gate at sunset over a tranquil sea. Such scenes take patience and should be worked in a quiet mood. The procedure used in making this drawing was to place the horizon line, then outline the clouds, place the sun, indicate the surrounding hills, work up distant ripples first and finish last with the foreground ripples. Shading was done in the same sequence.

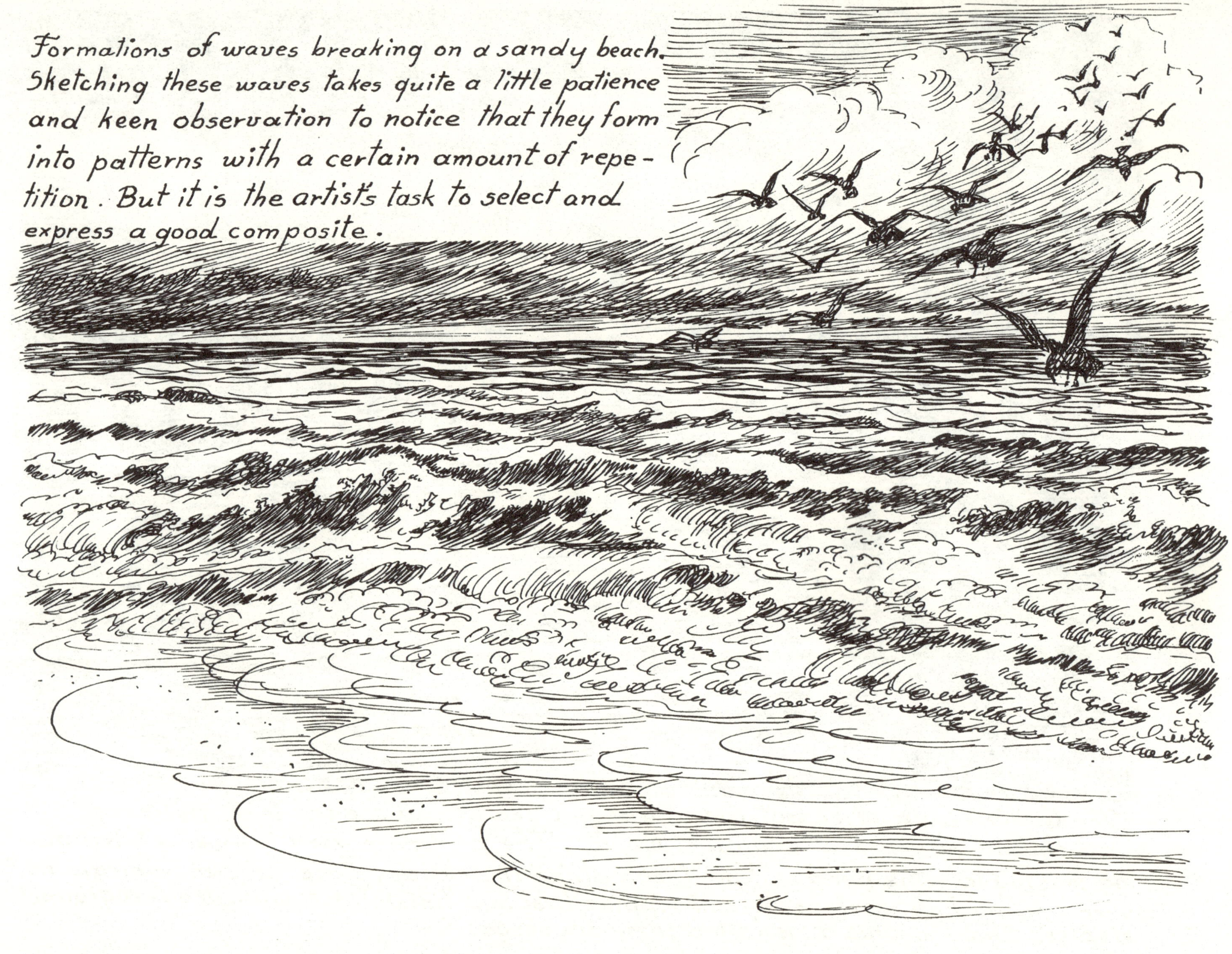

Formations of waves breaking on a sandy beach. Sketching these waves takes quite a little patience and keen observation to notice that they form into patterns with a certain amount of repetition. But it is the artist's task to select and express a good composite.

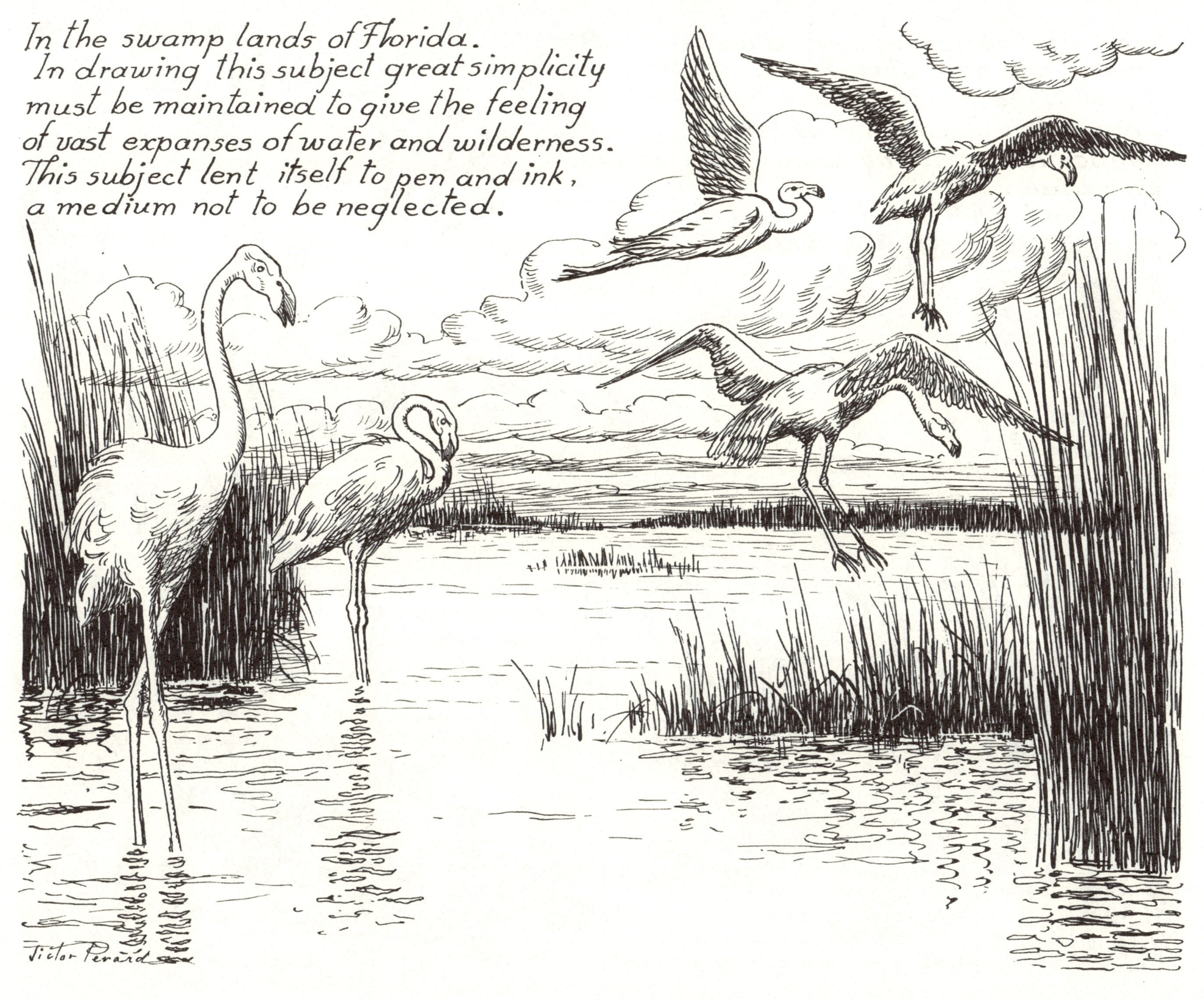

In the swamp lands of Florida.
In drawing this subject great simplicity must be maintained to give the feeling of vast expanses of water and wilderness. This subject lent itself to pen and ink, a medium not to be neglected.

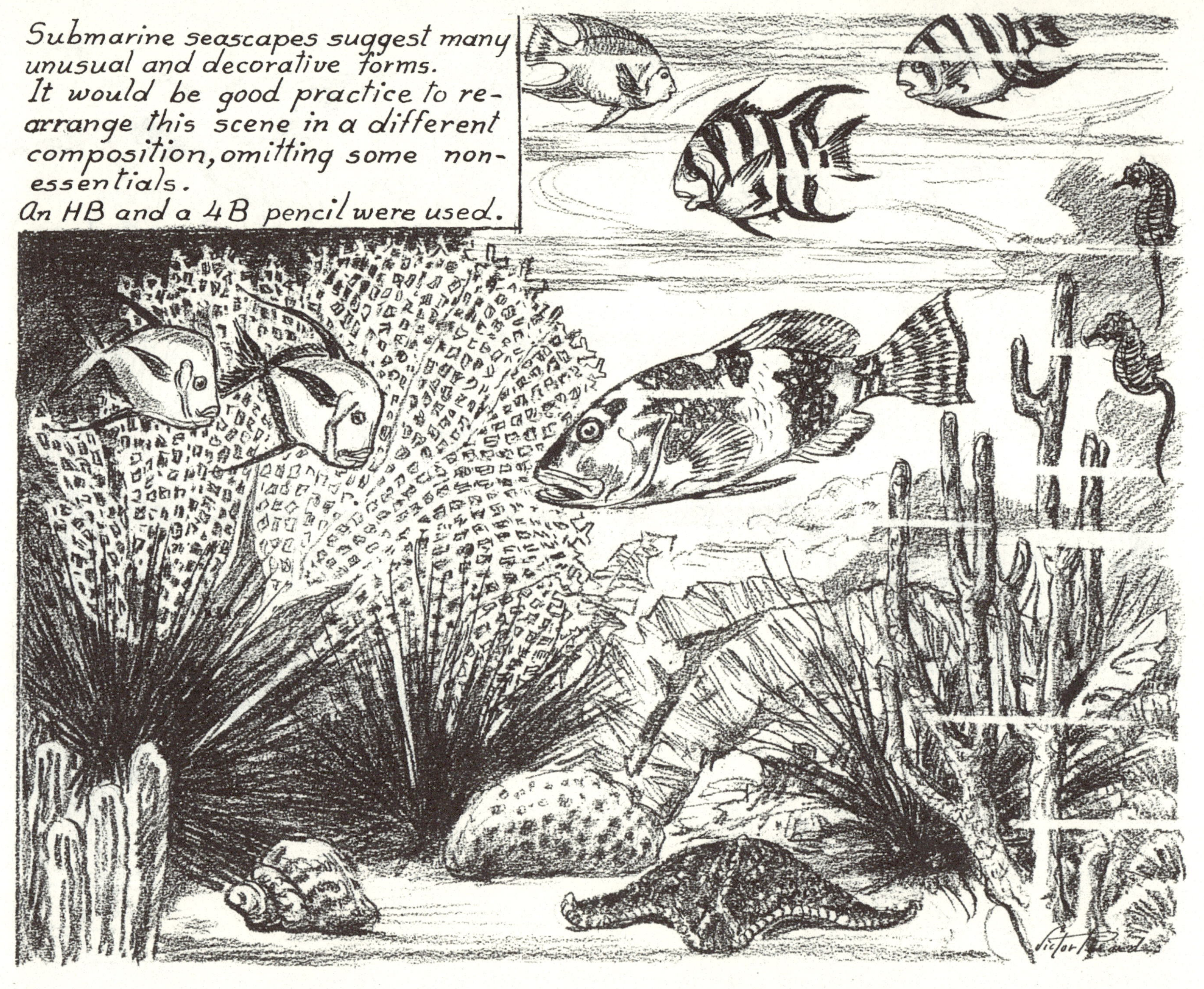

Submarine seascapes suggest many unusual and decorative forms.
It would be good practice to rearrange this scene in a different composition, omitting some nonessentials.
An HB and a 4B pencil were used.

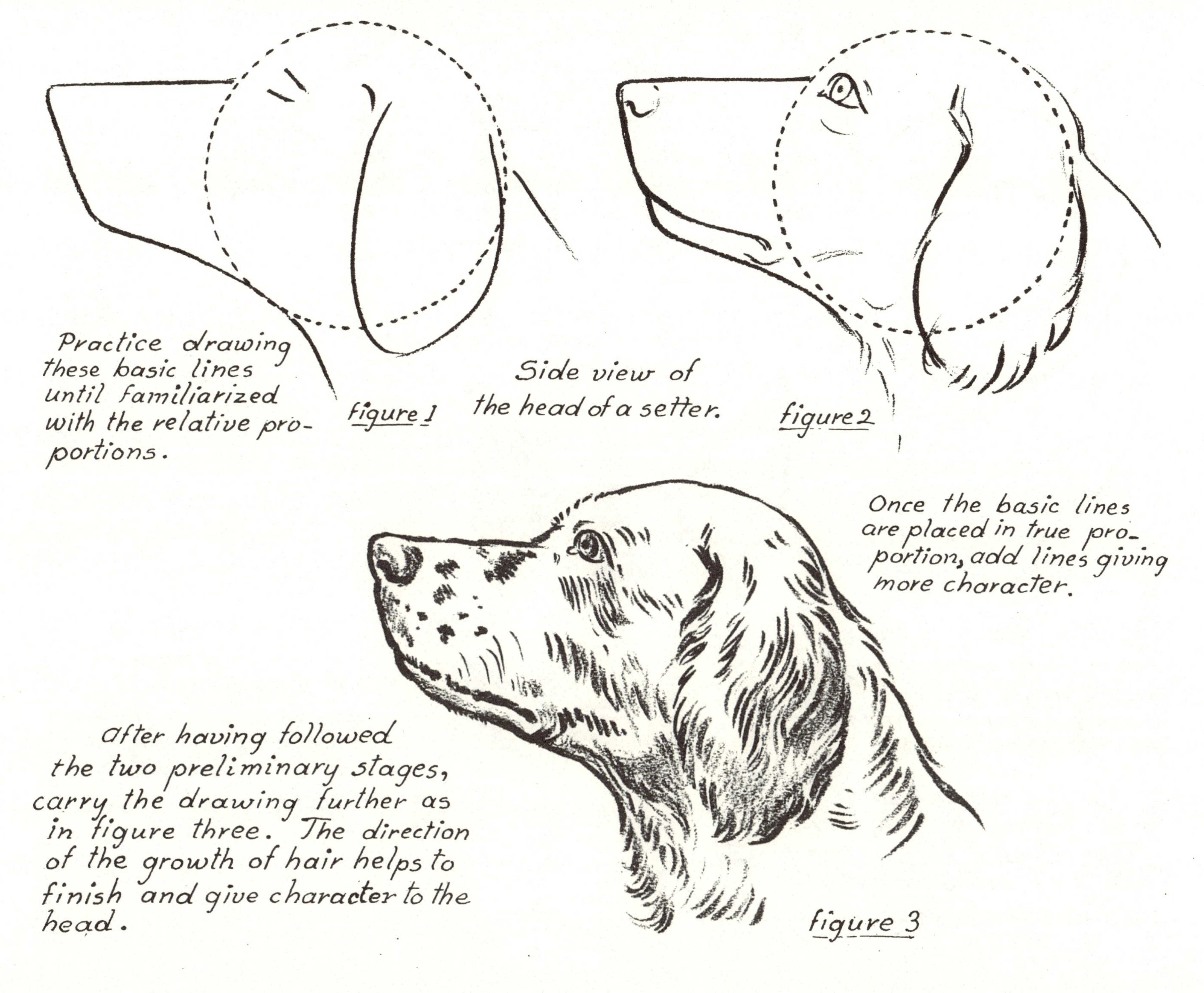
Practice drawing these basic lines until familiarized with the relative proportions.
figure 1
Side view of the head of a setter.
figure 2
Once the basic lines are placed in true proportion, add lines giving more character.
After having followed the two preliminary stages, carry the drawing further as in figure three. The direction of the growth of hair helps to finish and give character to the head.
figure 3

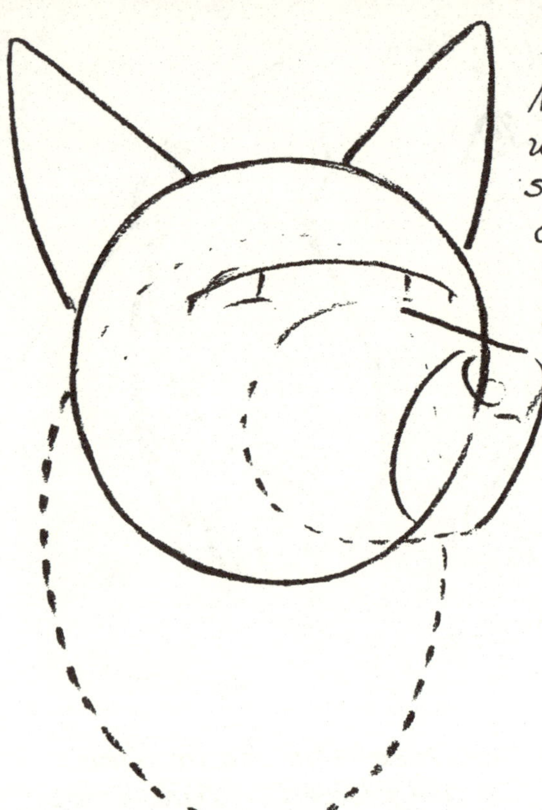

German Shepherd dog's head
Make a drawing of this whole page of the three stages of the drawing of this head.
It is important to form the habit of starting any subject with fundamental lines, as later it will be necessary to discover them yourself, on other subjects.

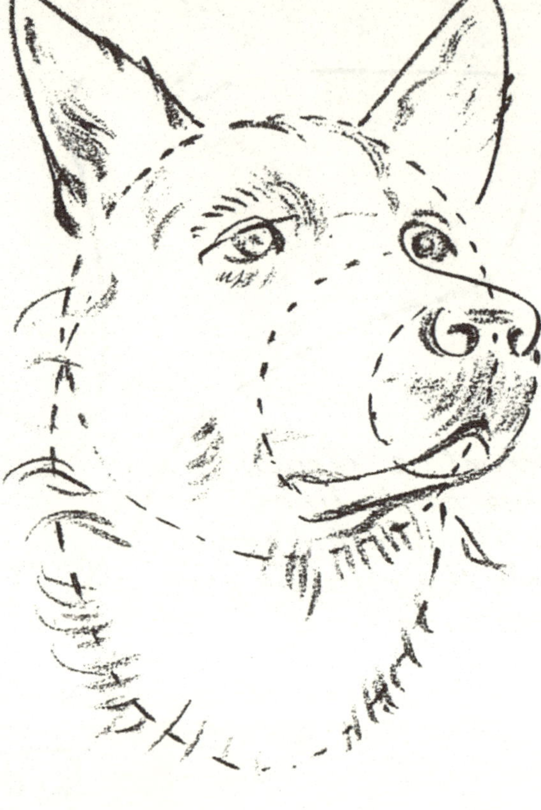

Practice drawing the above few lines on a separate piece of paper before starting on the final copy.

Draw the fundamental lines firmly but lightly. They should be lightened with a rubber before starting to finish the head.

Draw neatly so the work has a professional appearance.
Use the soft pencil to finish, and wear the point down to obtain broader strokes.

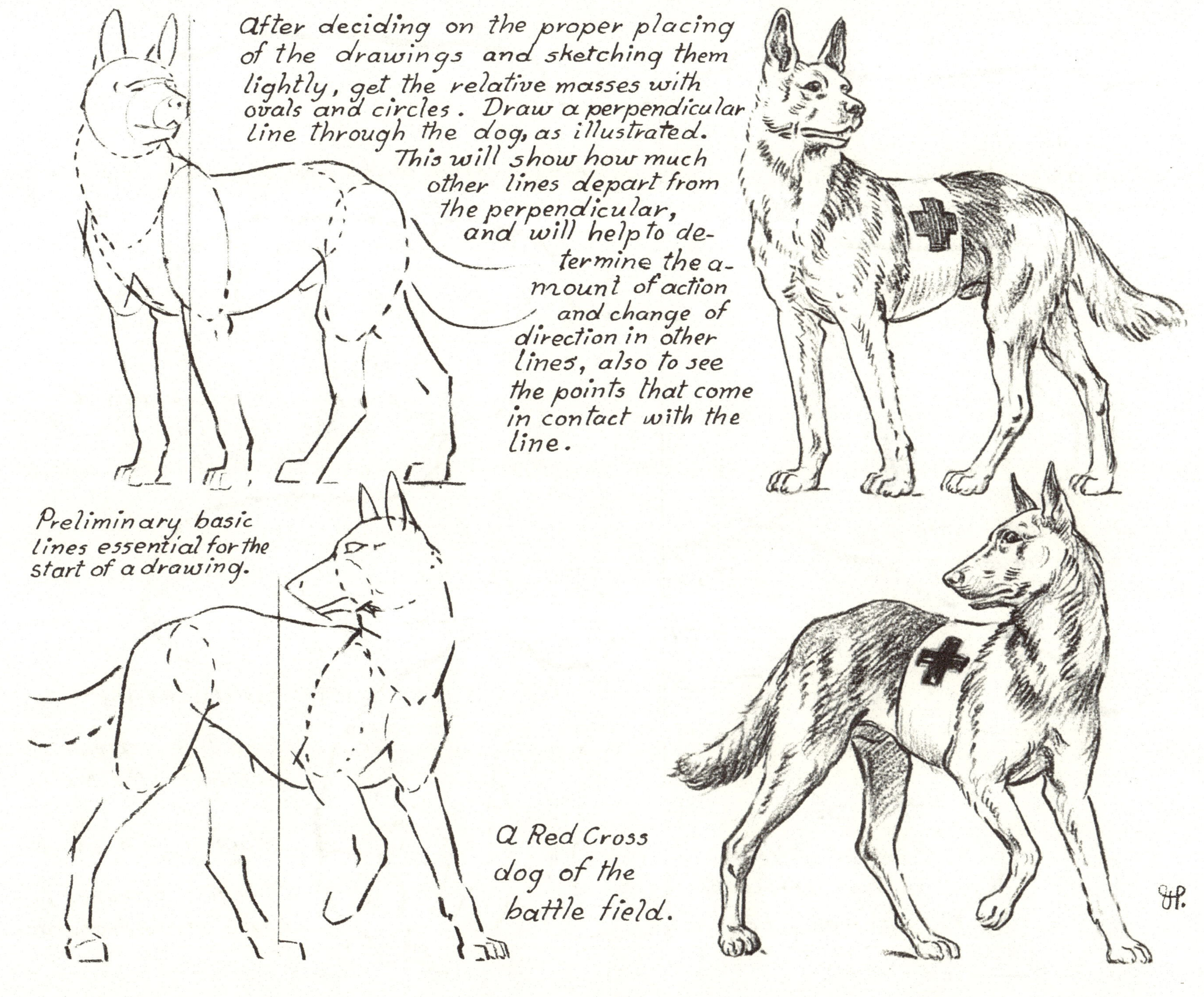
After deciding on the proper placing of the drawings and sketching them lightly, get the relative masses with ovals and circles. Draw a perpendicular line through the dog, as illustrated. This will show how much other lines depart from the perpendicular, and will help to determine the amount of action and change of direction in other lines, also to see the points that come in contact with the line.
Preliminary basic lines essential for the start of a drawing.
A Red Cross dog of the battle field.
J.P.

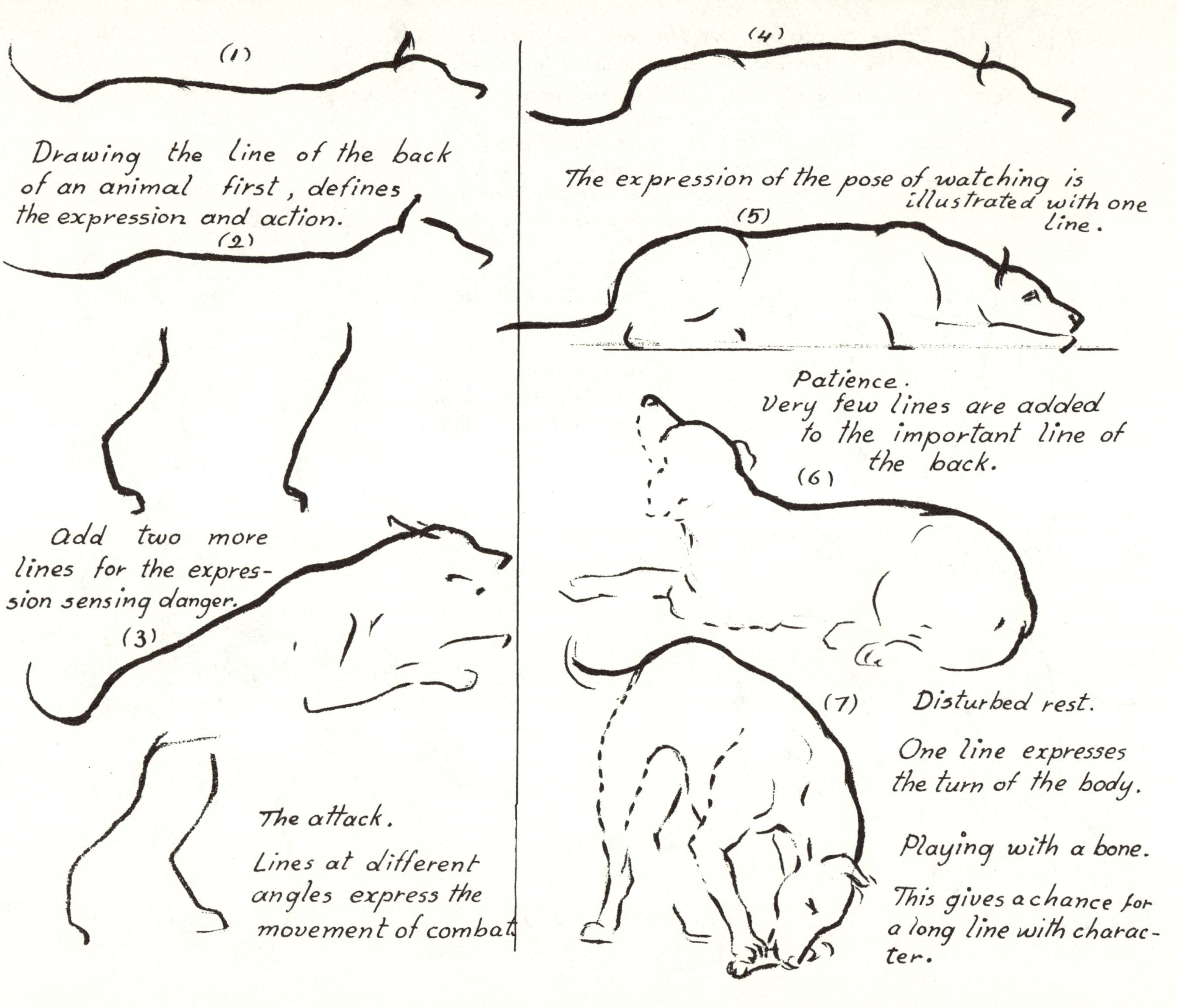
(1)
Drawing the line of the back of an animal first, defines the expression and action.
(2)
Add two more lines for the expression sensing danger.
(3)
The attack.
Lines at different angles express the movement of combat.
(4)
The expression of the pose of watching is illustrated with one line.
(5)
Patience.
Very few lines are added to the important line of the back.
(6)
(7)
Disturbed rest.
One line expresses the turn of the body.
Playing with a bone.
This gives a chance for a long line with character.

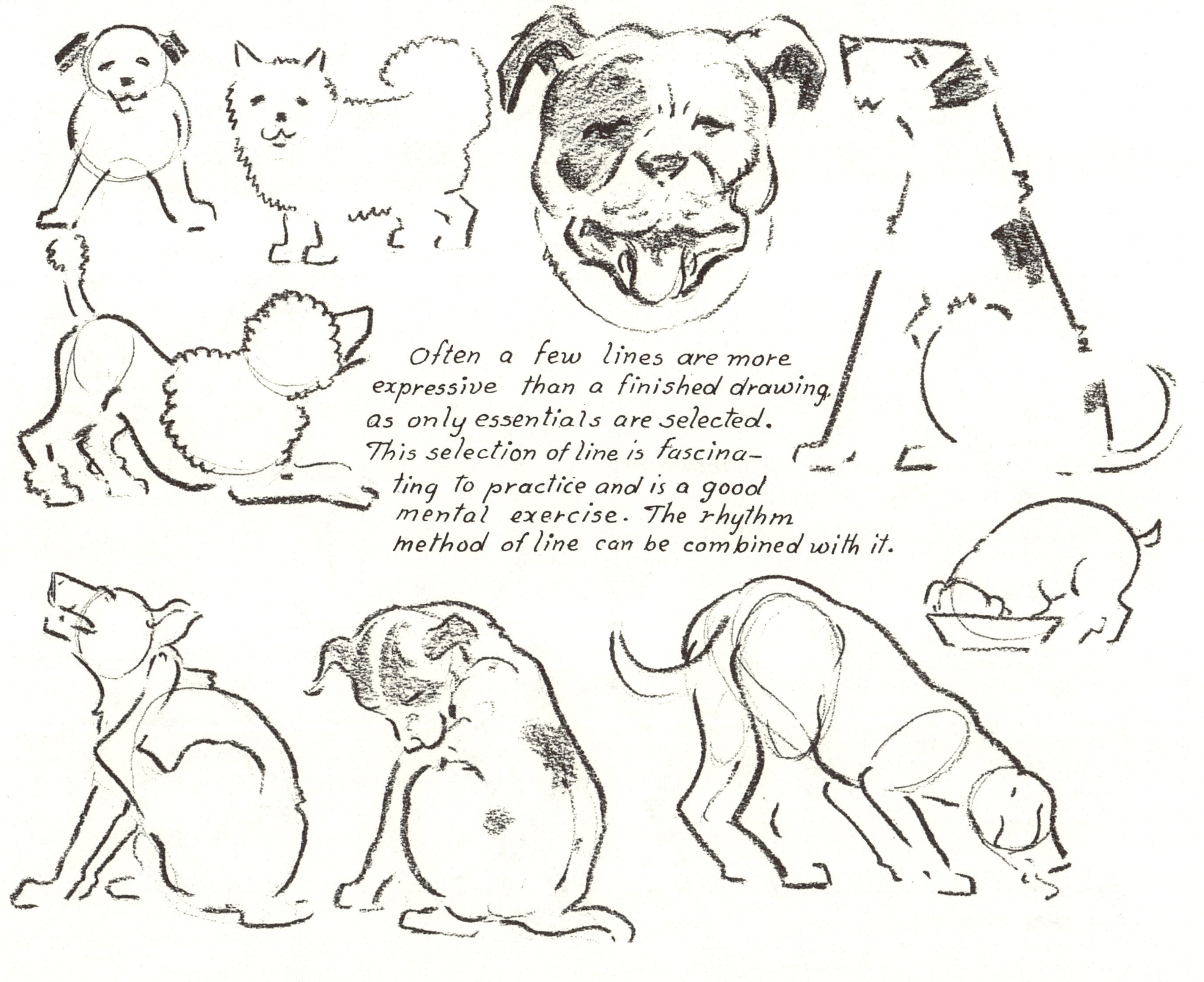
Often a few lines are more
expressive than a finished drawing,
as only essentials are selected.
This selection of line is fascinating to practice and is a good
mental exercise. The rhythm
method of line can be combined with it.

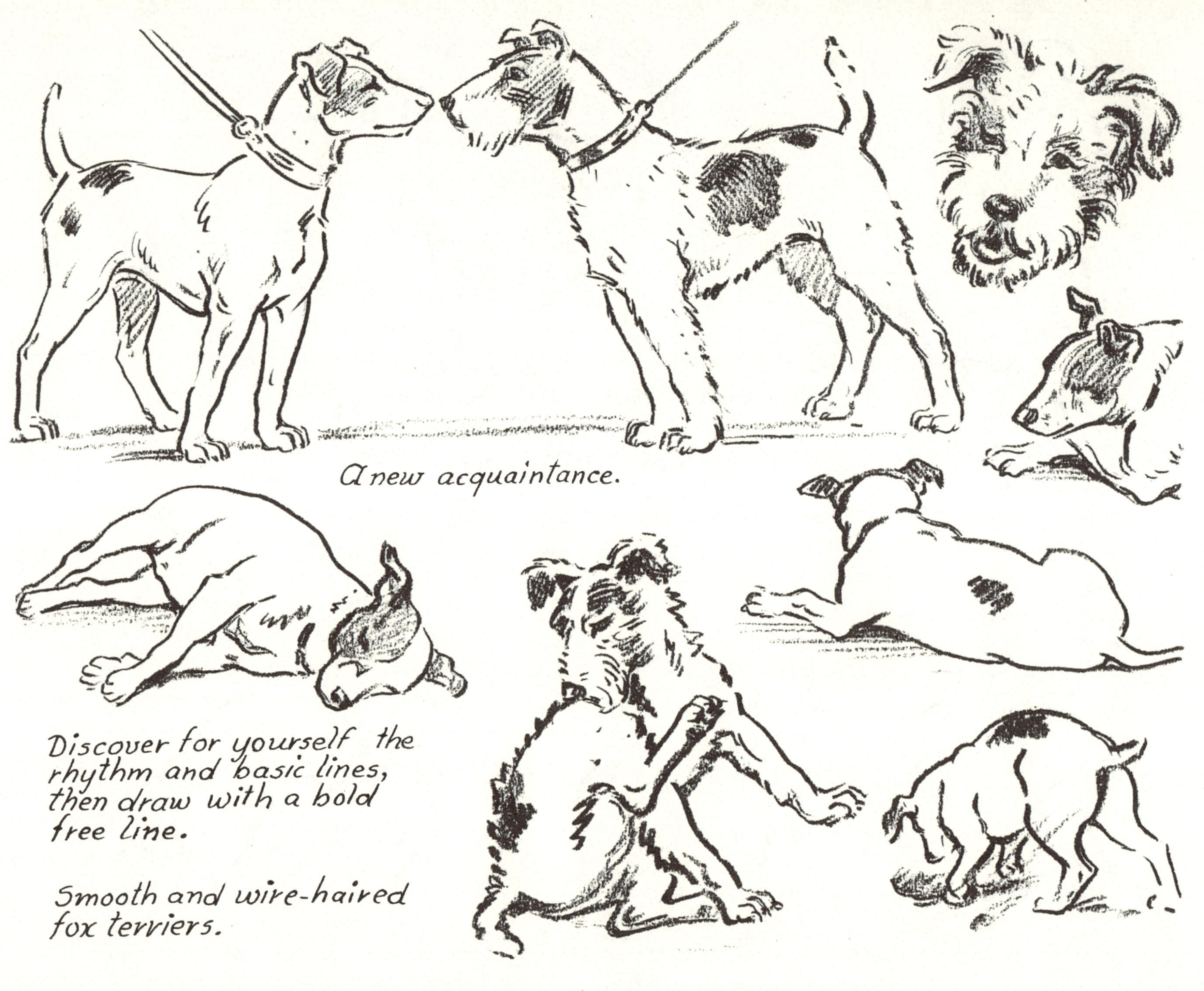

A new acquaintance.

Discover for yourself the rhythm and basic lines, then draw with a bold free line.

Smooth and wire-haired fox terriers.

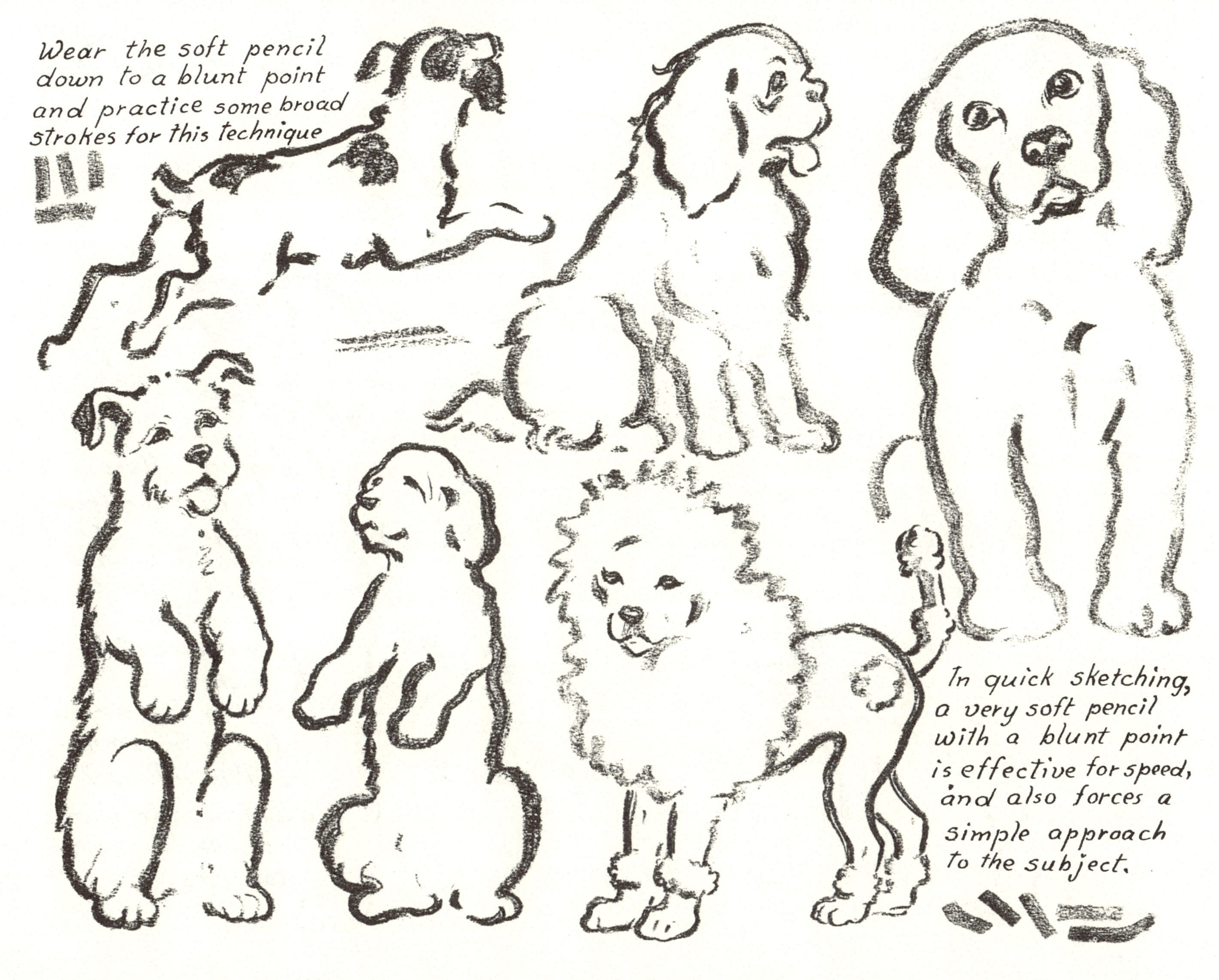
Wear the soft pencil down to a blunt point and practice some broad strokes for this technique
In quick sketching, a very soft pencil with a blunt point is effective for speed, and also forces a simple approach to the subject.

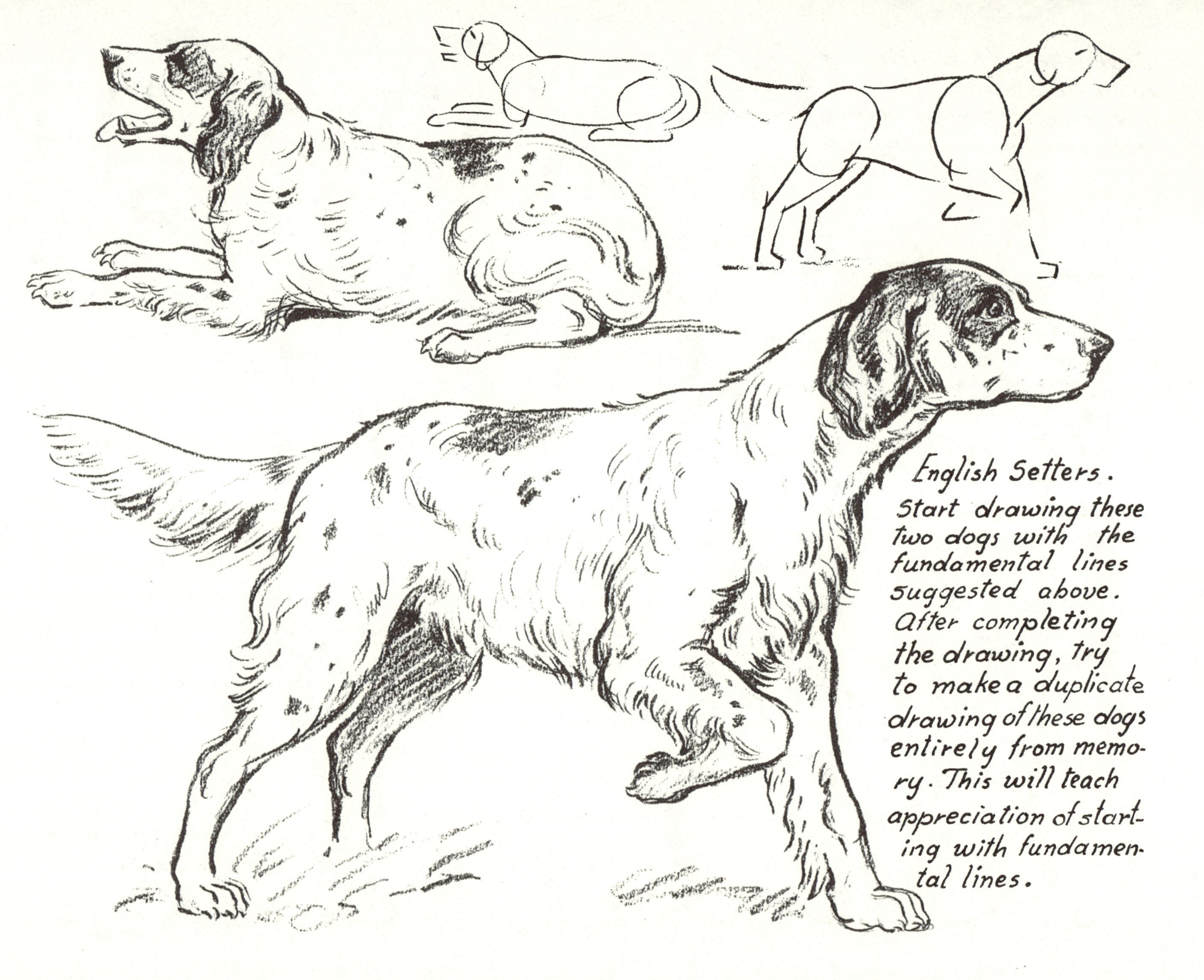
English Setters.
Start drawing these two dogs with the fundamental lines suggested above. After completing the drawing, try to make a duplicate drawing of these dogs entirely from memory. This will teach appreciation of starting with fundamental lines.

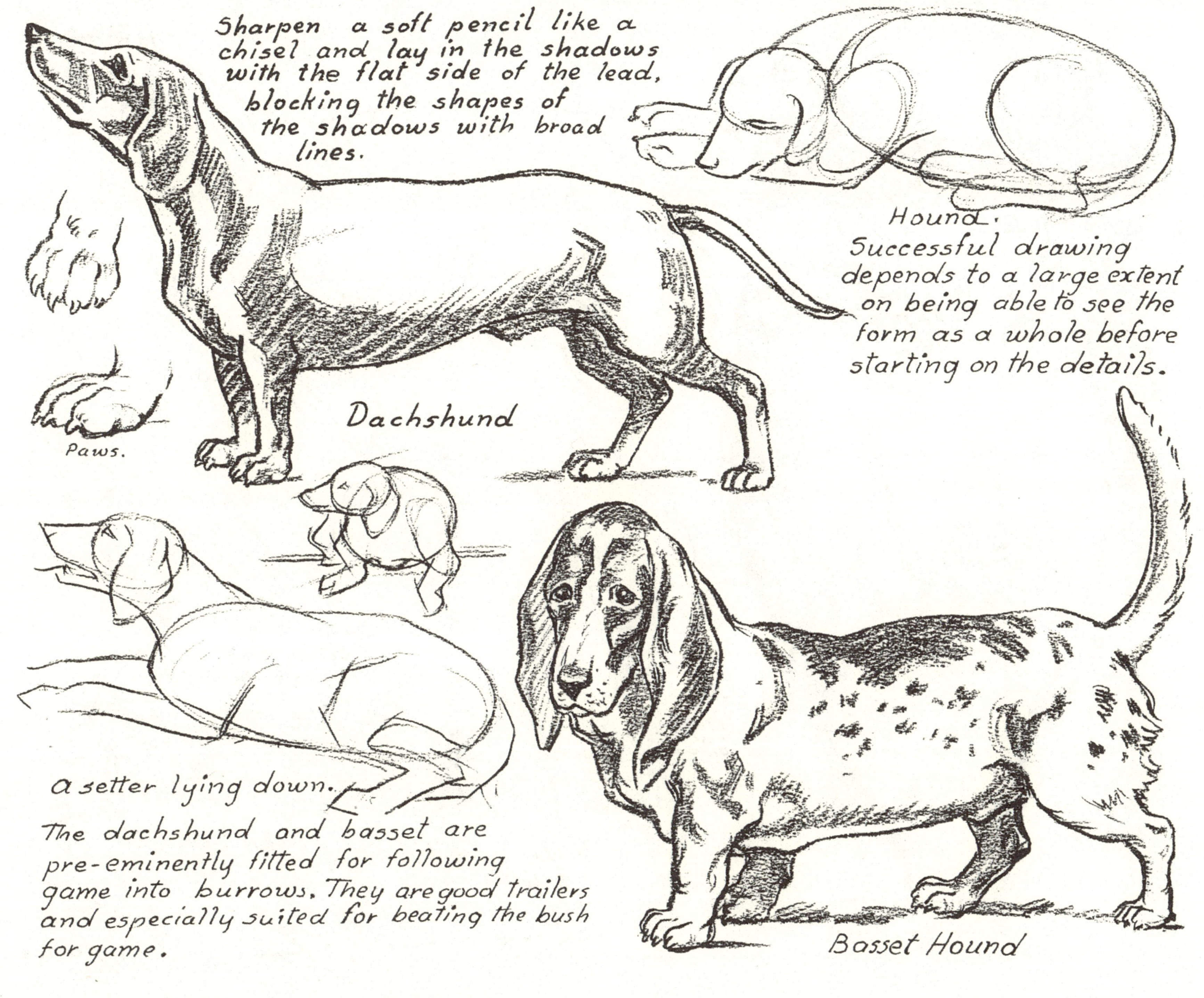
Sharpen a soft pencil like a chisel and lay in the shadows with the flat side of the lead, blocking the shapes of the shadows with broad lines.
Hound.
Successful drawing depends to a large extent on being able to see the form as a whole before starting on the details.
Paws.
Dachshund
a setter lying down.
The dachshund and basset are pre-eminently fitted for following game into burrows. They are good trailers and especially suited for beating the bush for game.
Basset Hound

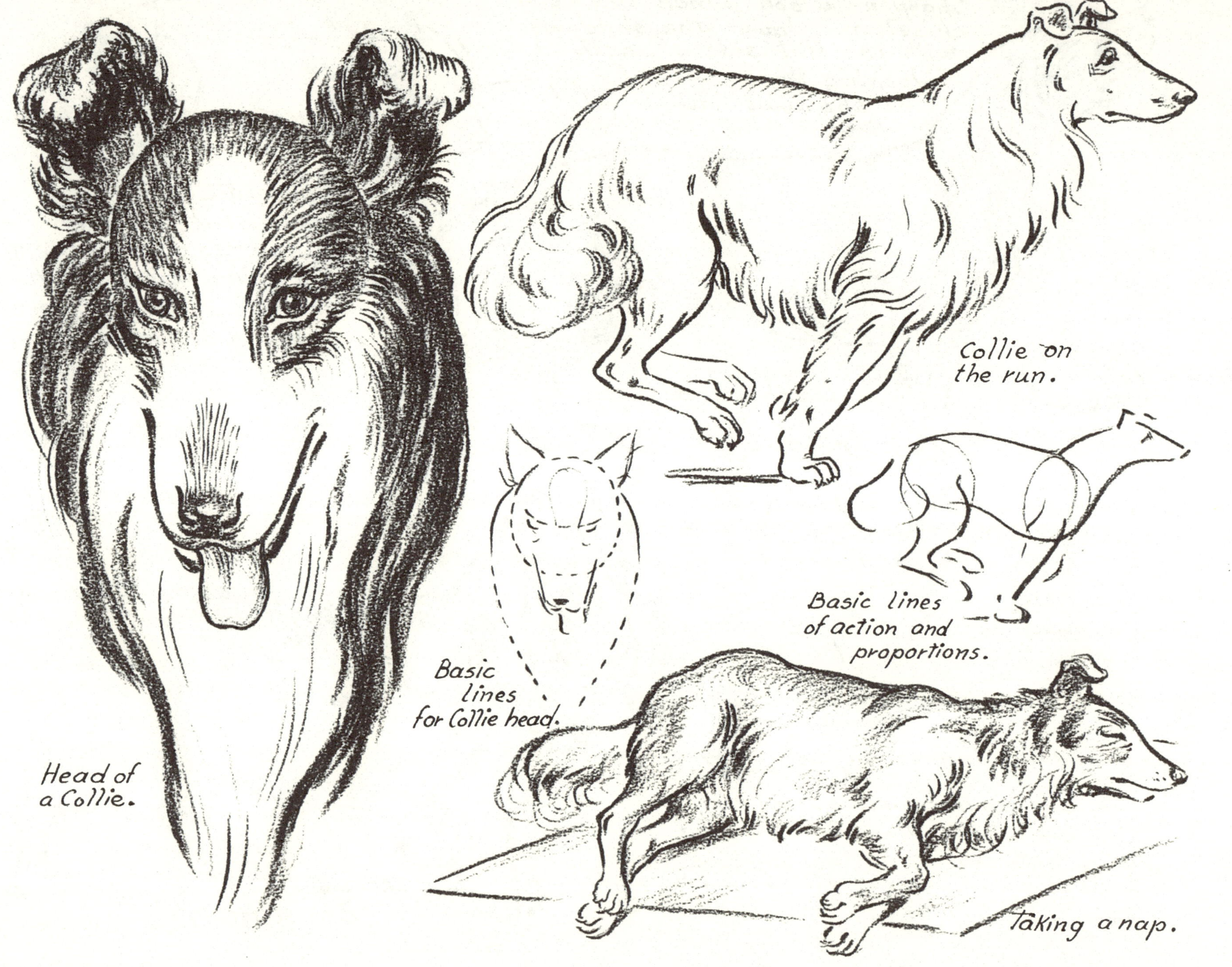
Collie on
the run.
Basic lines
of action and
proportions.
Basic
lines
for Collie head.
Head of
a Collie.
Taking a nap.

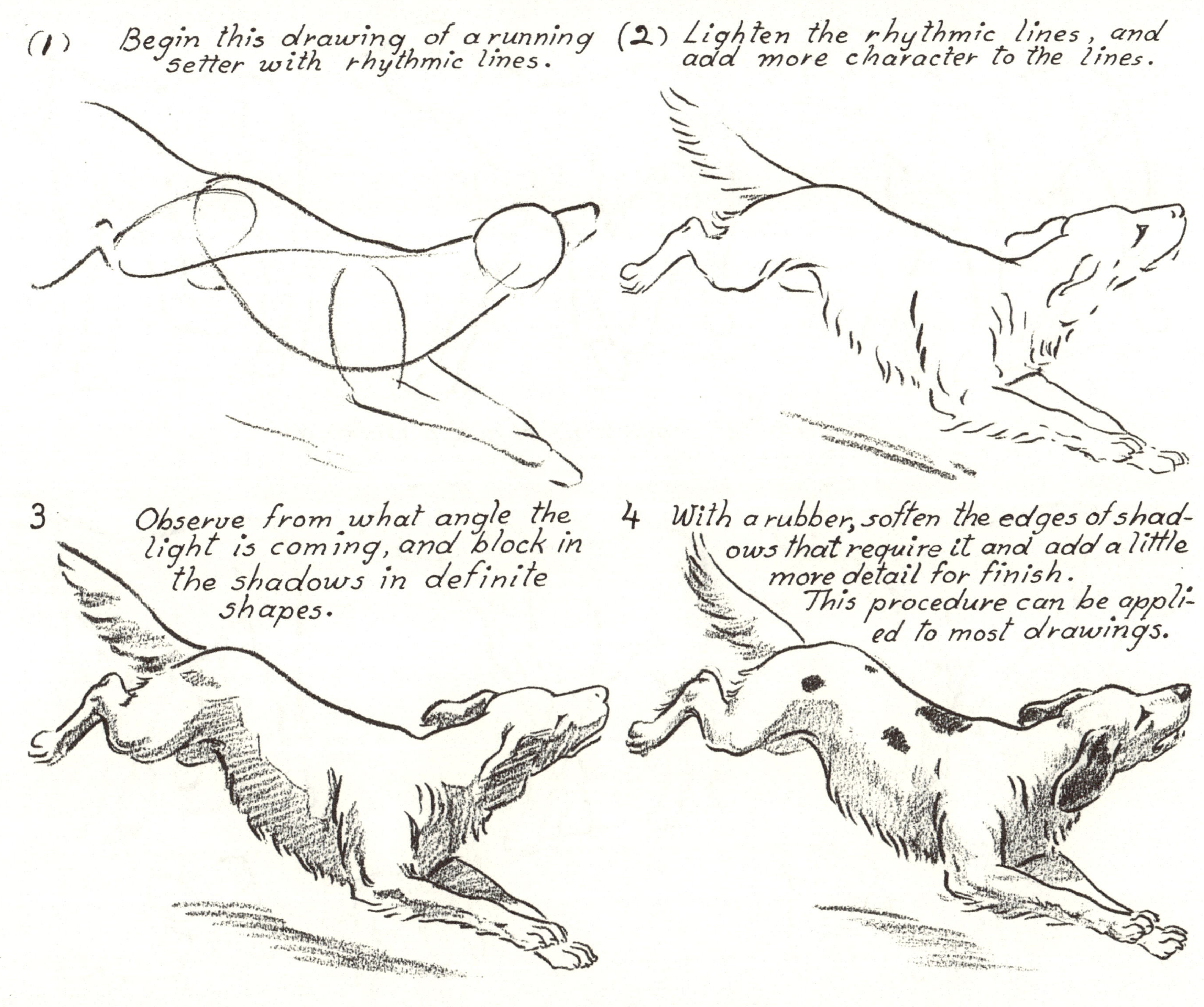
(1) Begin this drawing of a running setter with rhythmic lines.
(2) Lighten the rhythmic lines, and add more character to the lines.
3 Observe from what angle the light is coming, and block in the shadows in definite shapes.
4 With a rubber, soften the edges of shadows that require it and add a little more detail for finish.
This procedure can be applied to most drawings.

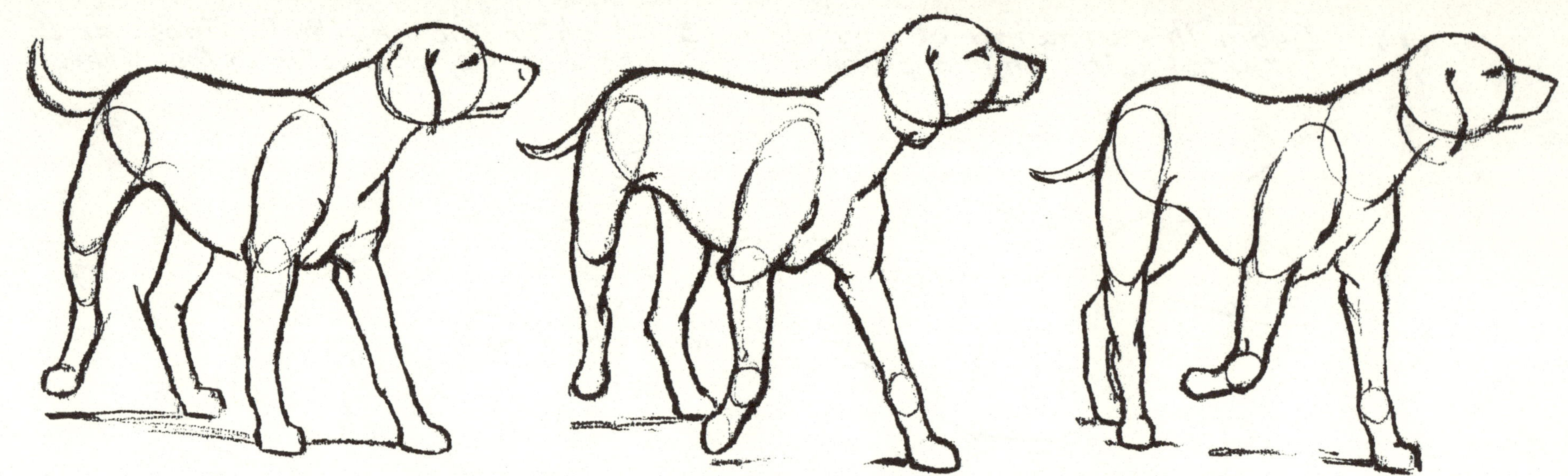

Progressive movements of a dog walking

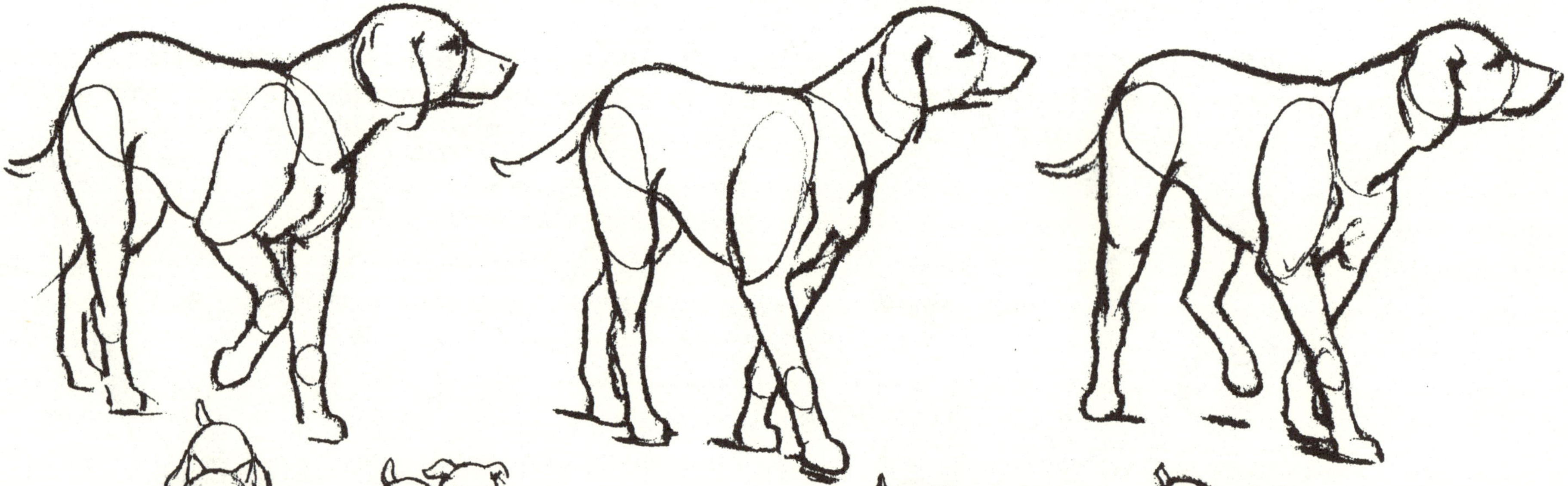

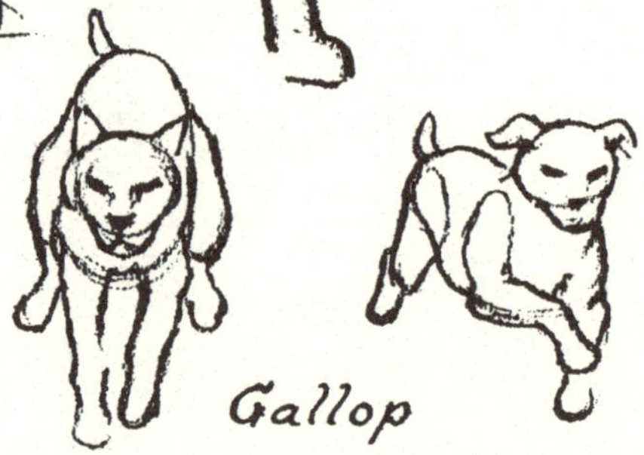

Gallop

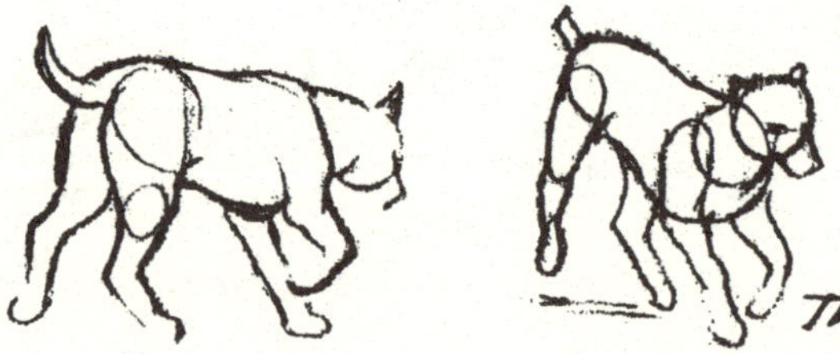

The trot

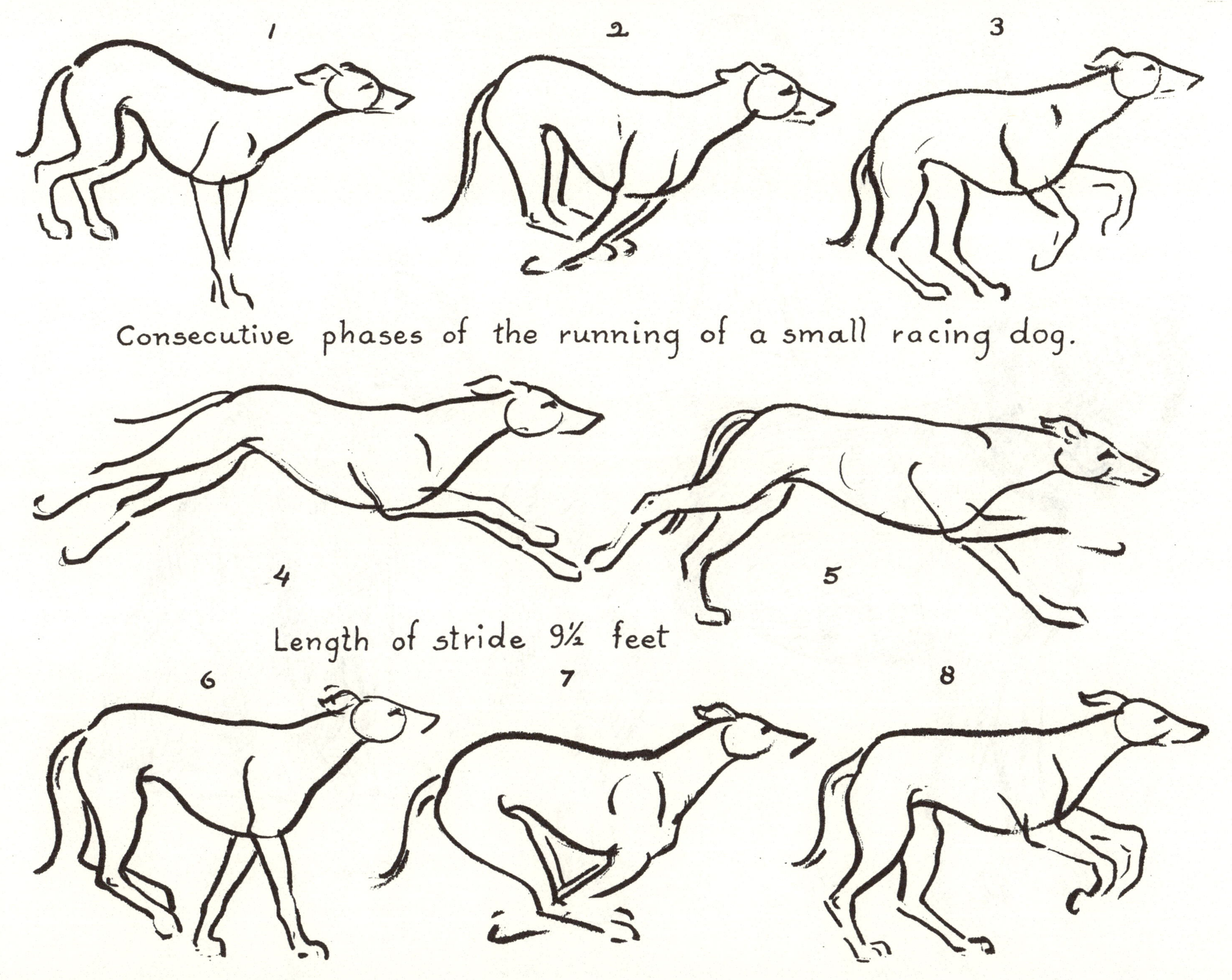

Consecutive phases of the running of a small racing dog.

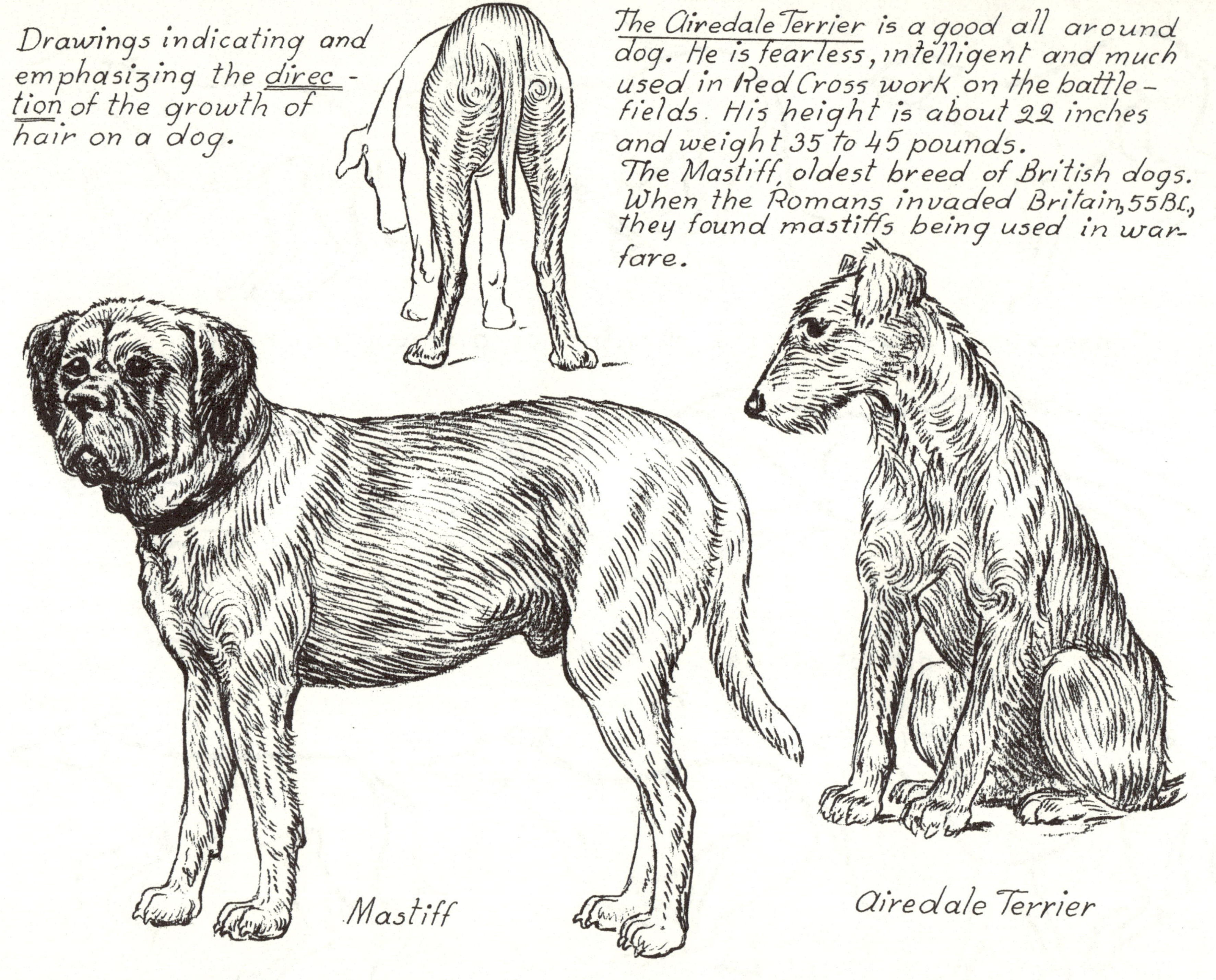

Mastiff

Airedale Terrier

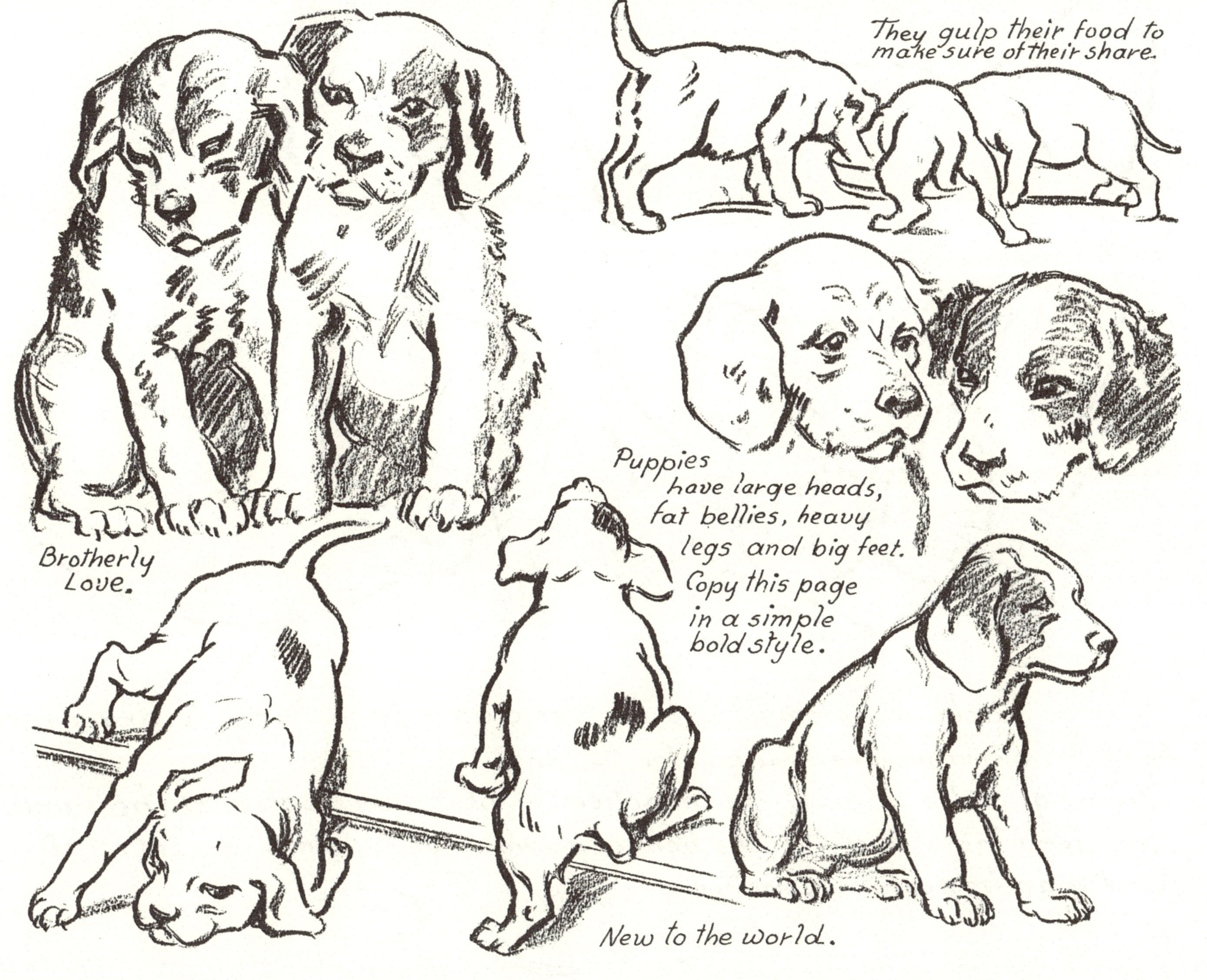
They gulp their food to make sure of their share.
Brotherly Love.
Puppies have large heads, fat bellies, heavy legs and big feet.
Copy this page in a simple bold style.
New to the world.

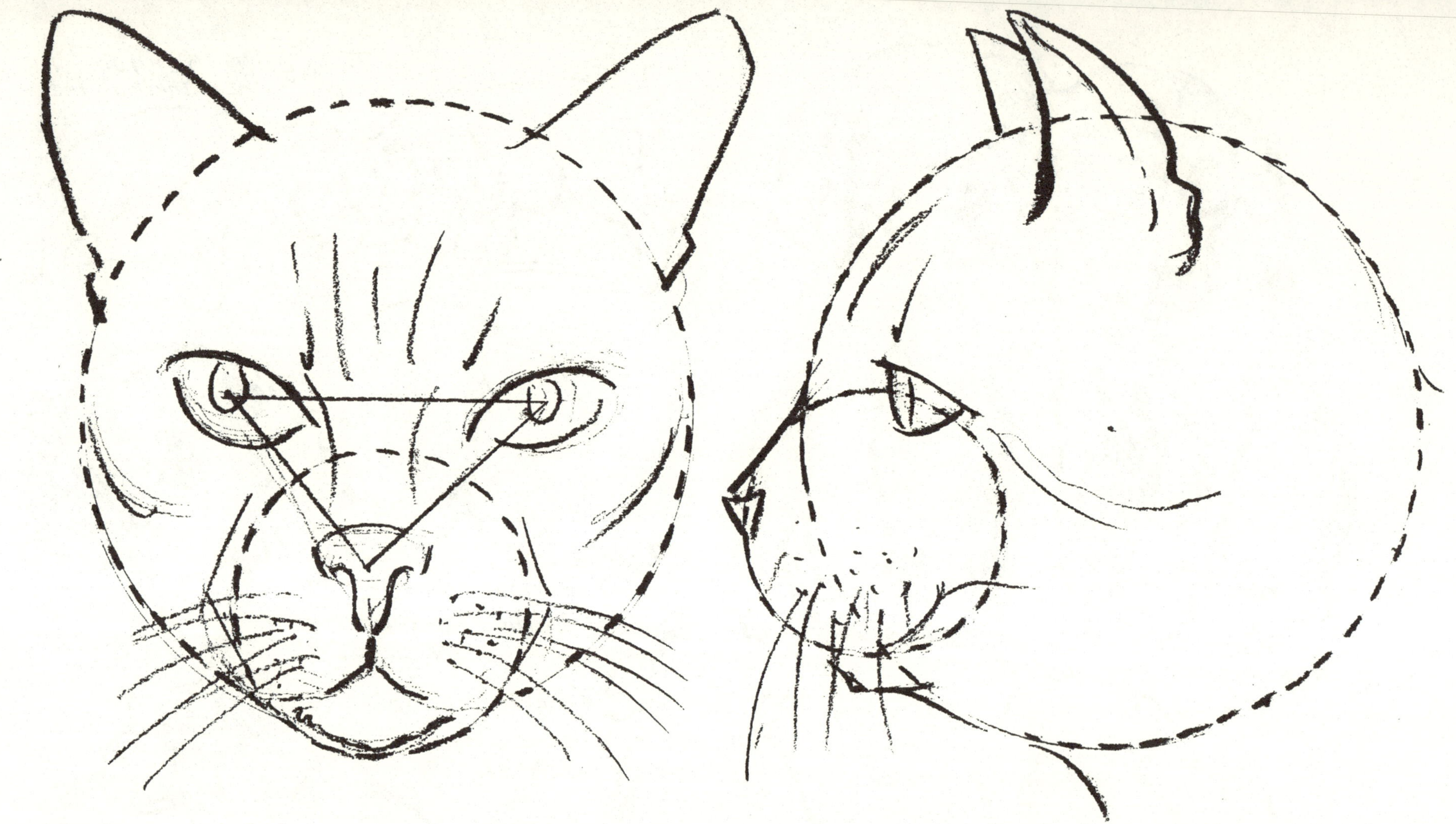

A large circle and a small one are basic lines in helping to draw a cat's head. The smaller one is used for the nose.
Drawing circles is excellent practice in obtaining control of the hand and drawing straight lines between two given points gives facility and is an important practice.

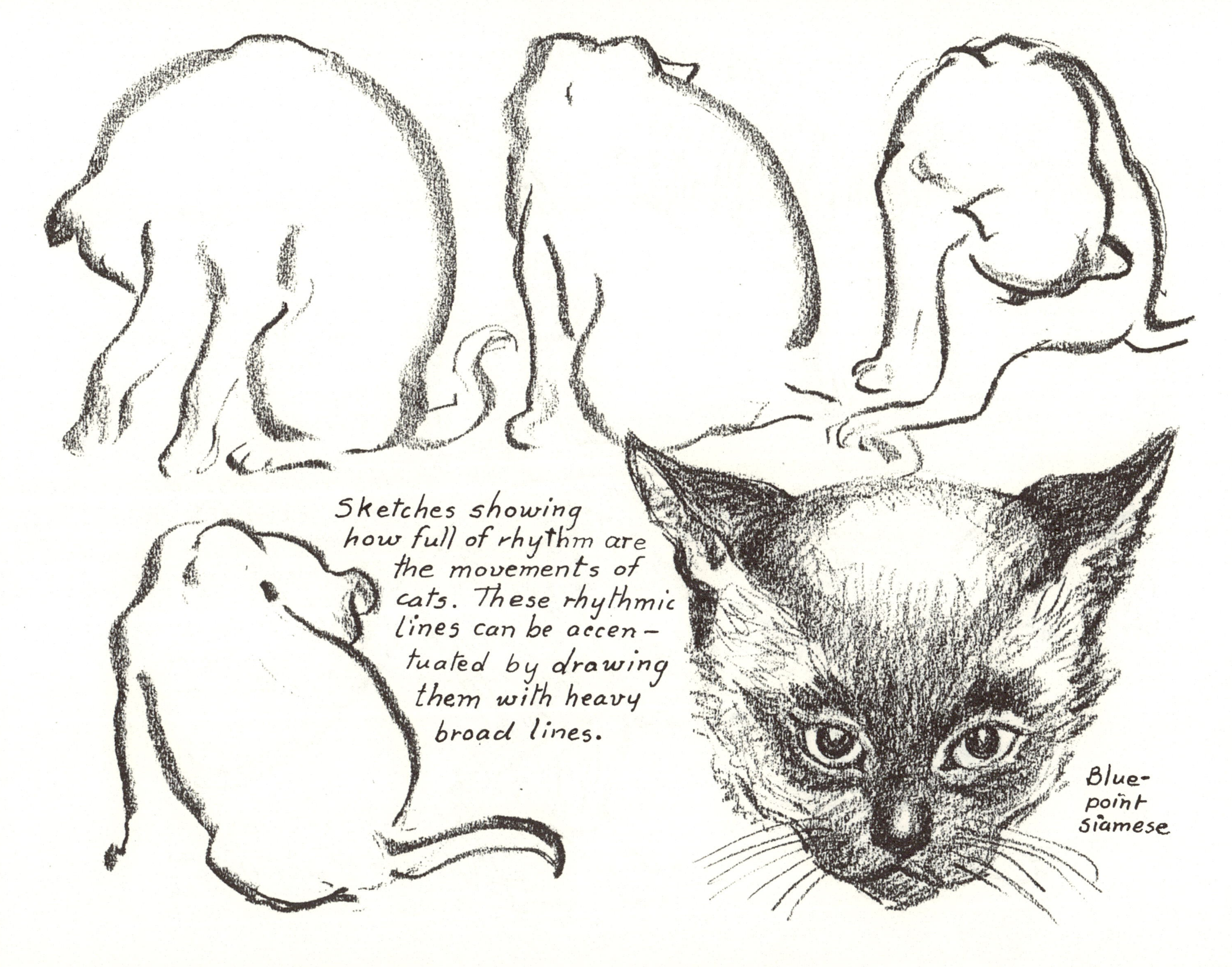
Sketches showing how full of rhythm are the movements of cats. These rhythmic lines can be accen-tuated by drawing them with heavy broad lines.
Blue-point Siamese

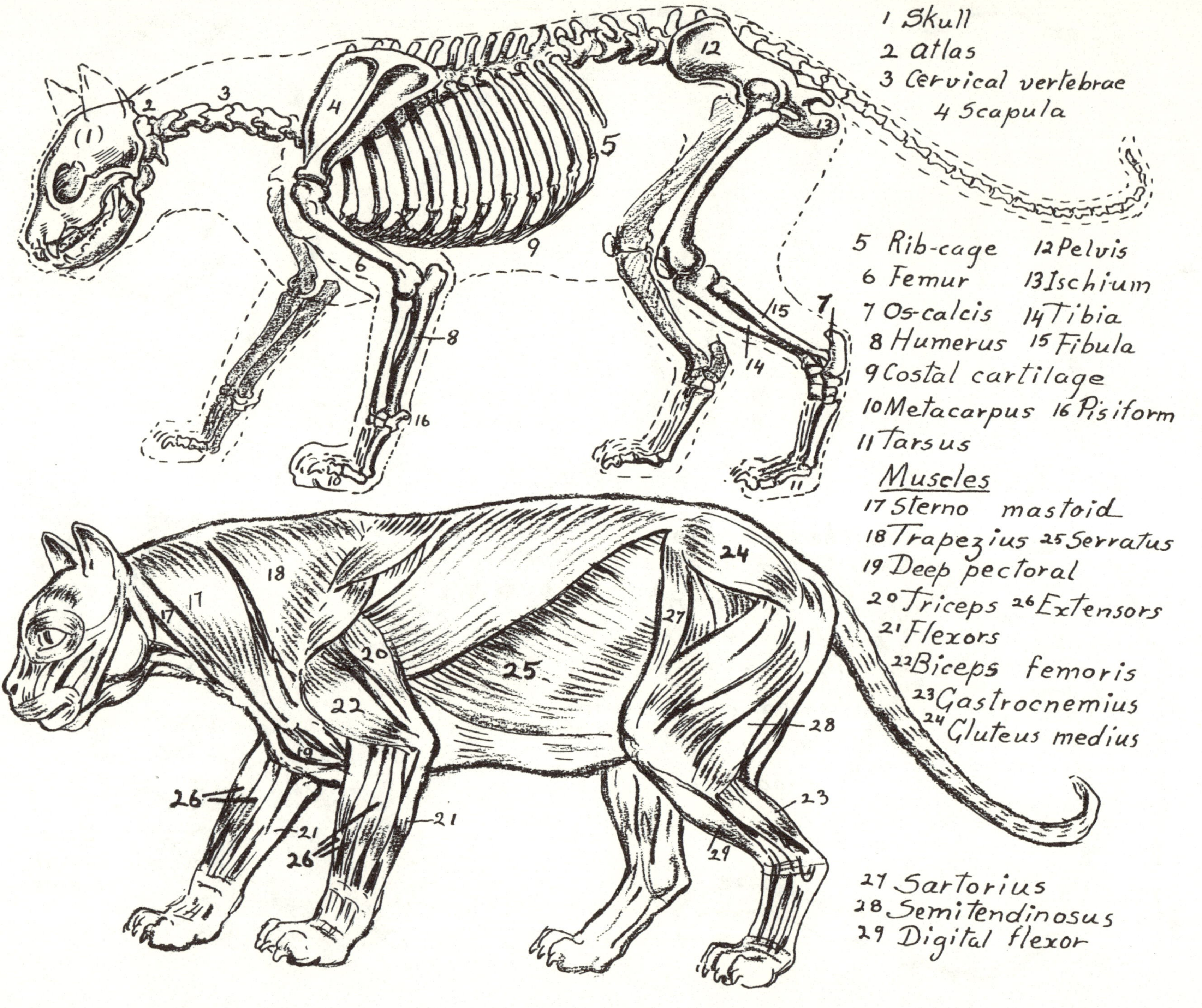
1 Skull
2 Atlas
3 Cervical vertebrae
4 Scapula
5 Rib-cage
12 Pelvis
6 Femur
13 Ischium
7 Os-calcis
14 Tibia
8 Humerus
15 Fibula
9 Costal cartilage
10 Metacarpus
16 Pisiform
11 Tarsus
Muscles
17 Sterno mastoid
18 Trapezius
25 Serratus
19 Deep pectoral
20 Triceps
26 Extensors
21 Flexors
22 Biceps femoris
23 Gastrocnemius
24 Gluteus medius
27 Sartorius
28 Semitendinosus
29 Digital flexor

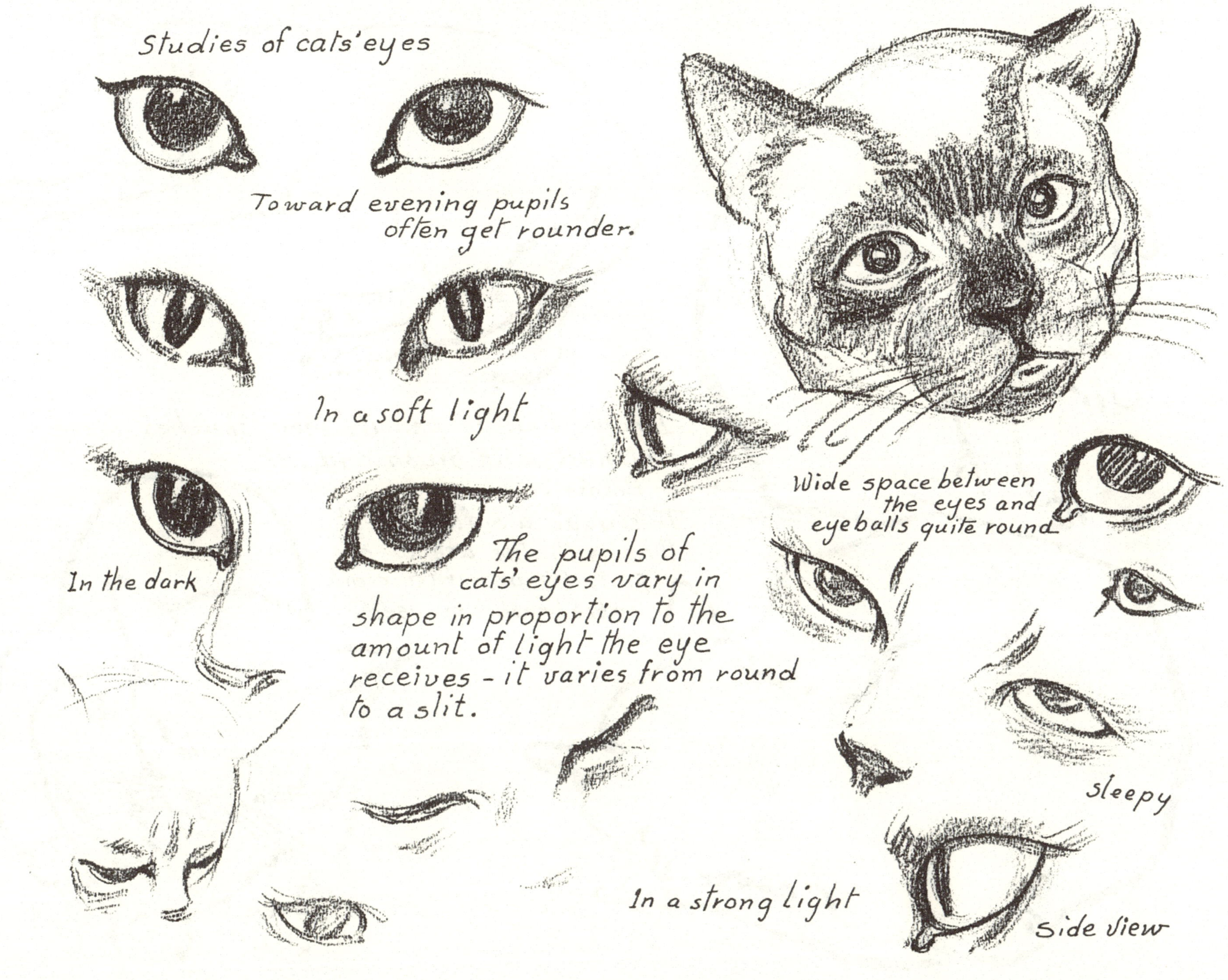
Studies of cats' eyes
Toward evening pupils often get rounder.
In a soft light
In the dark
The pupils of cats' eyes vary in shape in proportion to the amount of light the eye receives - it varies from round to a slit.
Wide space between the eyes and eyeballs quite round
sleepy
In a strong light
Side view

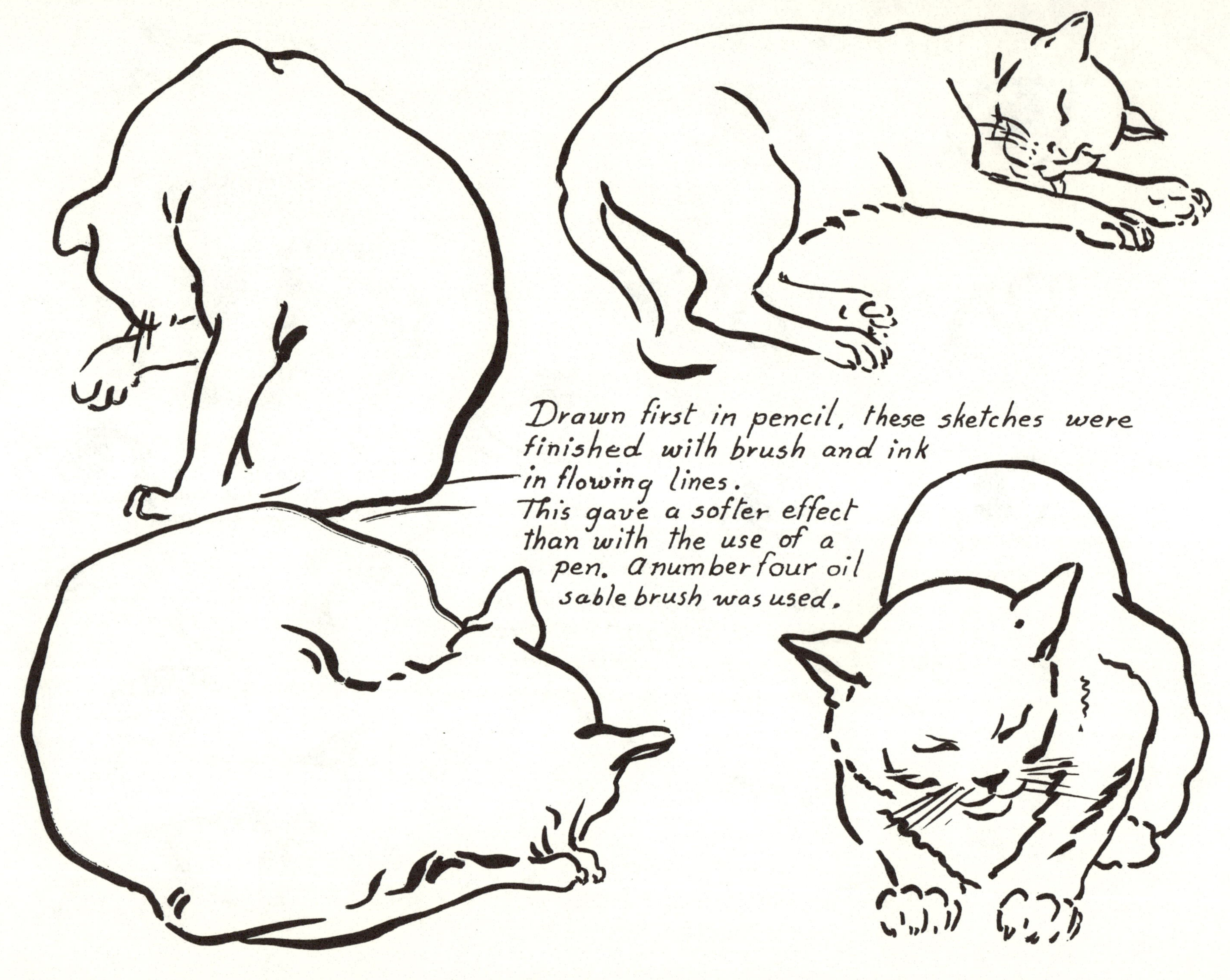
Drawn first in pencil, these sketches were
finished with brush and ink
in flowing lines.
This gave a softer effect
than with the use of a
pen. A number four oil
sable brush was used.

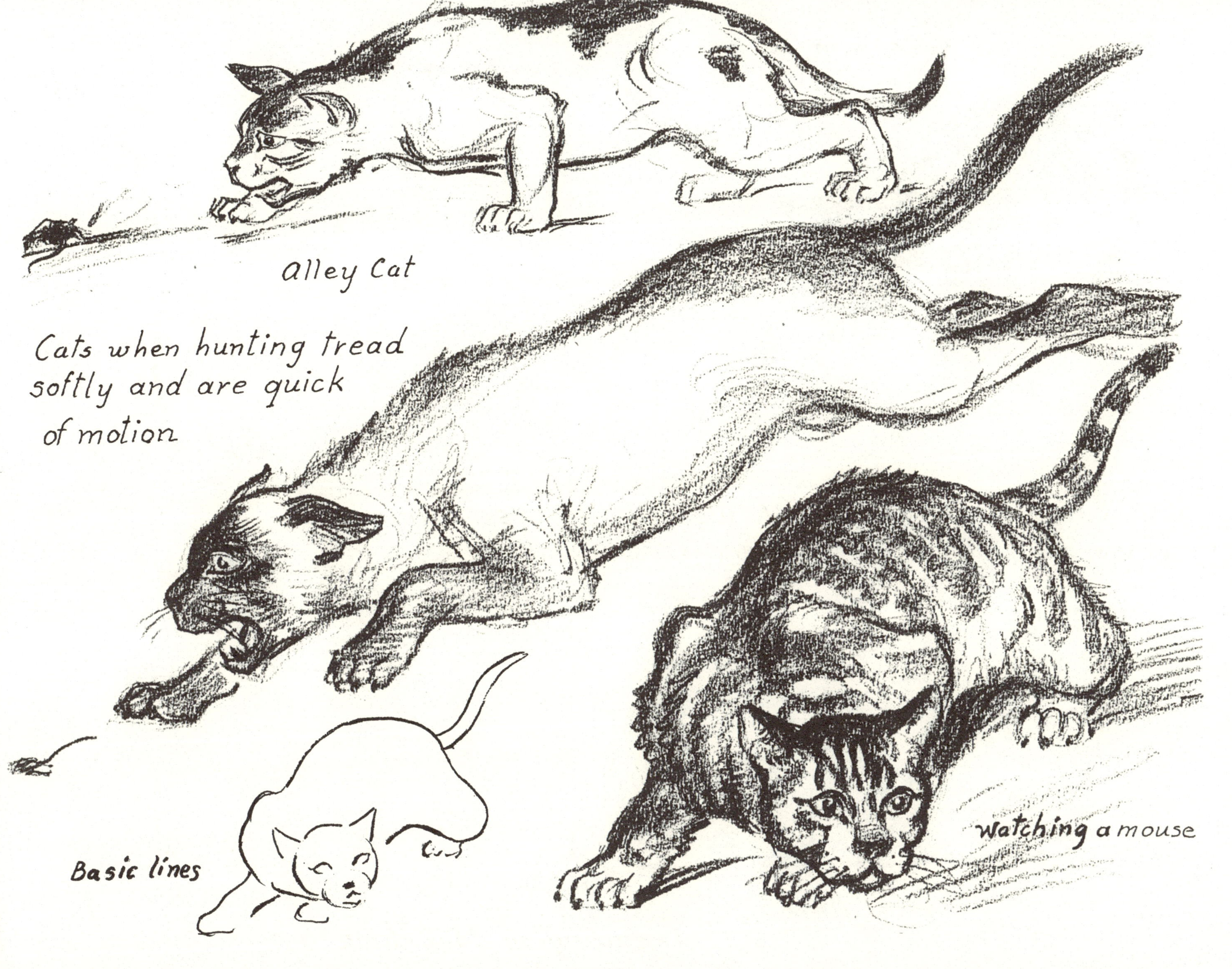
Alley Cat
Cats when hunting tread
softly and are quick
of motion
Basic lines
Watching a mouse

Kittens in action

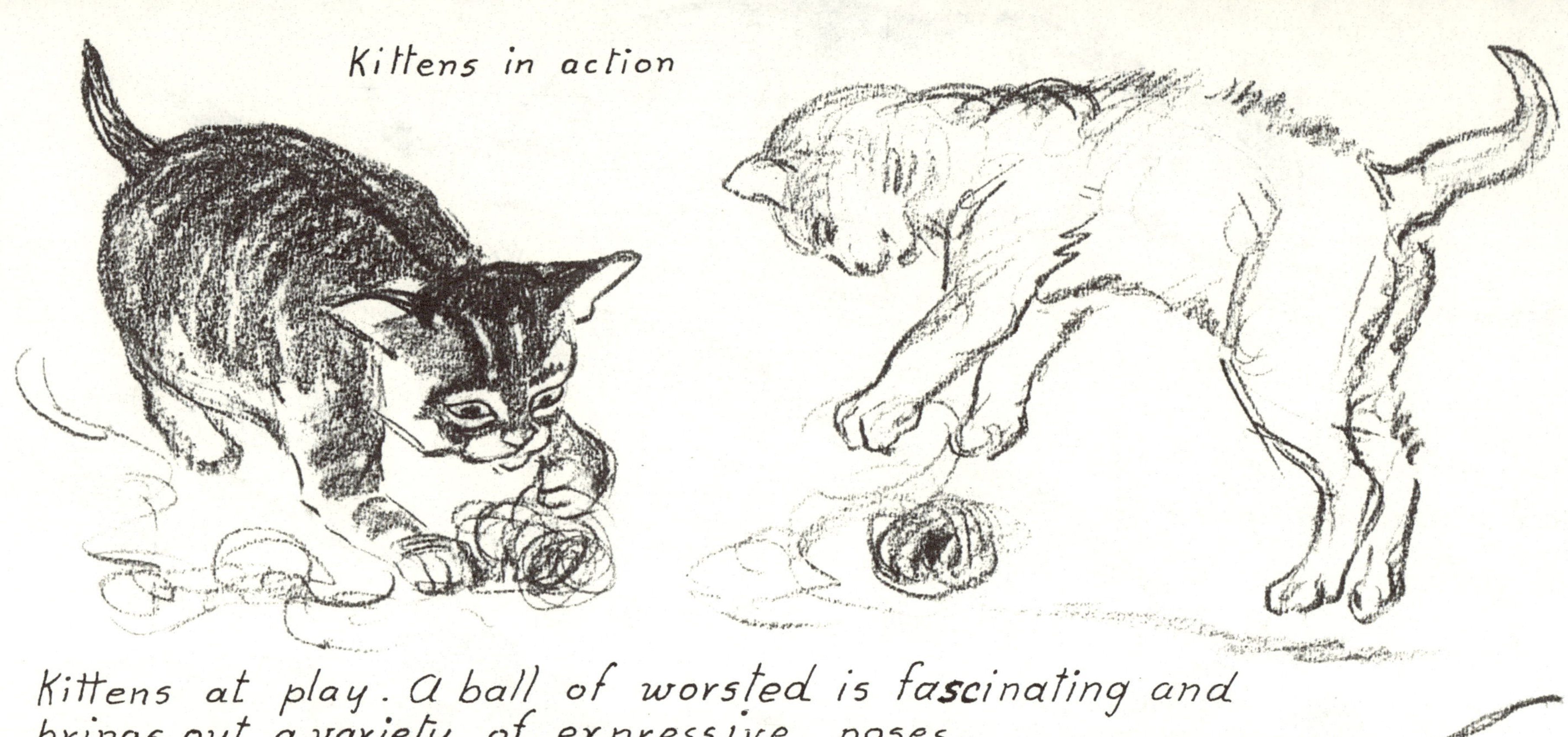

Kittens at play. A ball of worsted is fascinating and brings out a variety of expressive poses.

Treading on forbidden ground.

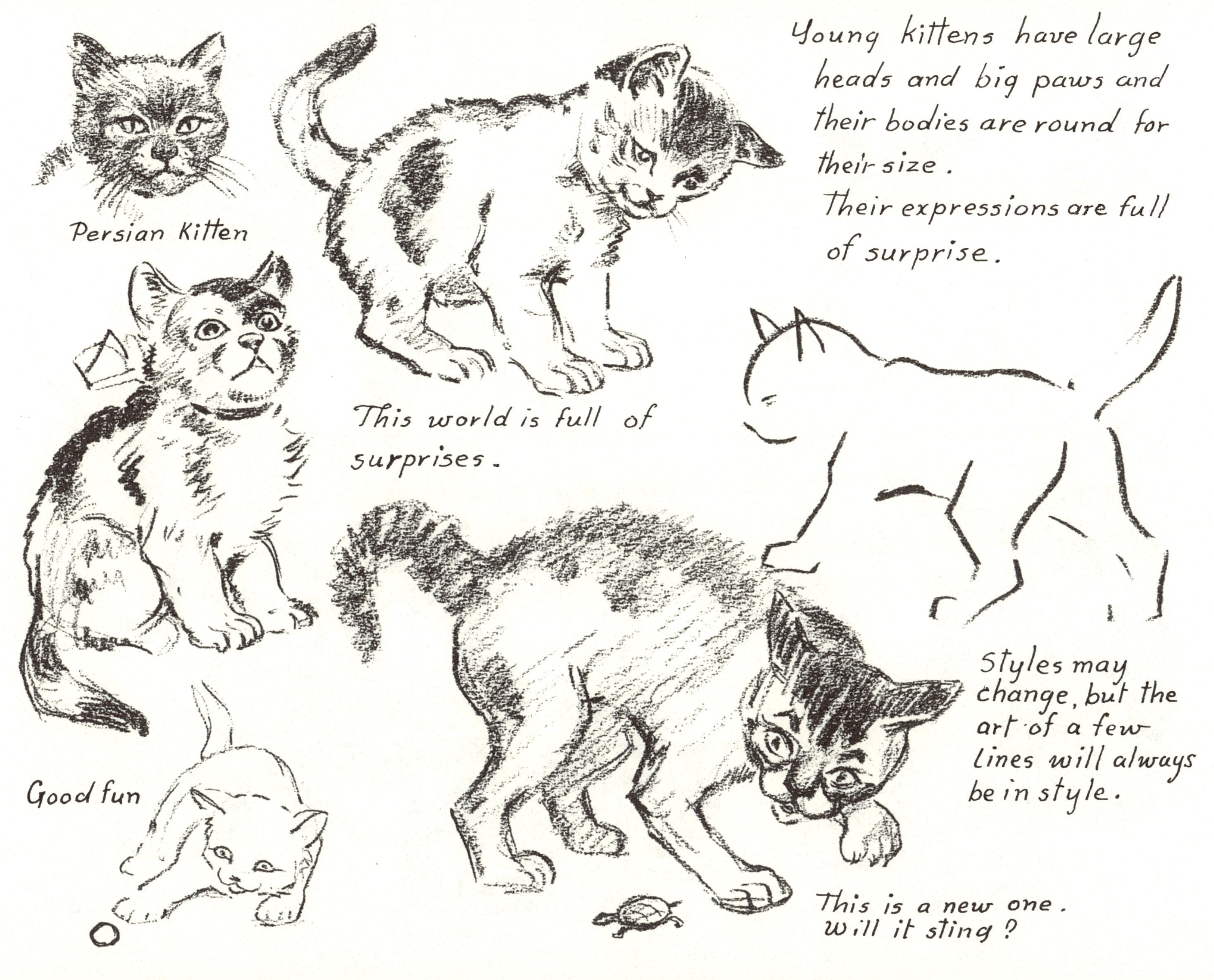
Young kittens have large heads and big paws and their bodies are round for their size.
Their expressions are full of surprise.
Persian Kitten
This world is full of surprises.
Styles may change, but the art of a few lines will always be in style.
Good fun
This is a new one. Will it sting?

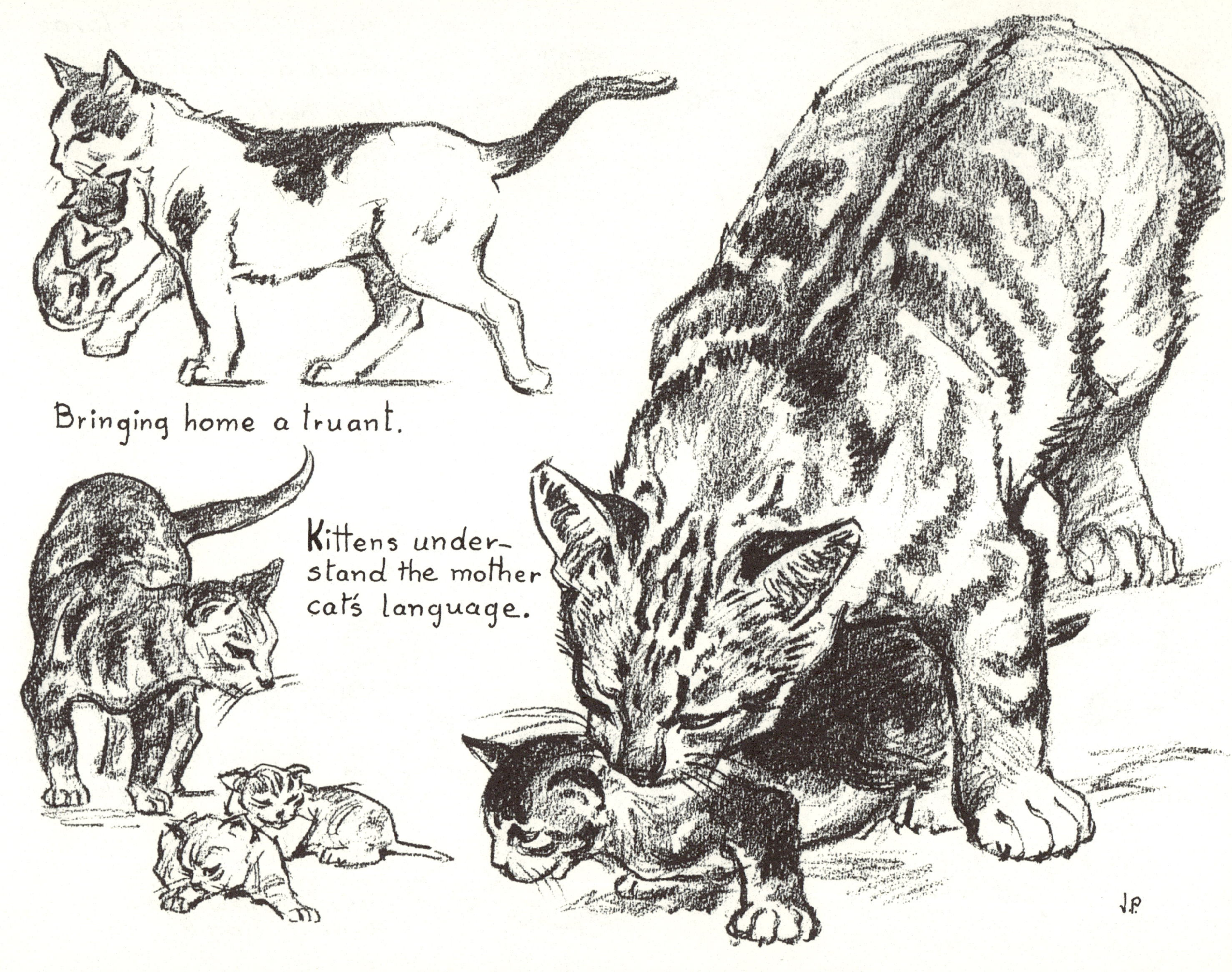

Bringing home a truant.

Kittens understand the mother cat's language.

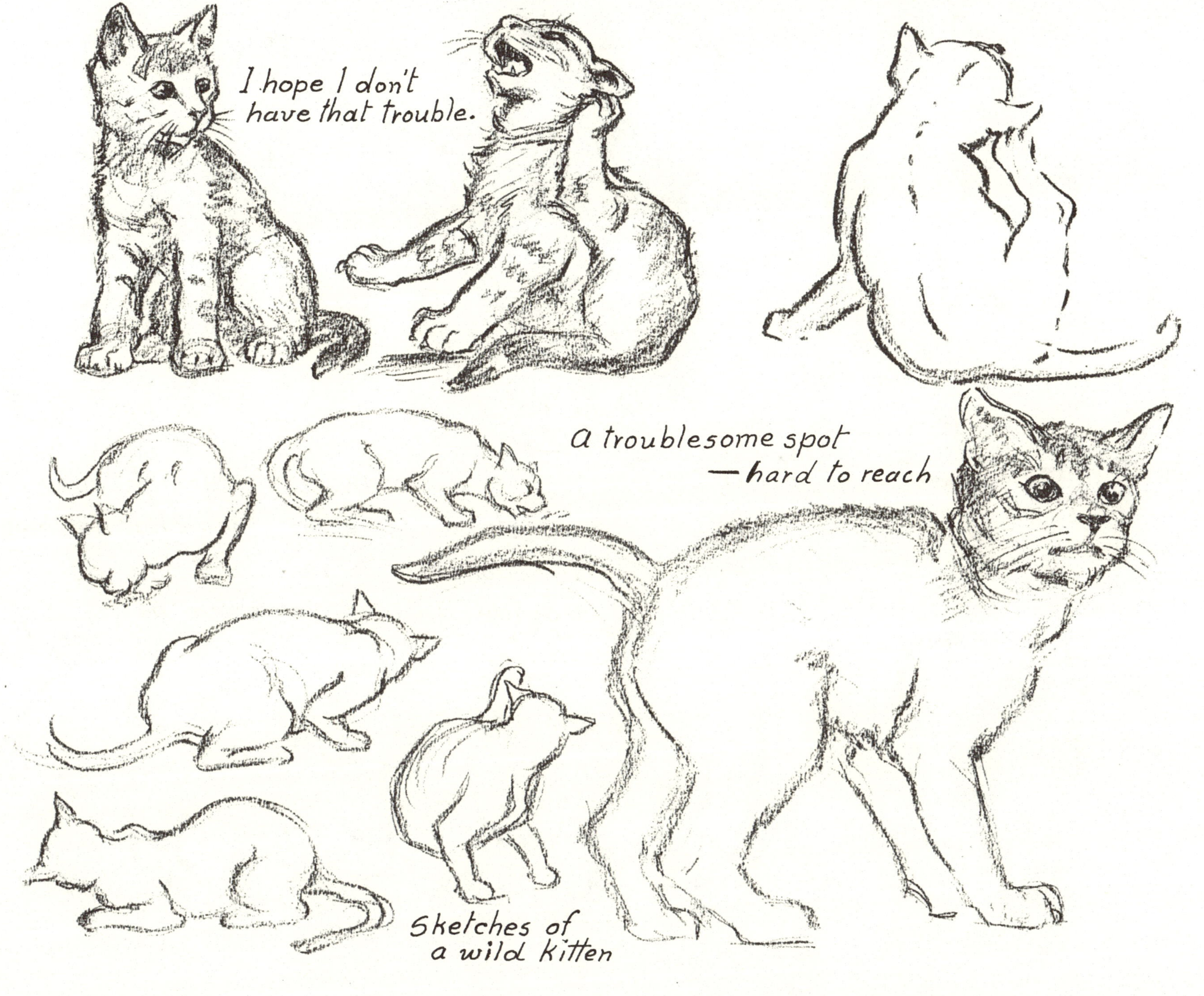
I hope I don't
have that trouble.
A troublesome spot
—hard to reach
Sketches of
a wild kitten

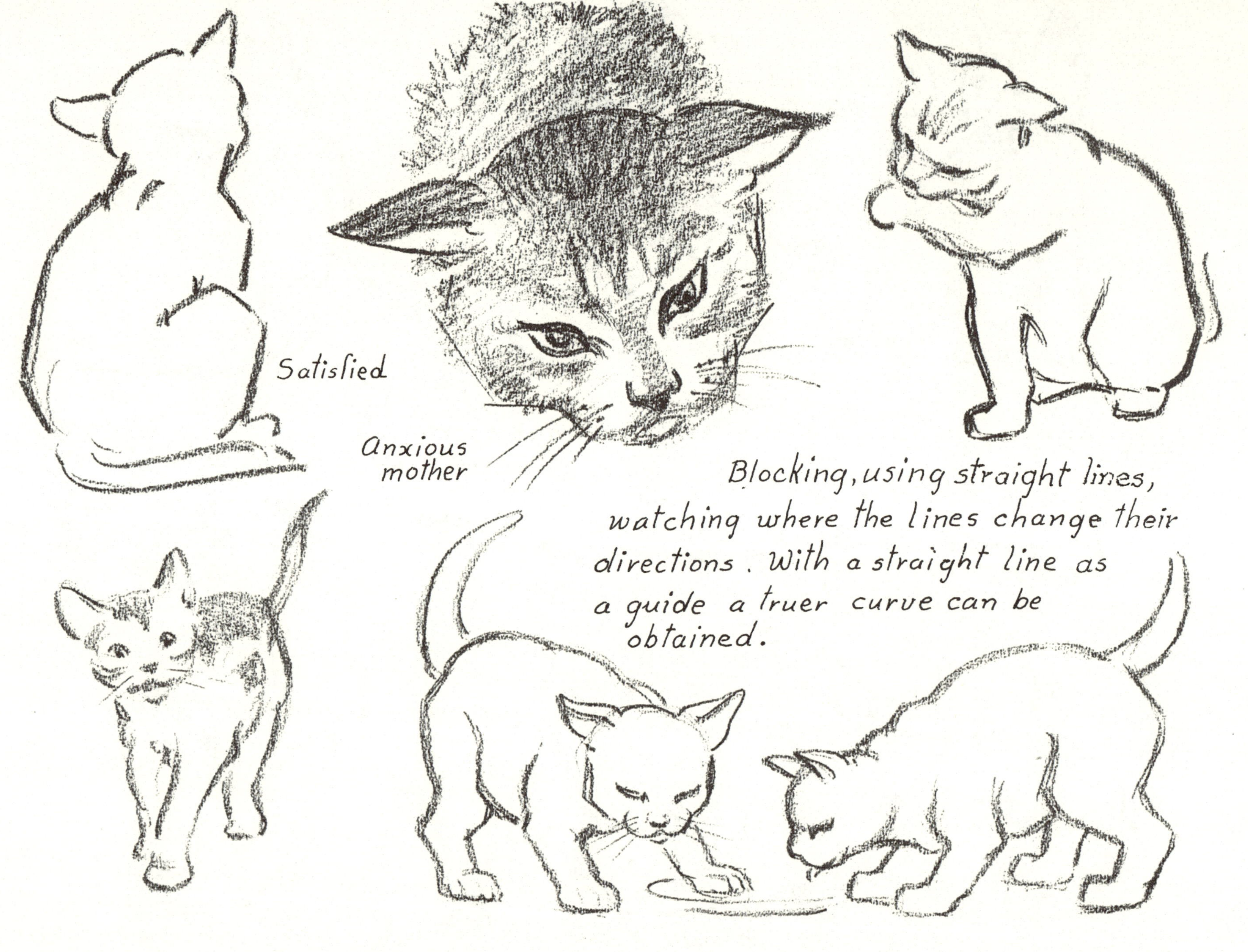
Satisfied
Anxious
mother
Blocking, using straight lines,
watching where the lines change their
directions. With a straight line as
a guide a truer curve can be
obtained.

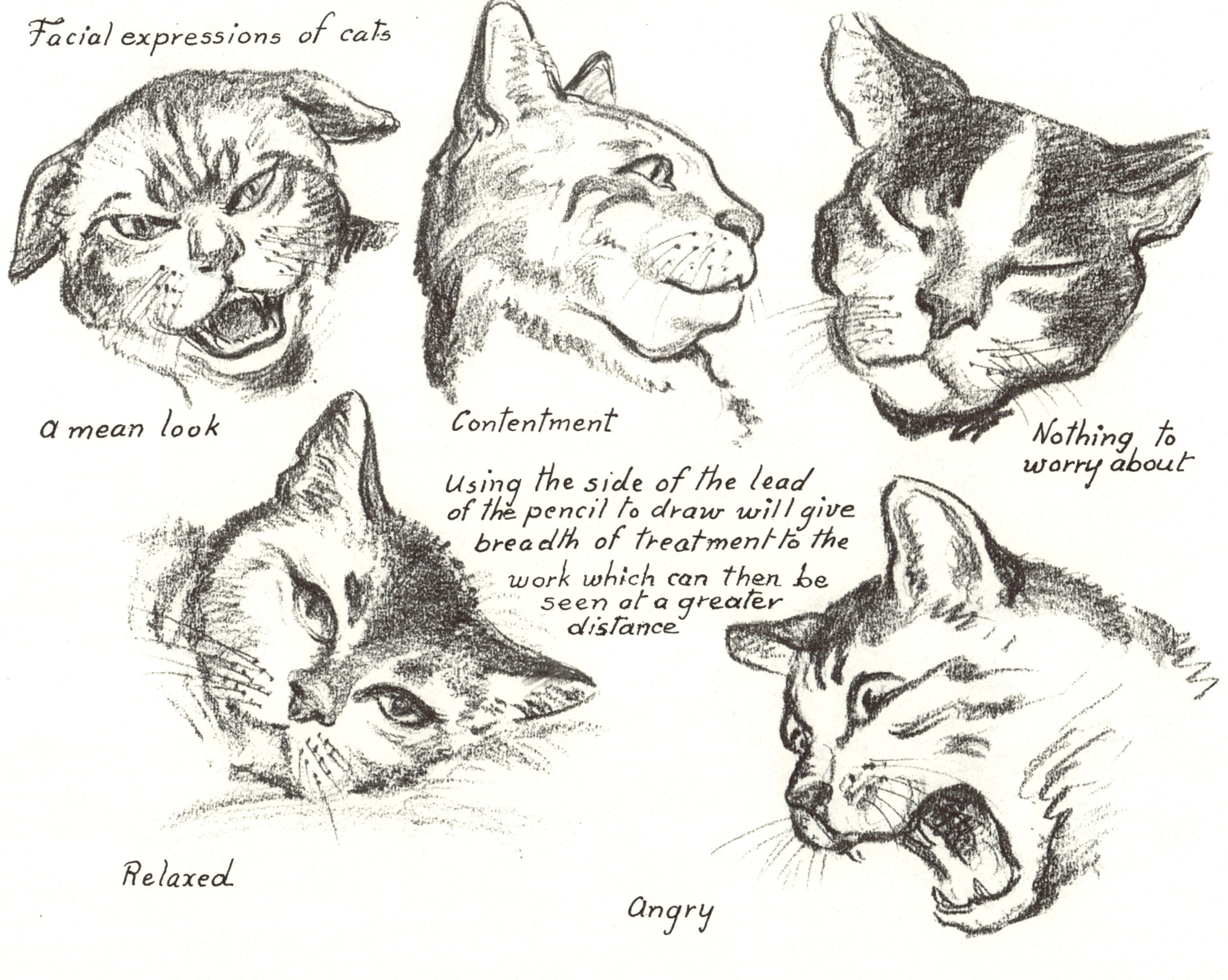
Facial expressions of cats
a mean look
Contentment
Nothing to
worry about
Using the side of the lead
of the pencil to draw will give
breadth of treatment to the
work which can then be
seen at a greater
distance
Relaxed
angry

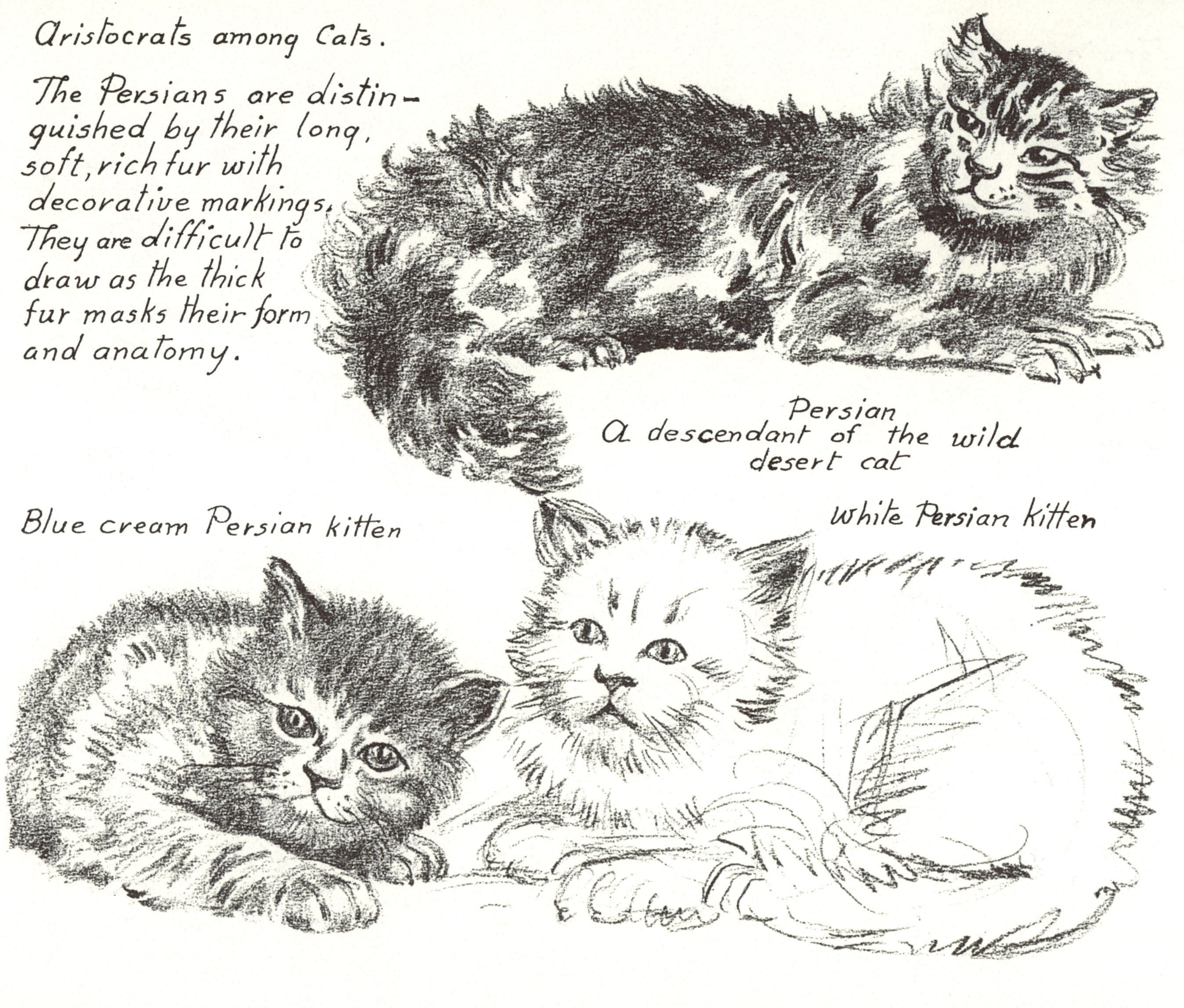
Aristocrats among Cats.
The Persians are distinguished by their long, soft, rich fur with decorative markings. They are difficult to draw as the thick fur masks their form and anatomy.
Persian
A descendant of the wild desert cat
Blue cream Persian kitten
White Persian kitten

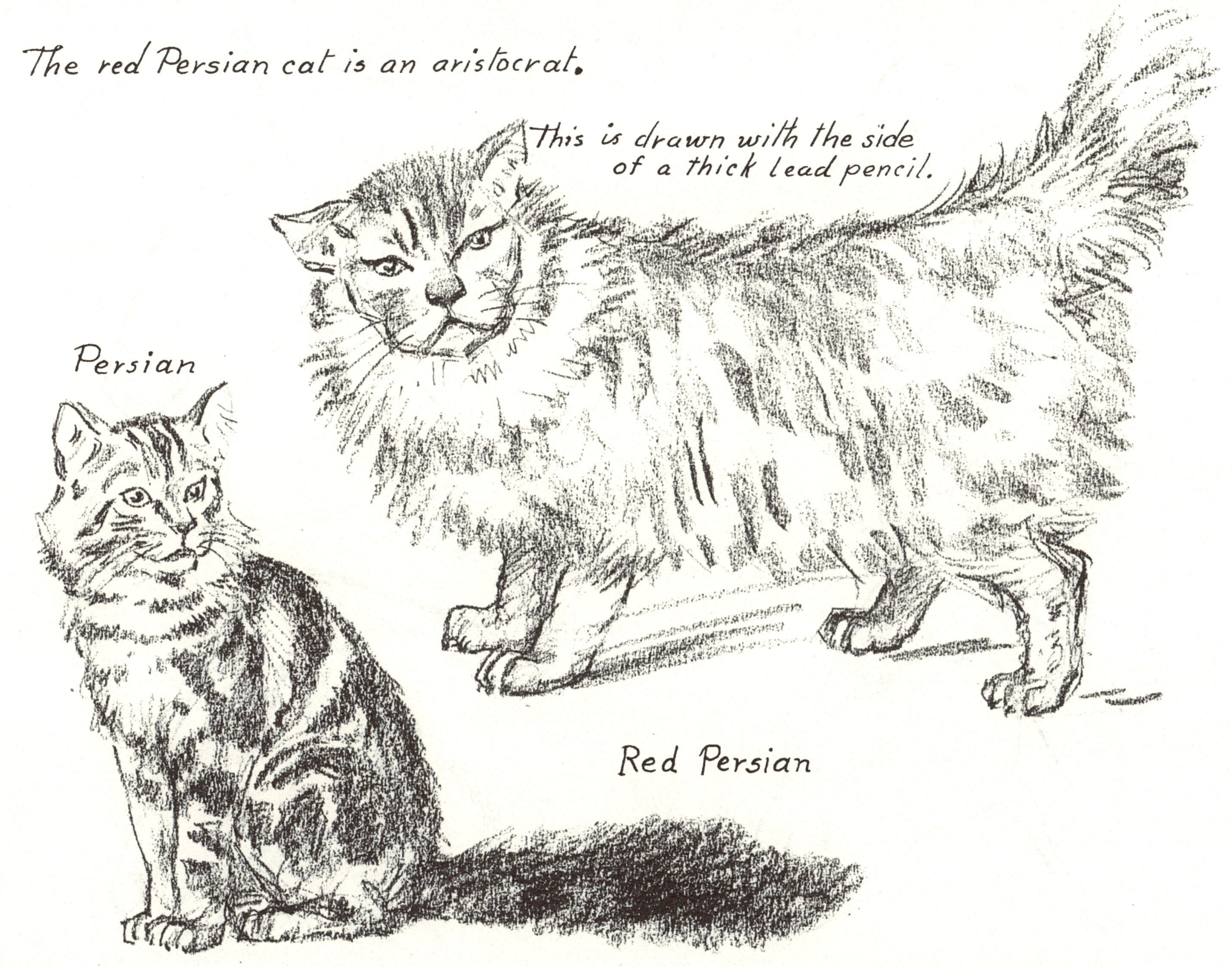
The red Persian cat is an aristocrat.
This is drawn with the side of a thick lead pencil.
Persian
Red Persian

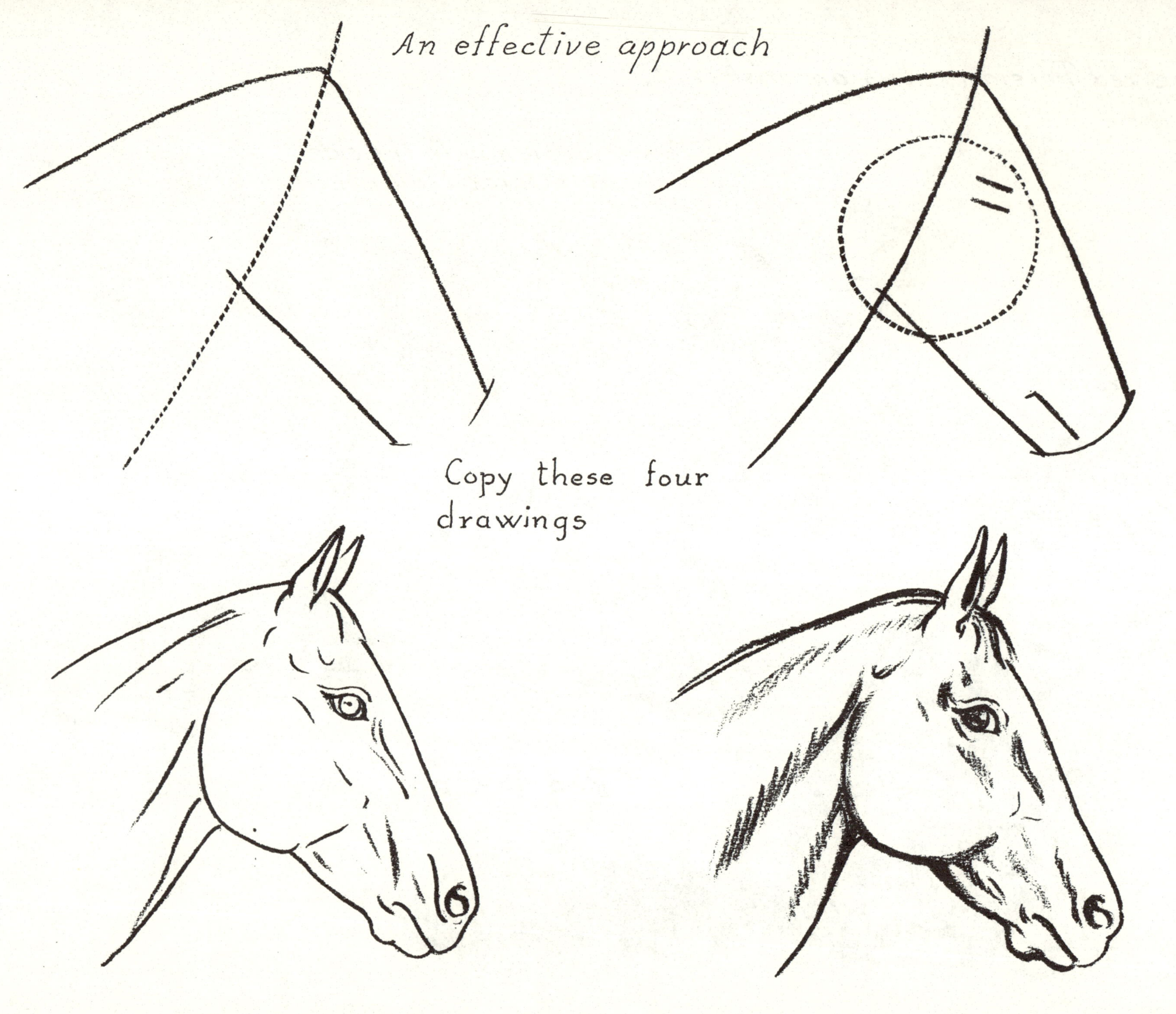
An effective approach
Copy these four
drawings

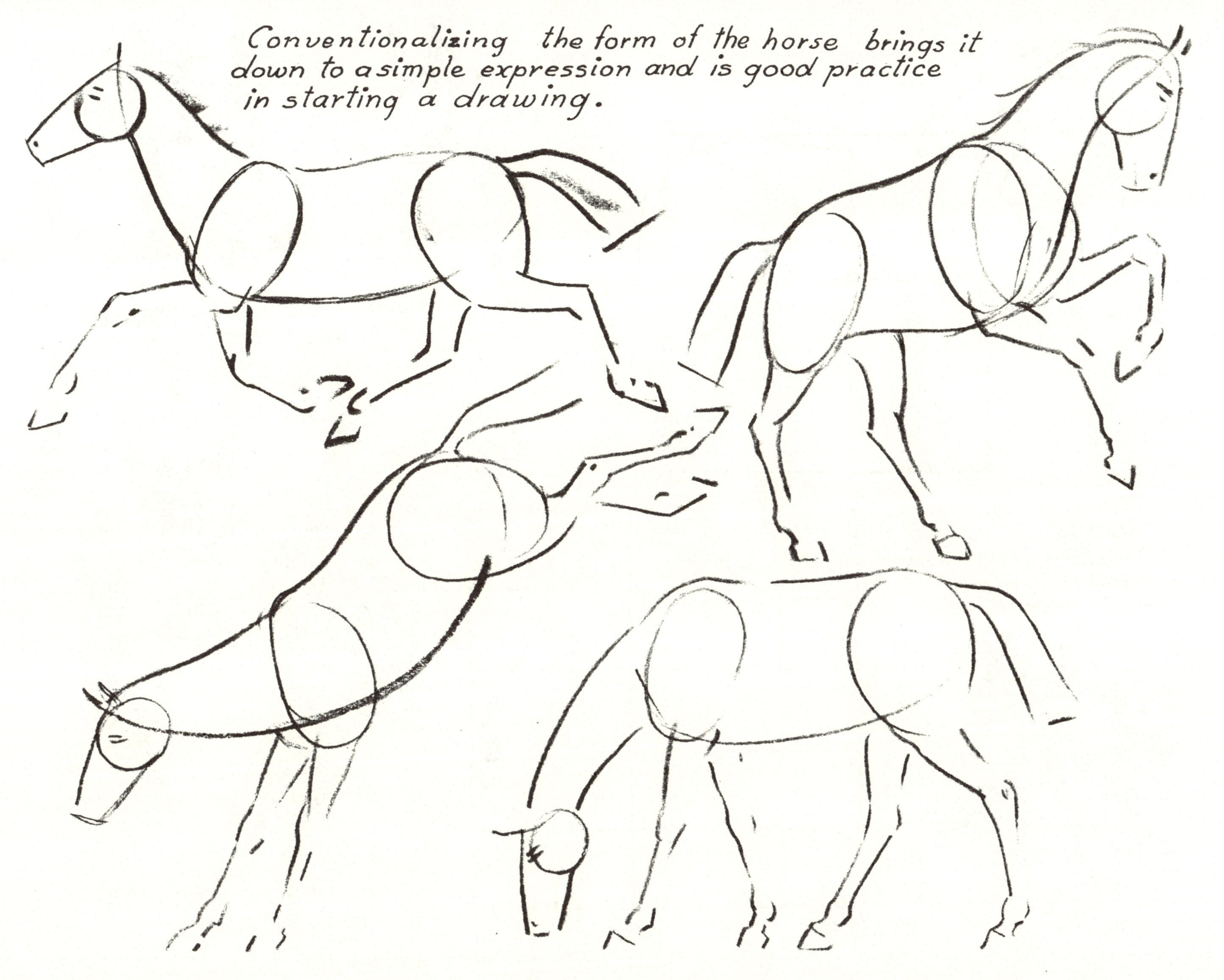
Conventionalizing the form of the horse brings it down to a simple expression and is good practice in starting a drawing.

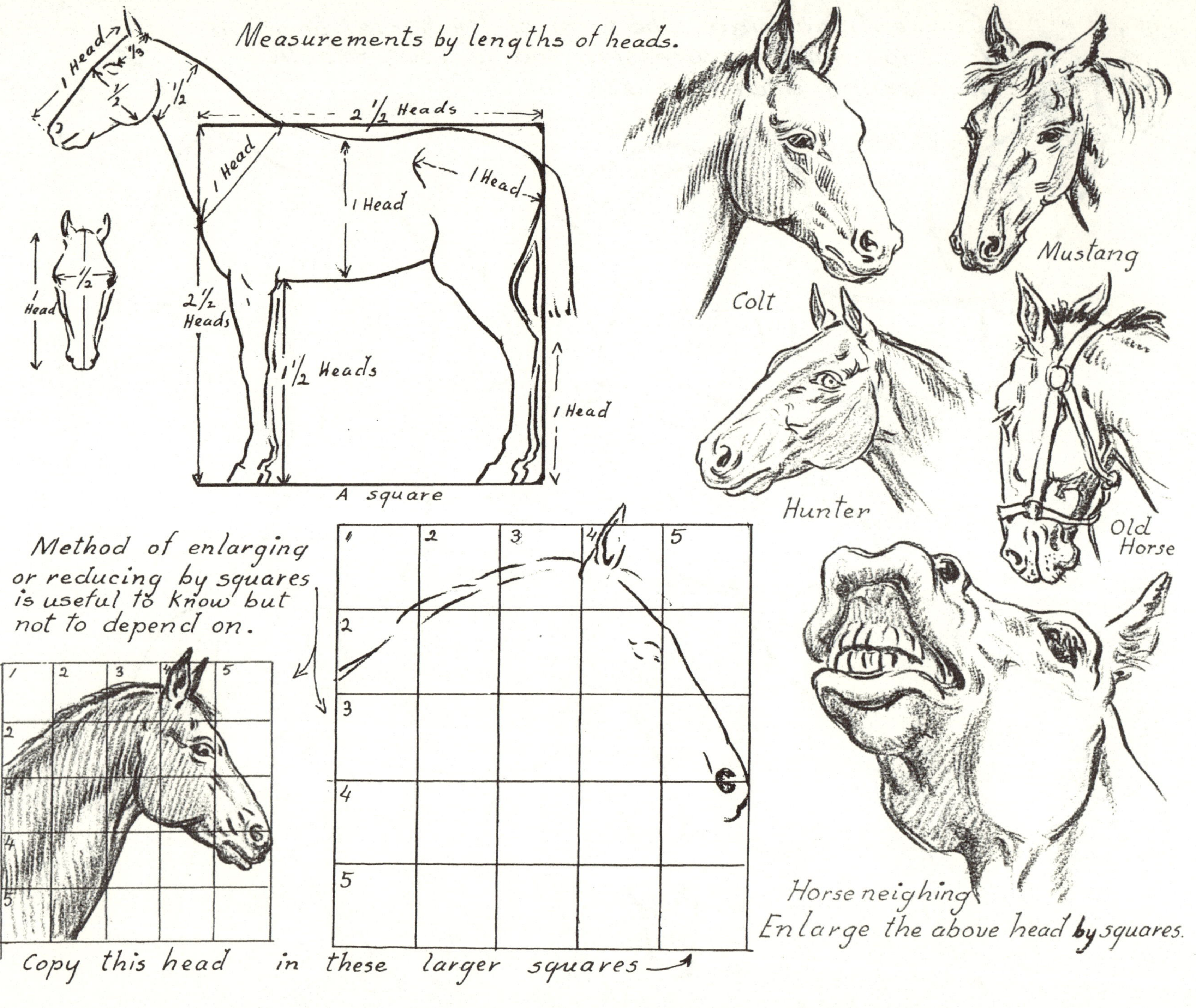
Measurements by lengths of heads.
1 Head
1/3
1/2
1/2
2 1/2 Heads
1 Head
1 Head
1 Head
1/2
1 Head
2 1/2 Heads
1 1/2 Heads
1 Head
A square
Colt
Mustang
Hunter
Old Horse
Method of enlarging or reducing by squares is useful to know but not to depend on.
1
2
3
4
5
Copy this head in these larger squares
Horse neighing
Enlarge the above head by squares.

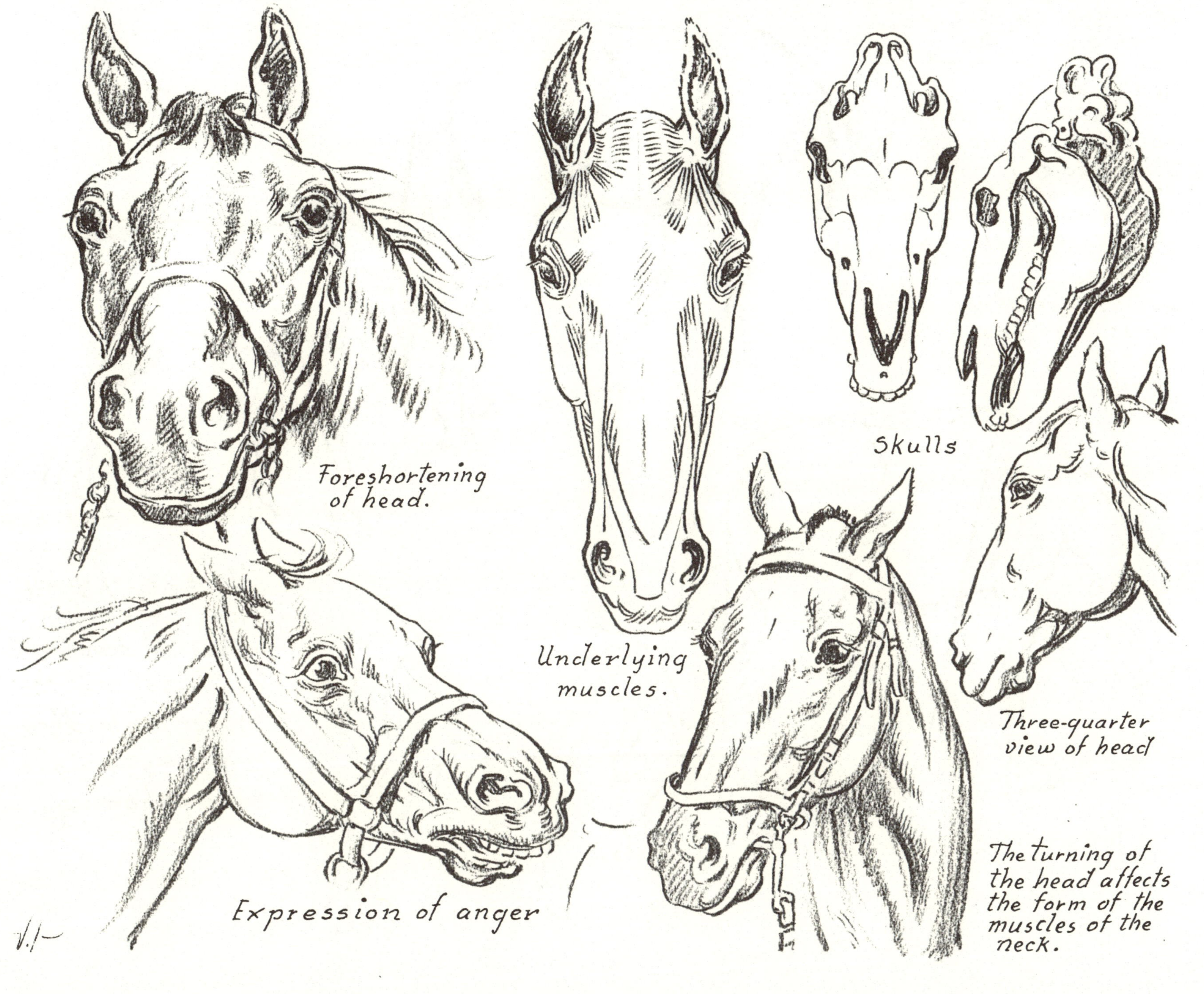
Foreshortening of head.
Underlying muscles.
Skulls
Three-quarter view of head
Expression of anger
The turning of the head affects the form of the muscles of the neck.

See with how few lines the subject may be expressed at the start. Care at first will save trouble later. It is easier to make changes at the start than later on when there is detail to cope with.

Colts have short necks, long ears and rounded foreheads.

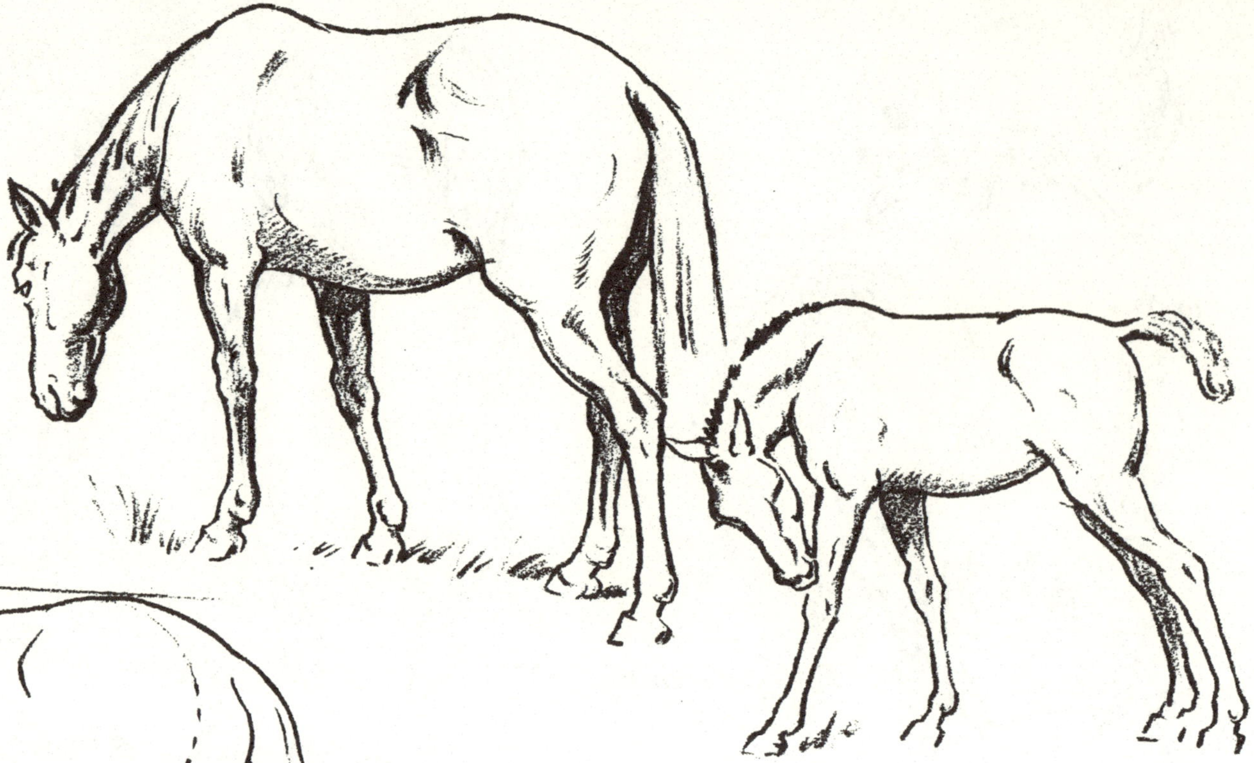

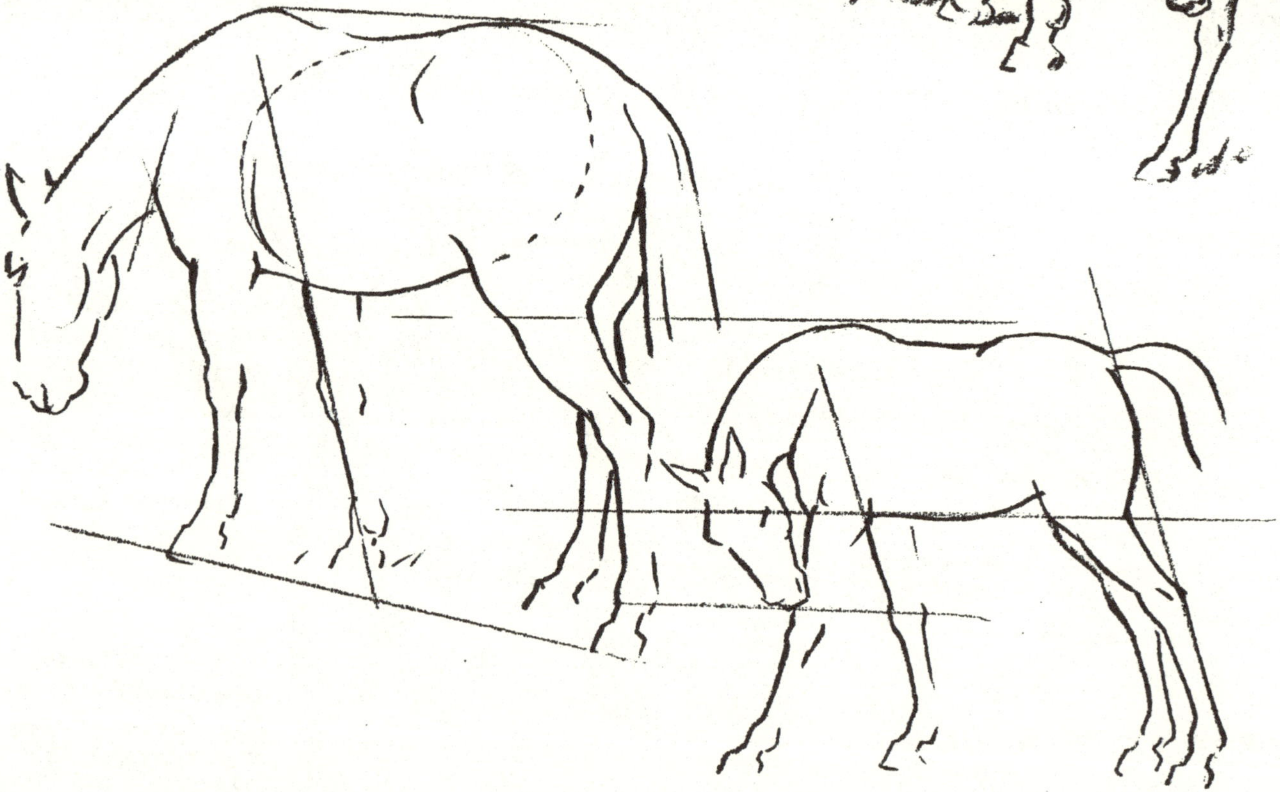

Make use of guide lines, they help place the drawing on the paper at the proper angle. They can be rubbed out before shading.

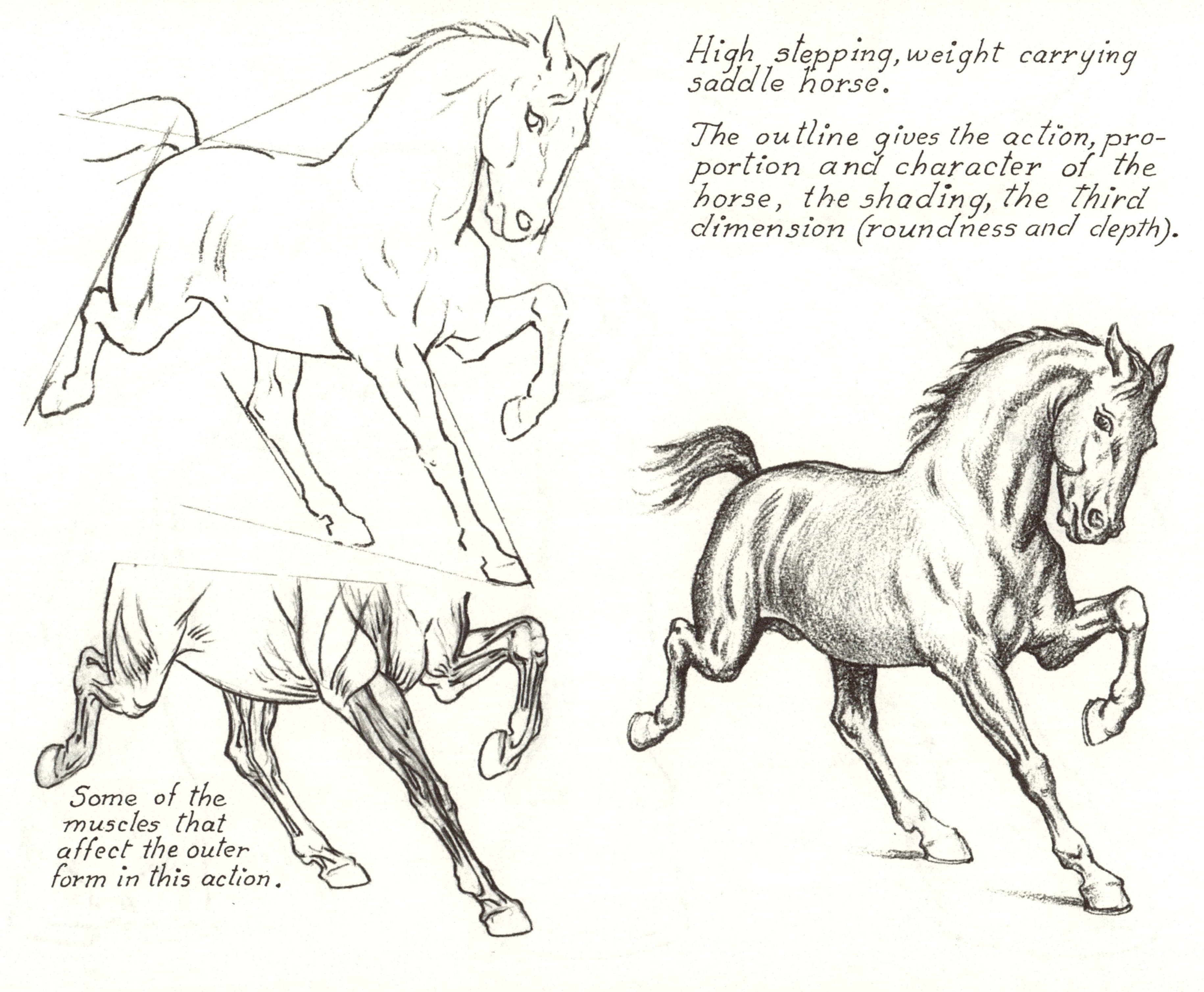

High stepping, weight carrying saddle horse.

The outline gives the action, proportion and character of the horse, the shading, the third dimension (roundness and depth).

Some of the muscles that affect the outer form in this action.

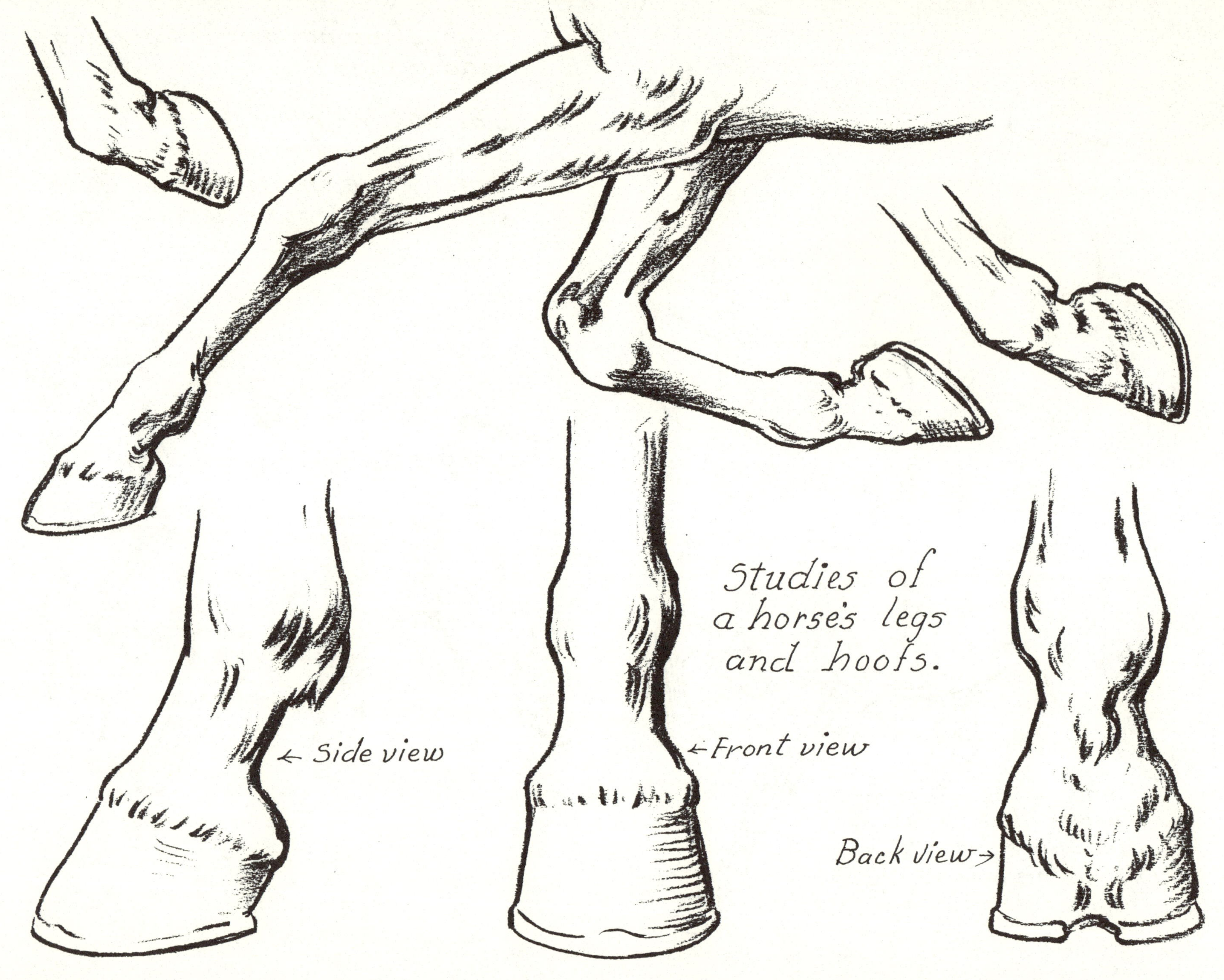
Studies of
a horse's legs
and hoofs.
← Side view
← Front view
Back view →

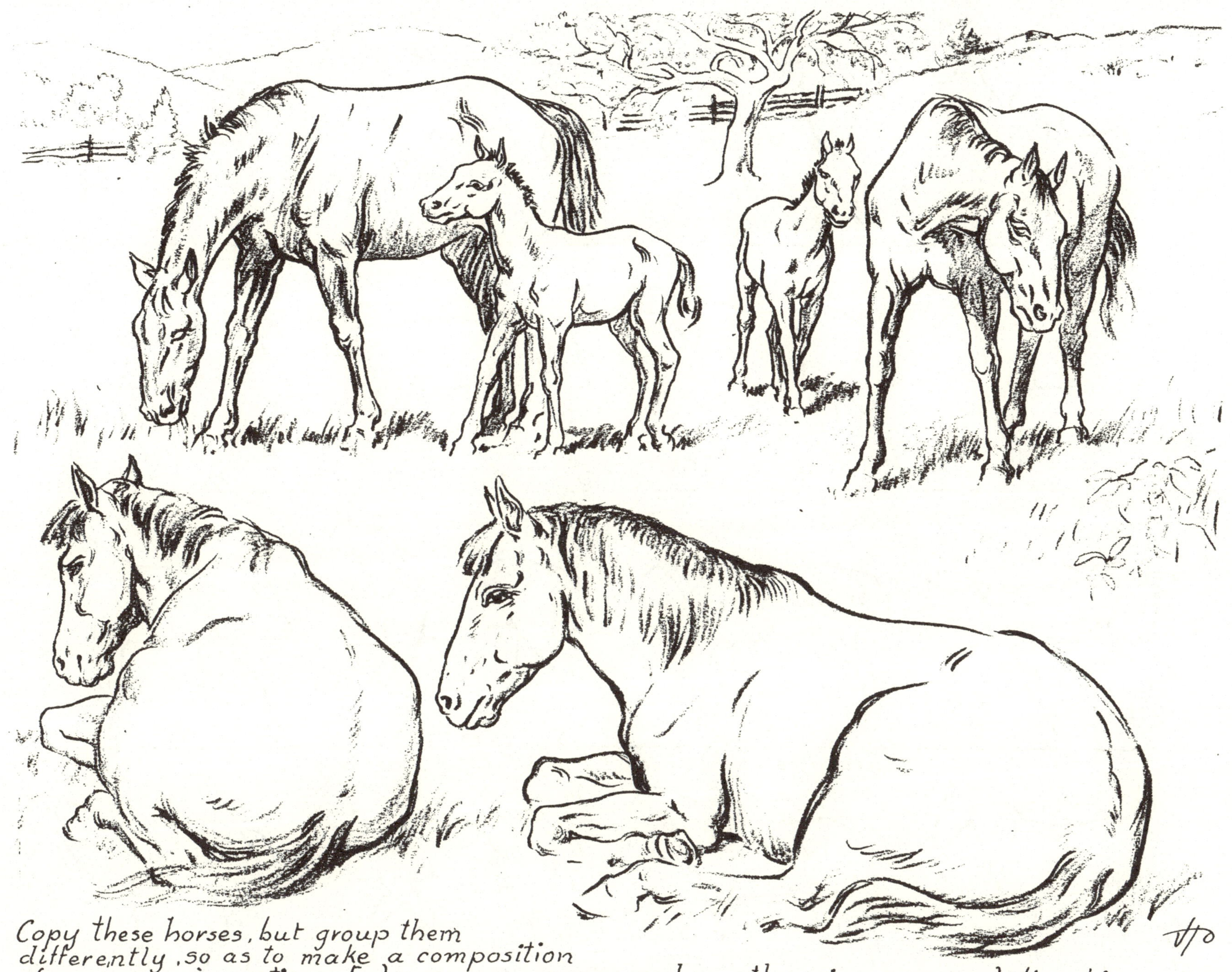

Copy these horses, but group them
differently, so as to make a composition
of your own invention. Enlarge some groups, reduce others in proper relationship.

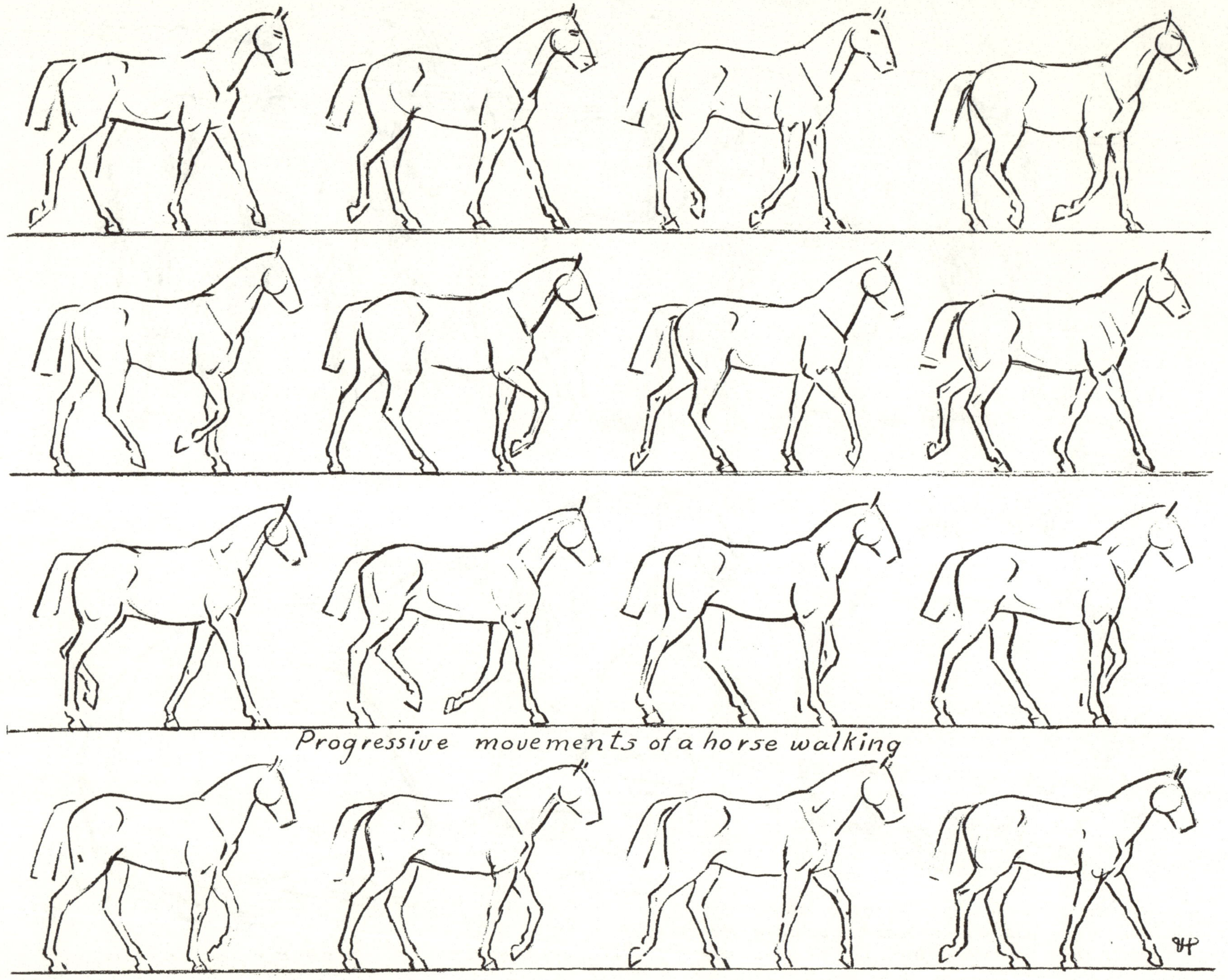

Progressive movements of a horse walking

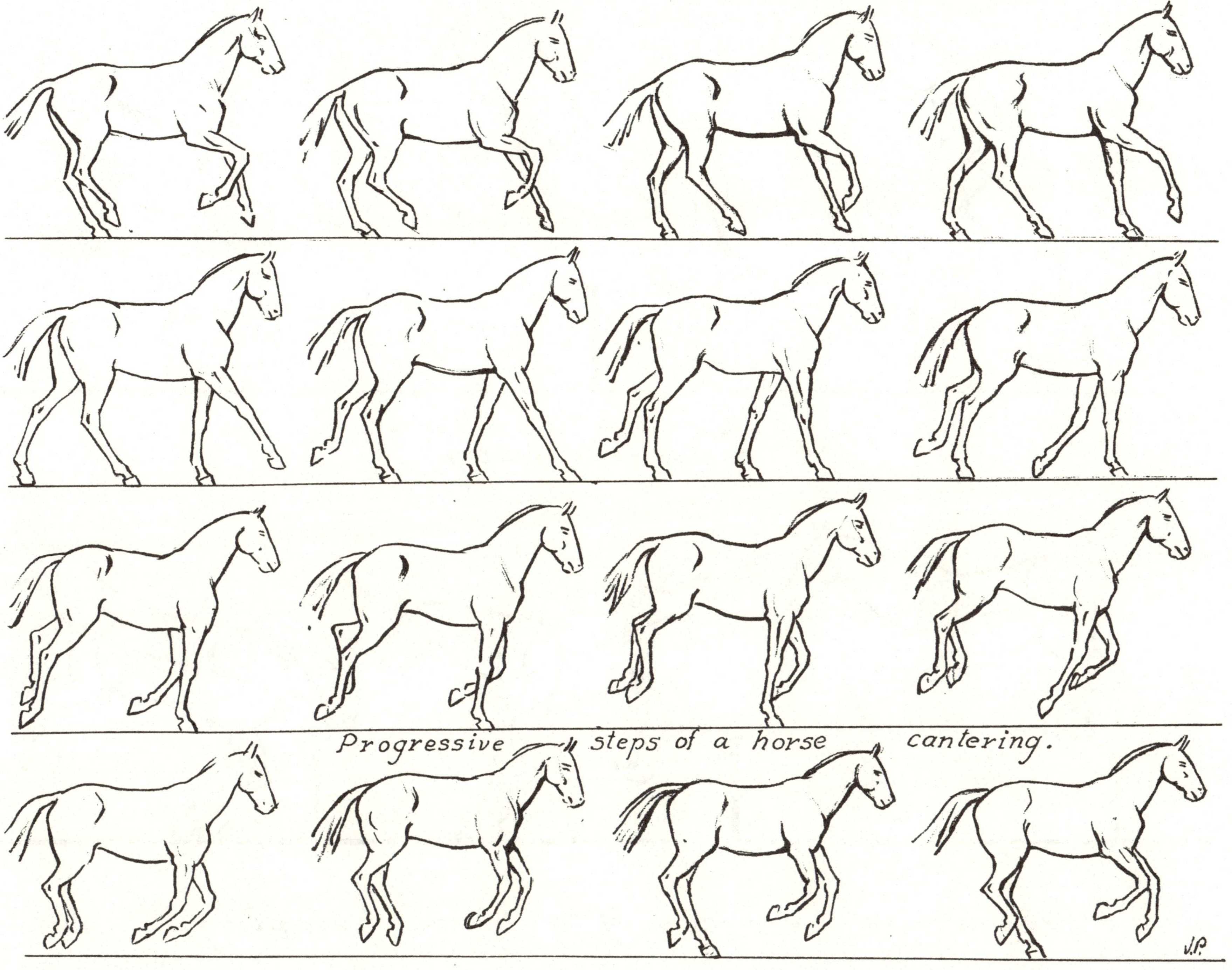

Progressive steps of a horse cantering.

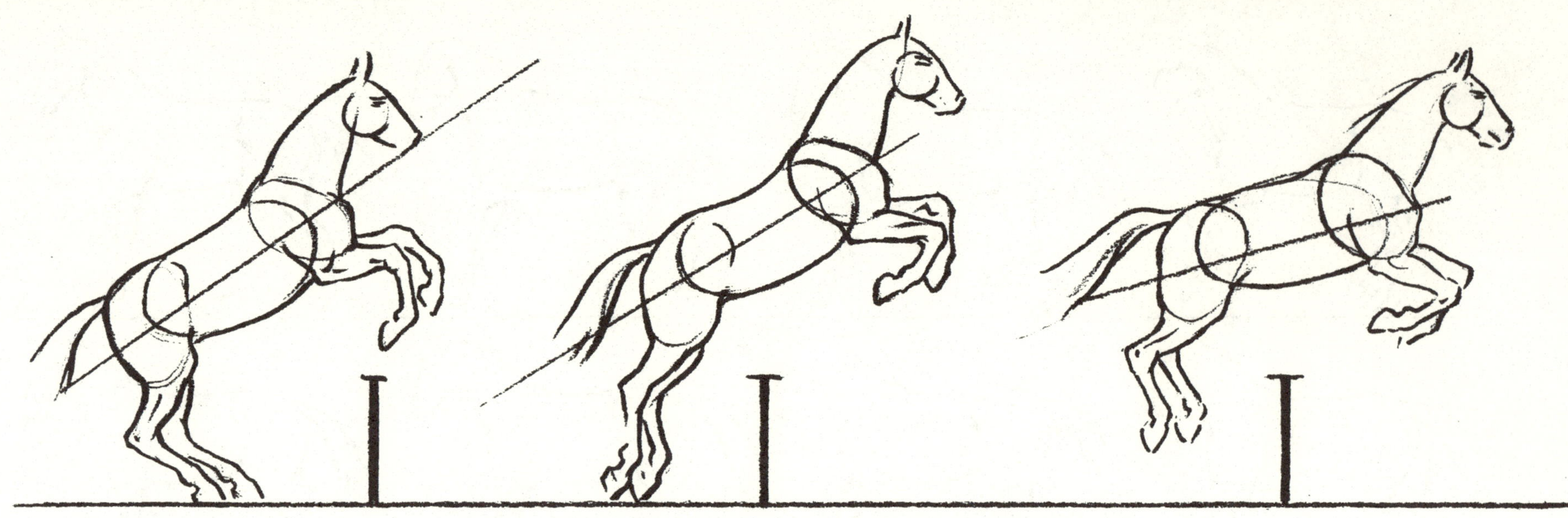

Use a center line on the horse to show angle of action.

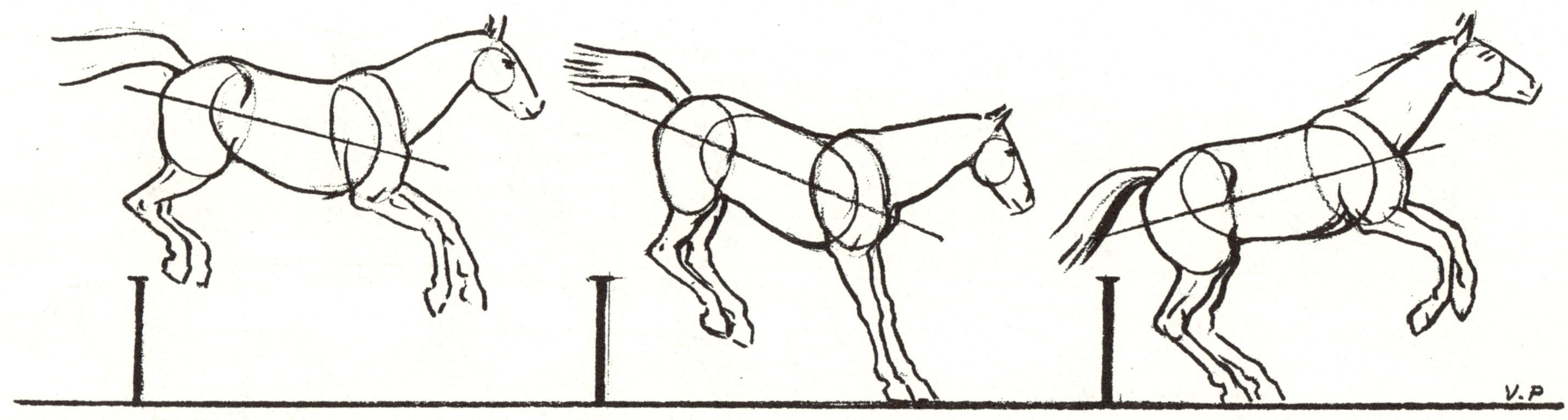

Progressive actions of a horse jumping.

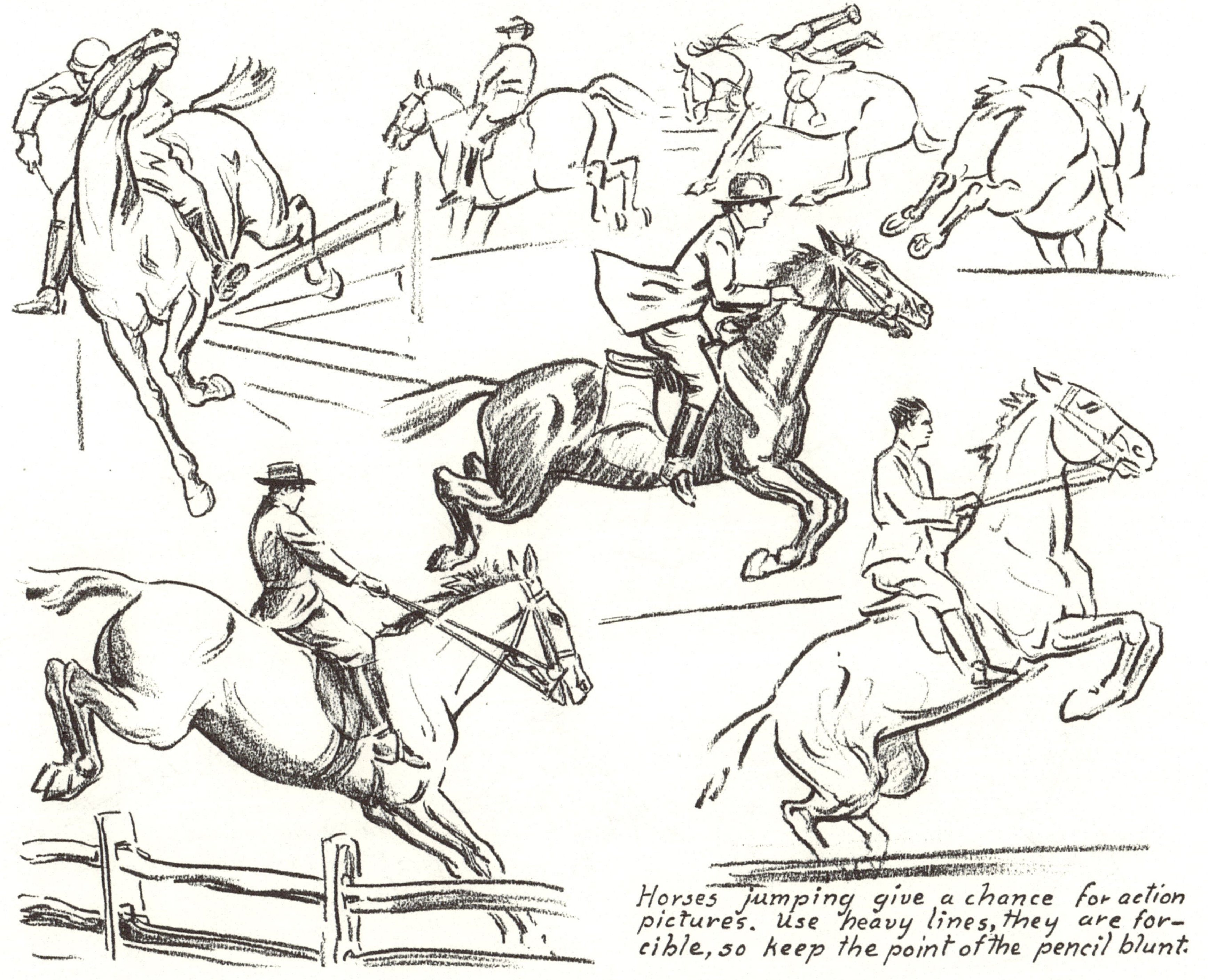

Horses jumping give a chance for action pictures. Use heavy lines, they are forcible, so keep the point of the pencil blunt.

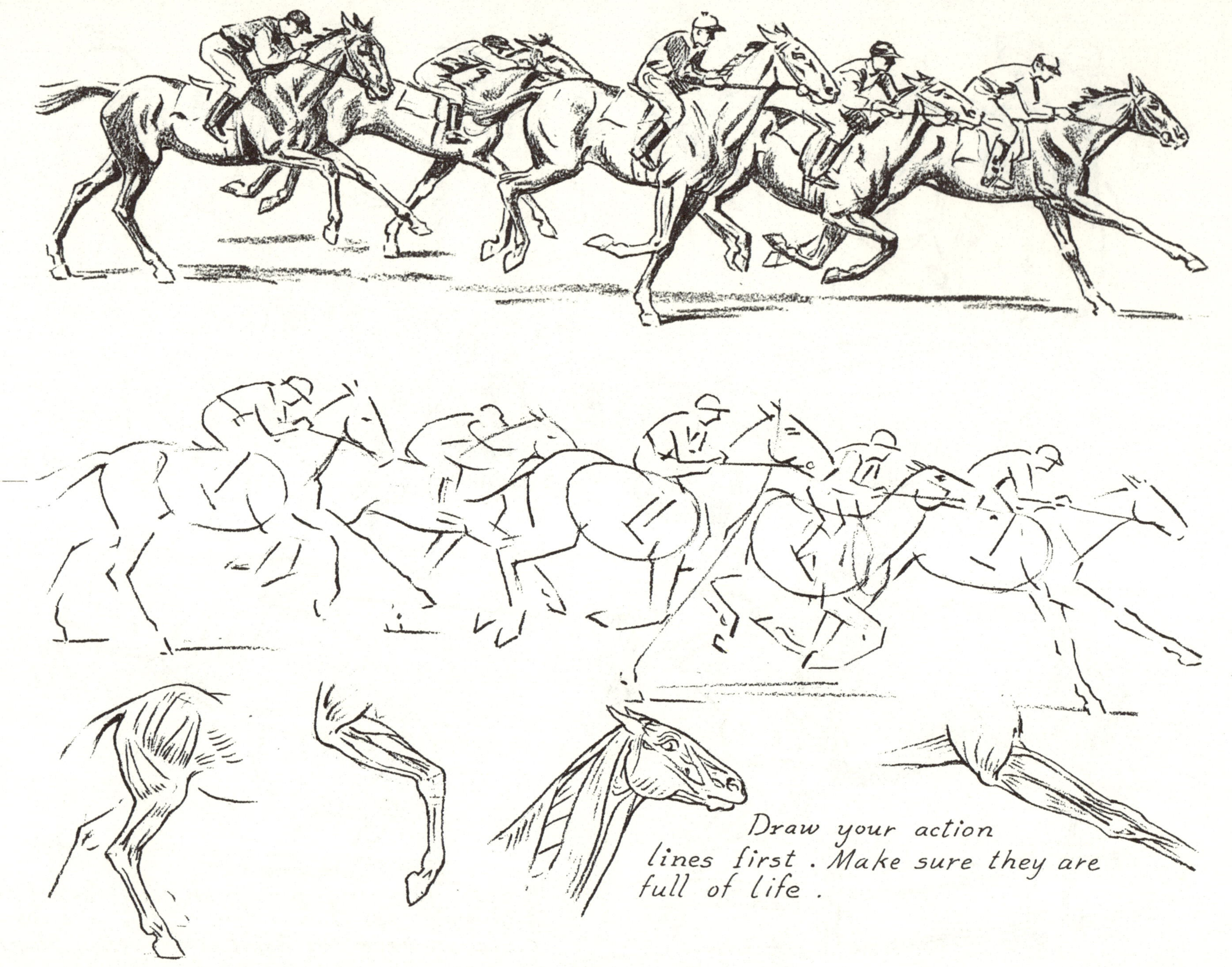

Draw your action lines first. Make sure they are full of life.

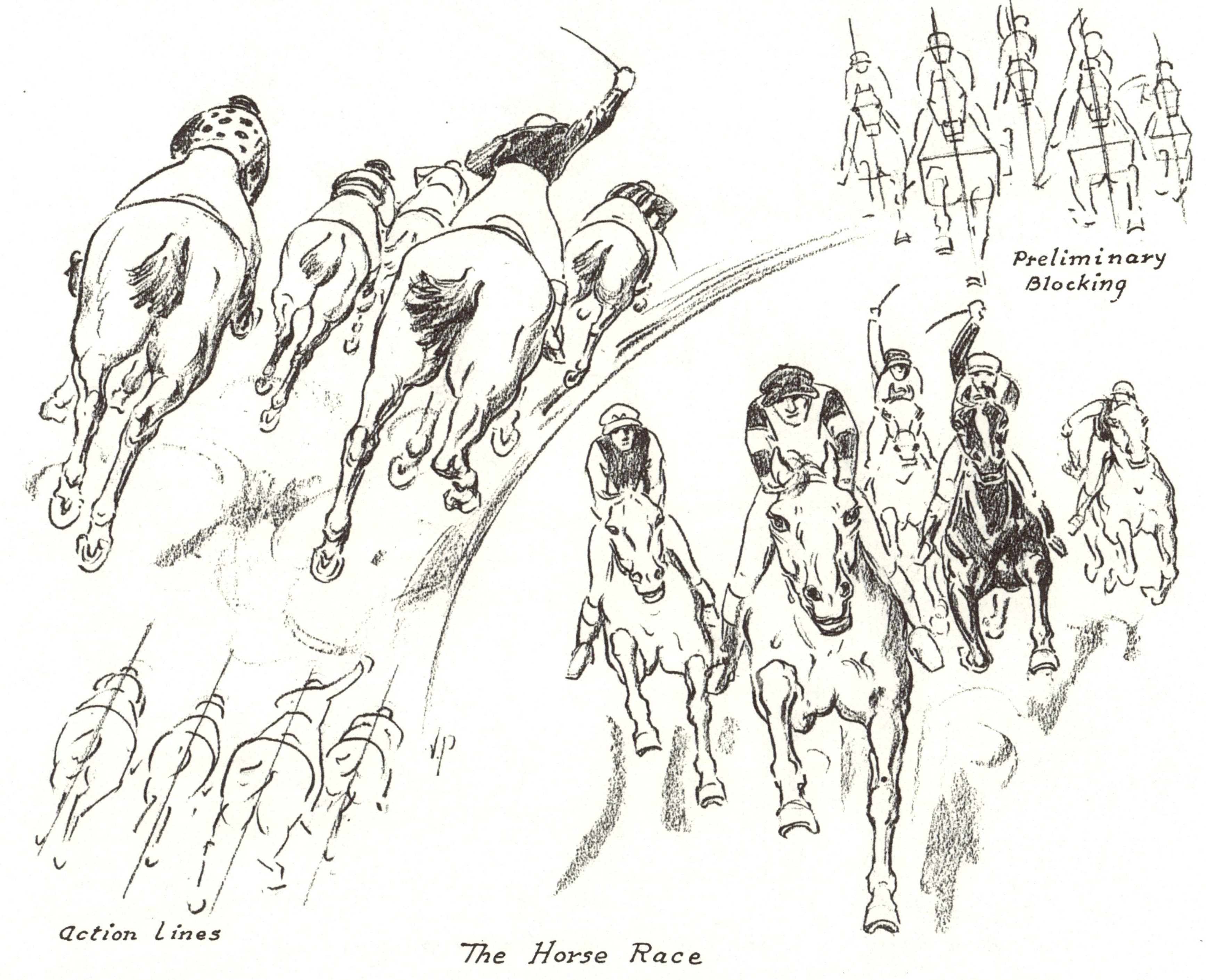

The Horse Race

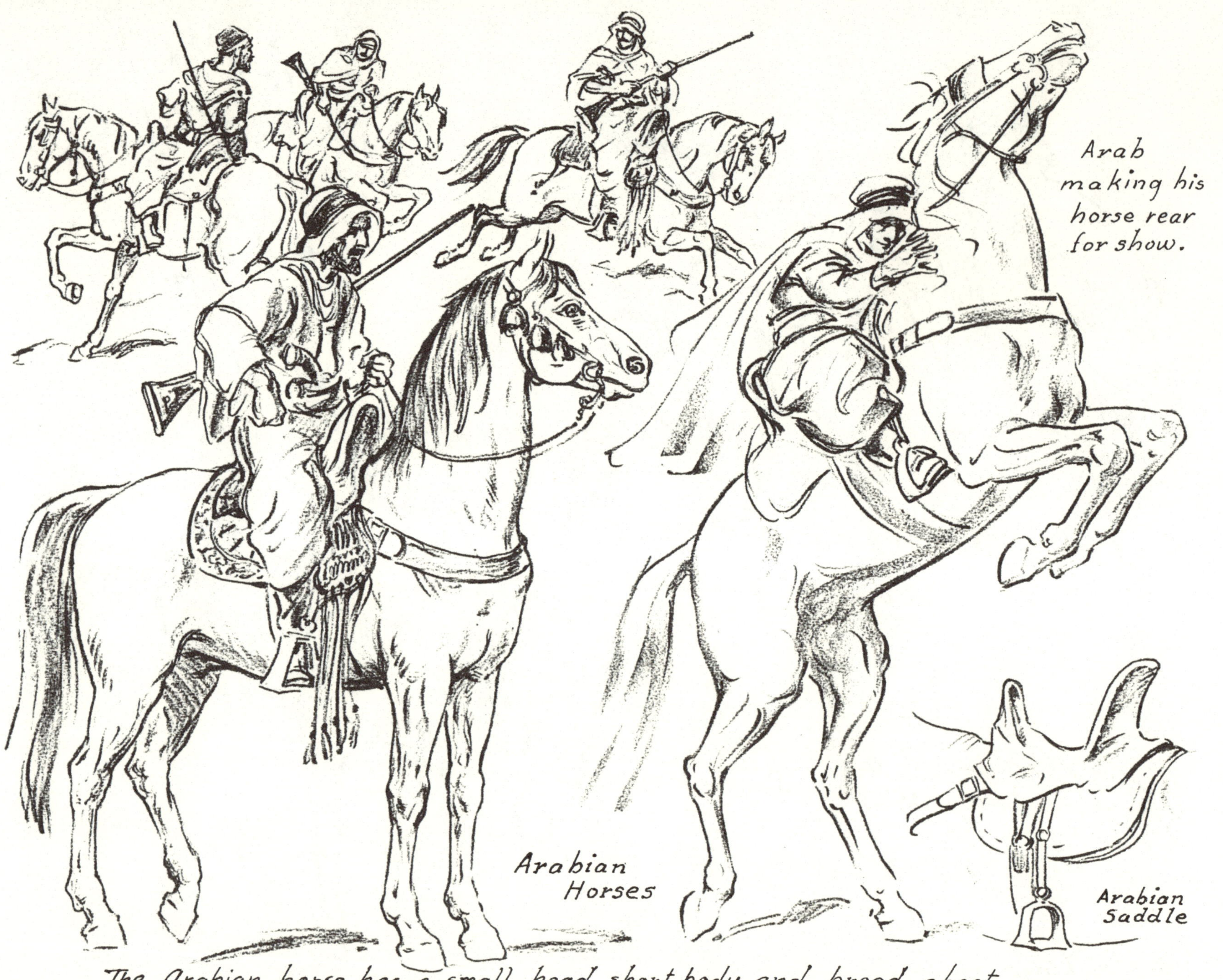

The Arabian horse has a small head short body and broad chest

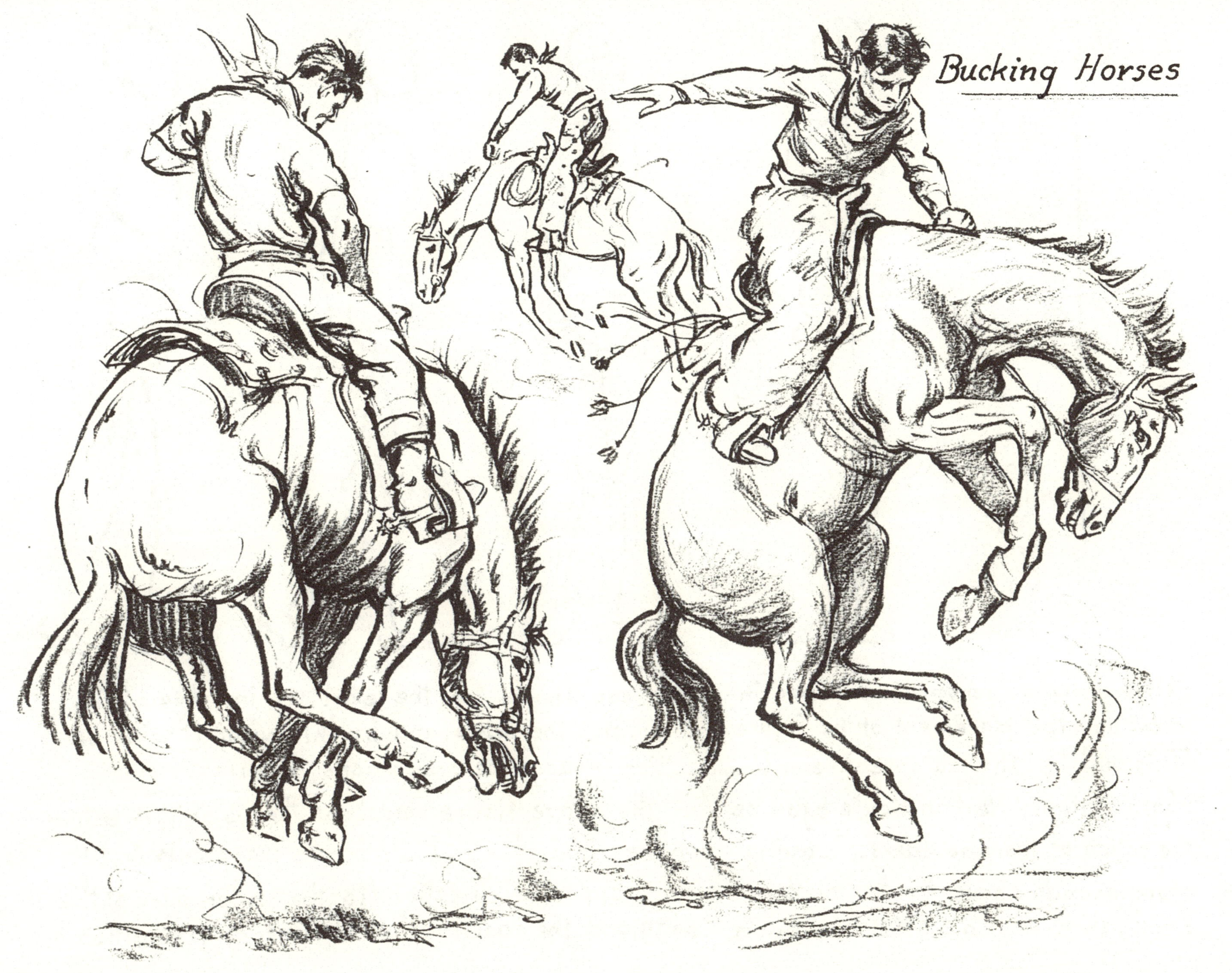
Bucking Horses

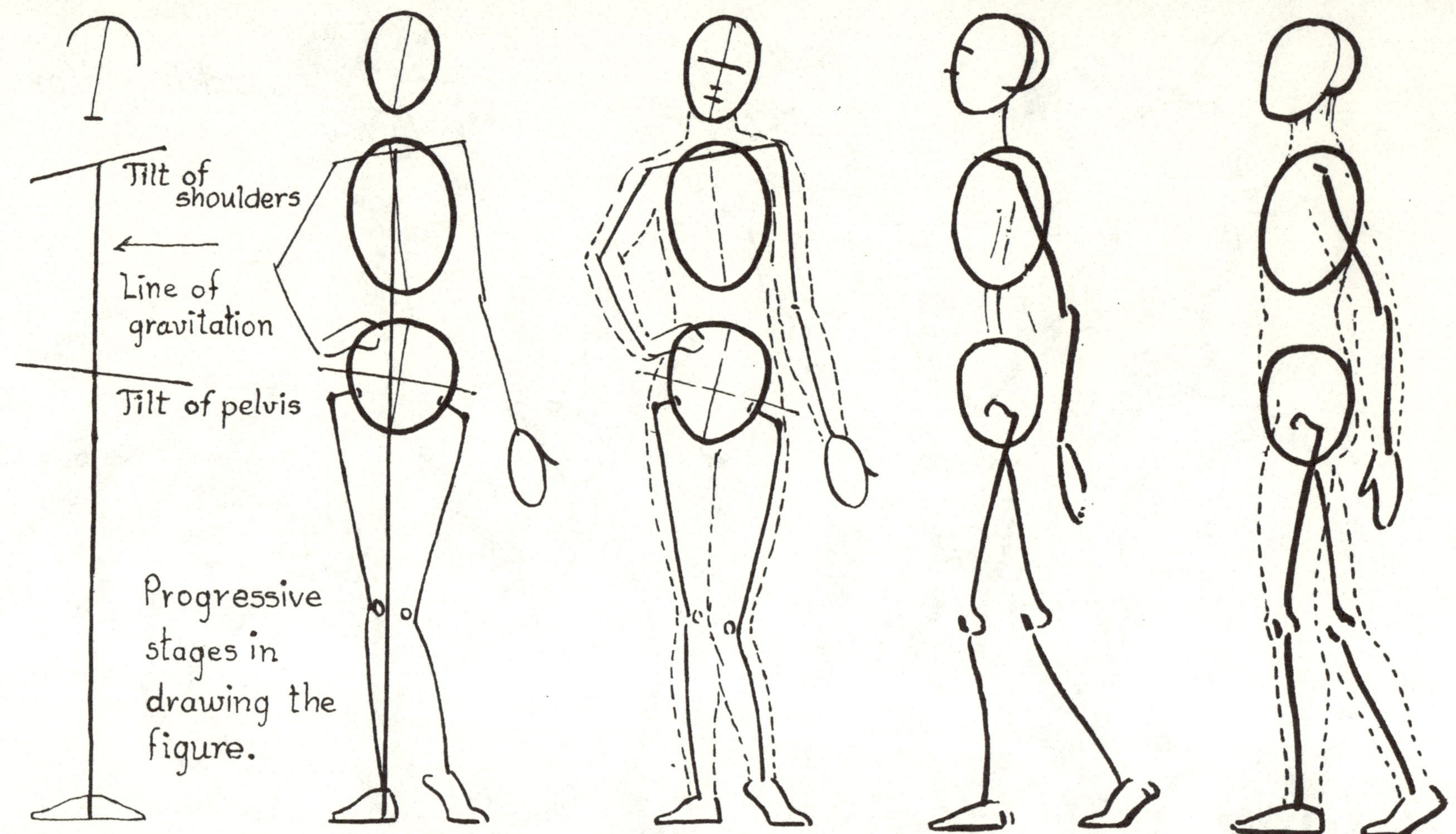

First draw a perpendicular line indicating the placement of the figure. This will be the balance line or line of gravitation. Next indicate by a line the action of the shoulders, leaving room enough above for the neck and head, then indicate the tilt of pelvis.

Use egg shapes for the start of the head, the torso, and the pelvis, and in this way it will be easier to judge the proportions by eye.

In the above figure, most of the weight is resting on the right leg, which forces the pelvis to tilt in an opposite direction to the upper part of the body, and the foot touches the line of gravitation.

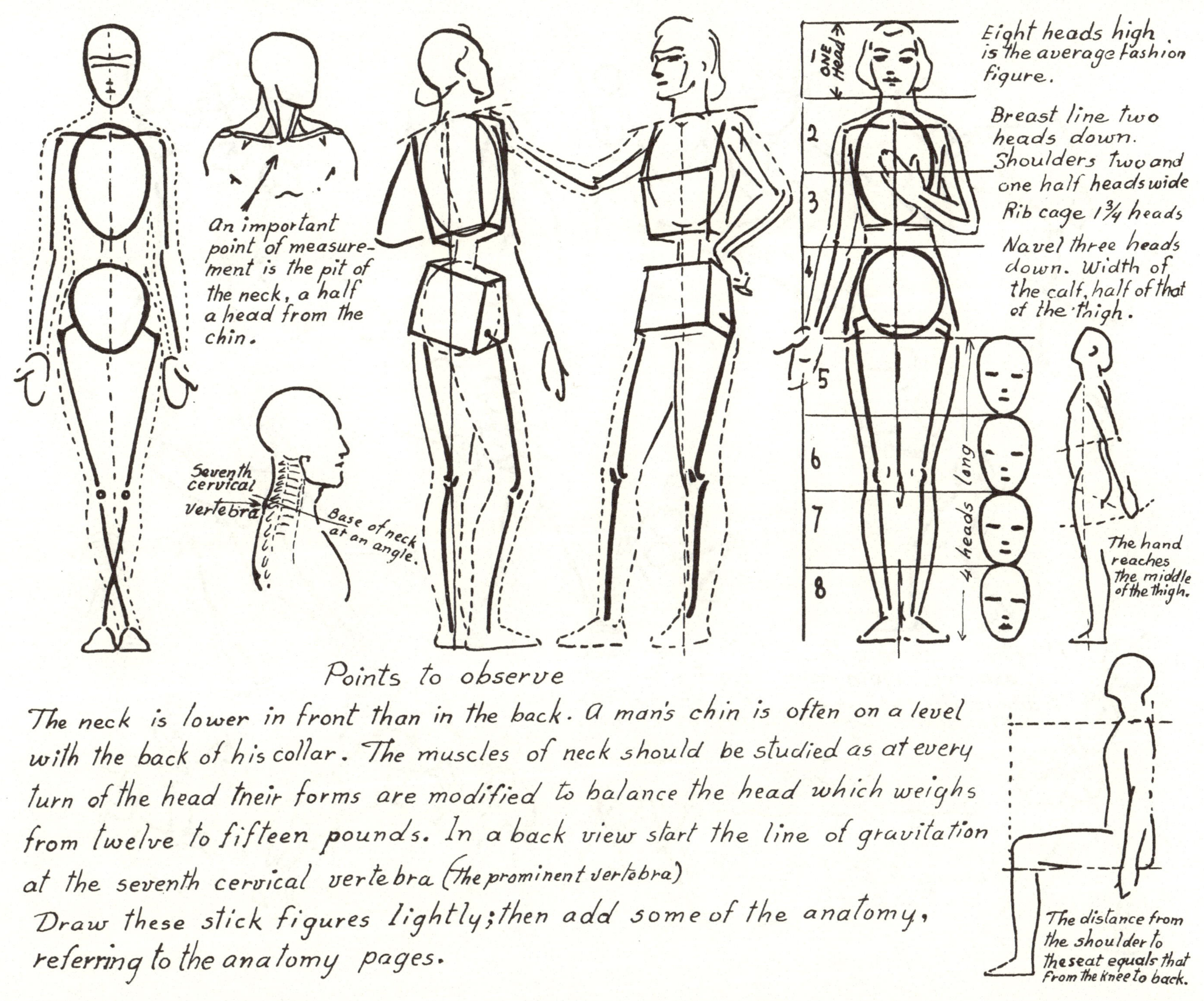

An important point of measurement is the pit of the neck, a half a head from the chin.
Seventh cervical vertebra
Base of neck at an angle.
ONE HEAD
1
2
3
4
5
6
7
8
Eight heads high is the average fashion figure.
Breast line two heads down. Shoulders two and one half heads wide
Rib cage 1¾ heads
Navel three heads down. Width of the calf, half of that of the thigh.
4 heads long
The hand reaches the middle of the thigh.
Points to observe
The neck is lower in front than in the back. A man's chin is often on a level with the back of his collar. The muscles of neck should be studied as at every turn of the head their forms are modified to balance the head which weighs from twelve to fifteen pounds. In a back view start the line of gravitation at the seventh cervical vertebra (the prominent vertebra)
Draw these stick figures lightly; then add some of the anatomy, referring to the anatomy pages.
The distance from the shoulder to the seat equals that from the knee to back.

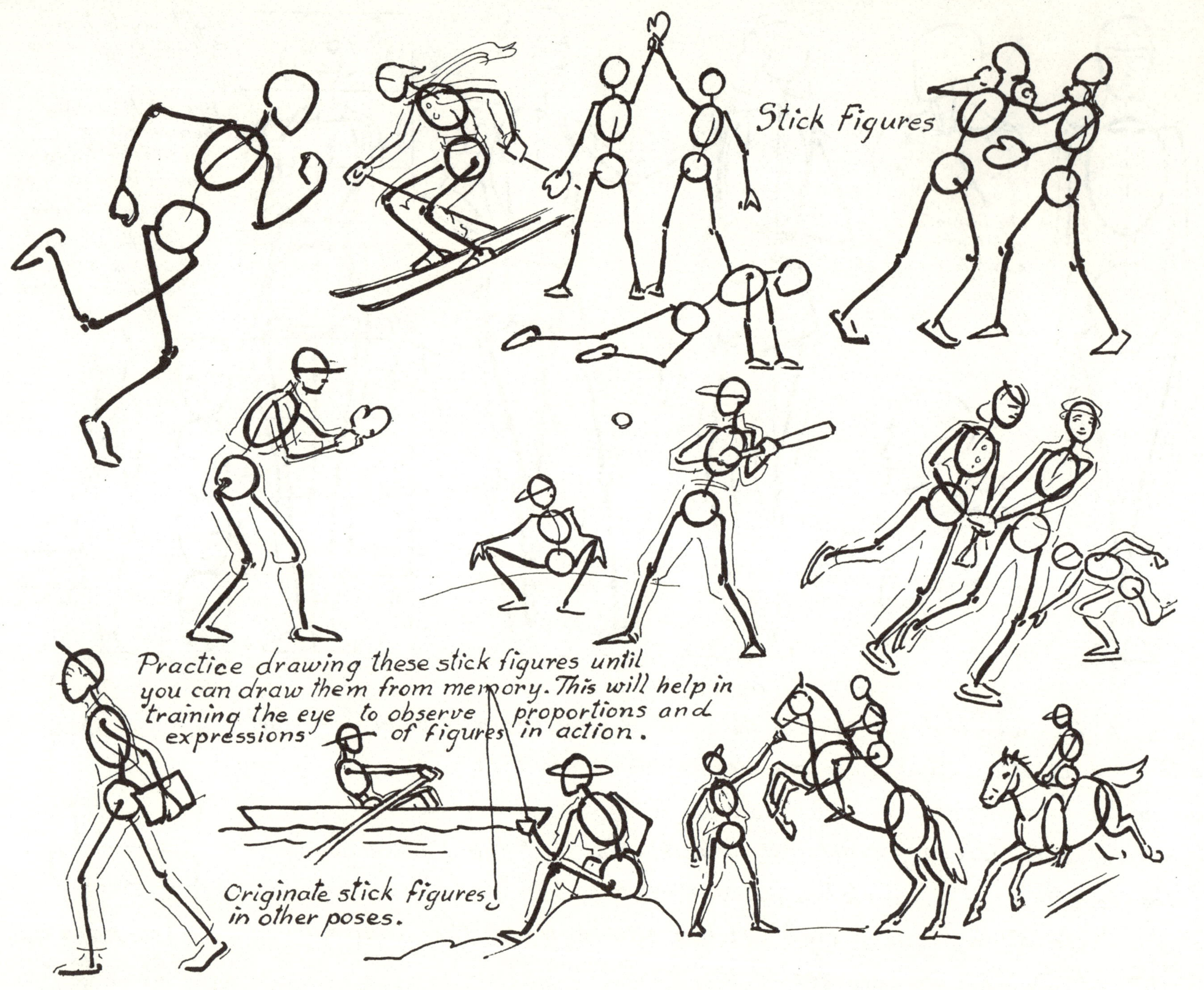
Stick Figures
Practice drawing these stick figures until you can draw them from memory. This will help in training the eye to observe proportions and expressions of figures in action.
Originate stick figures in other poses.

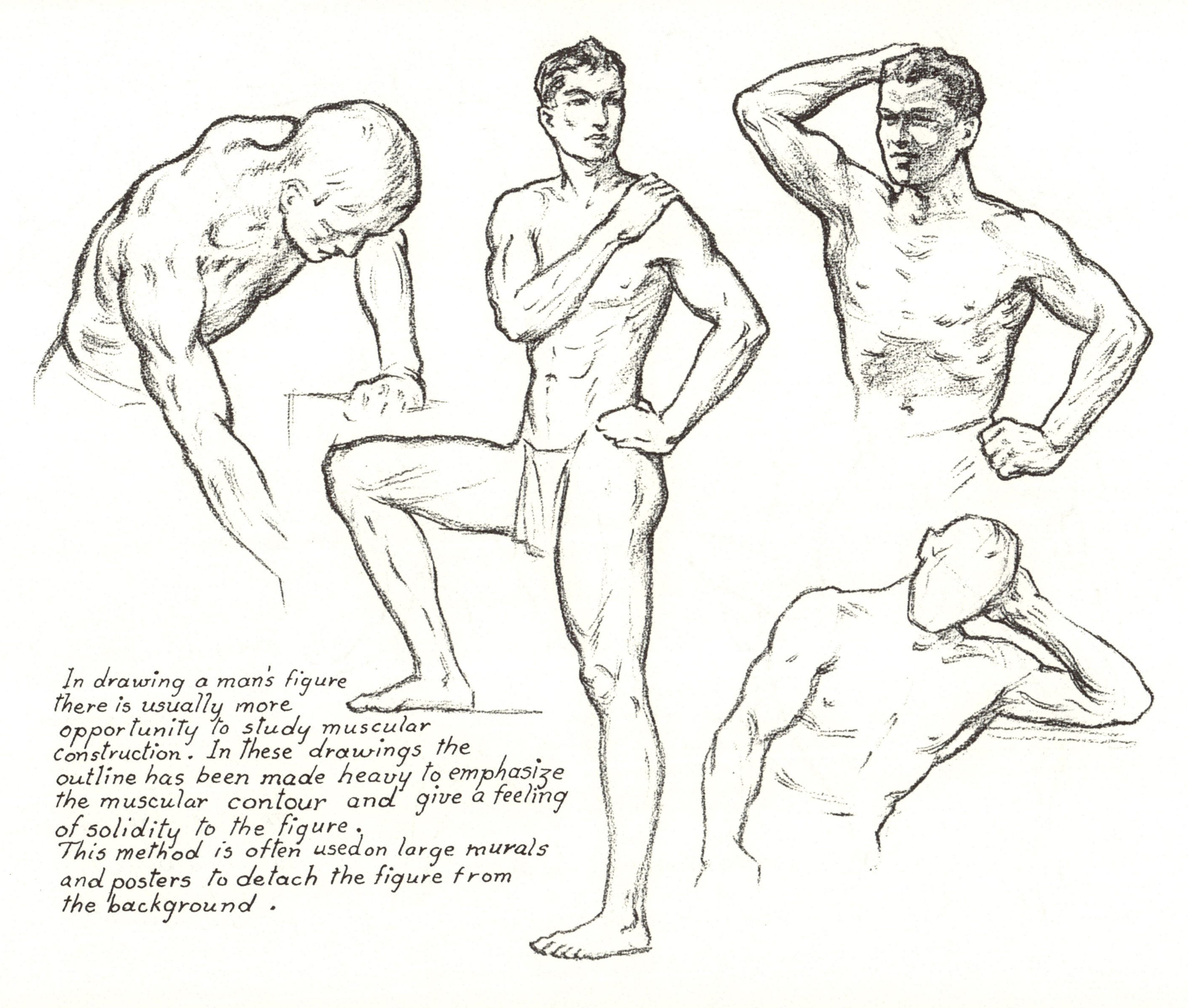

In drawing a man's figure there is usually more opportunity to study muscular construction. In these drawings the outline has been made heavy to emphasize the muscular contour and give a feeling of solidity to the figure.
This method is often usedon large murals and posters to detach the figure from the background.

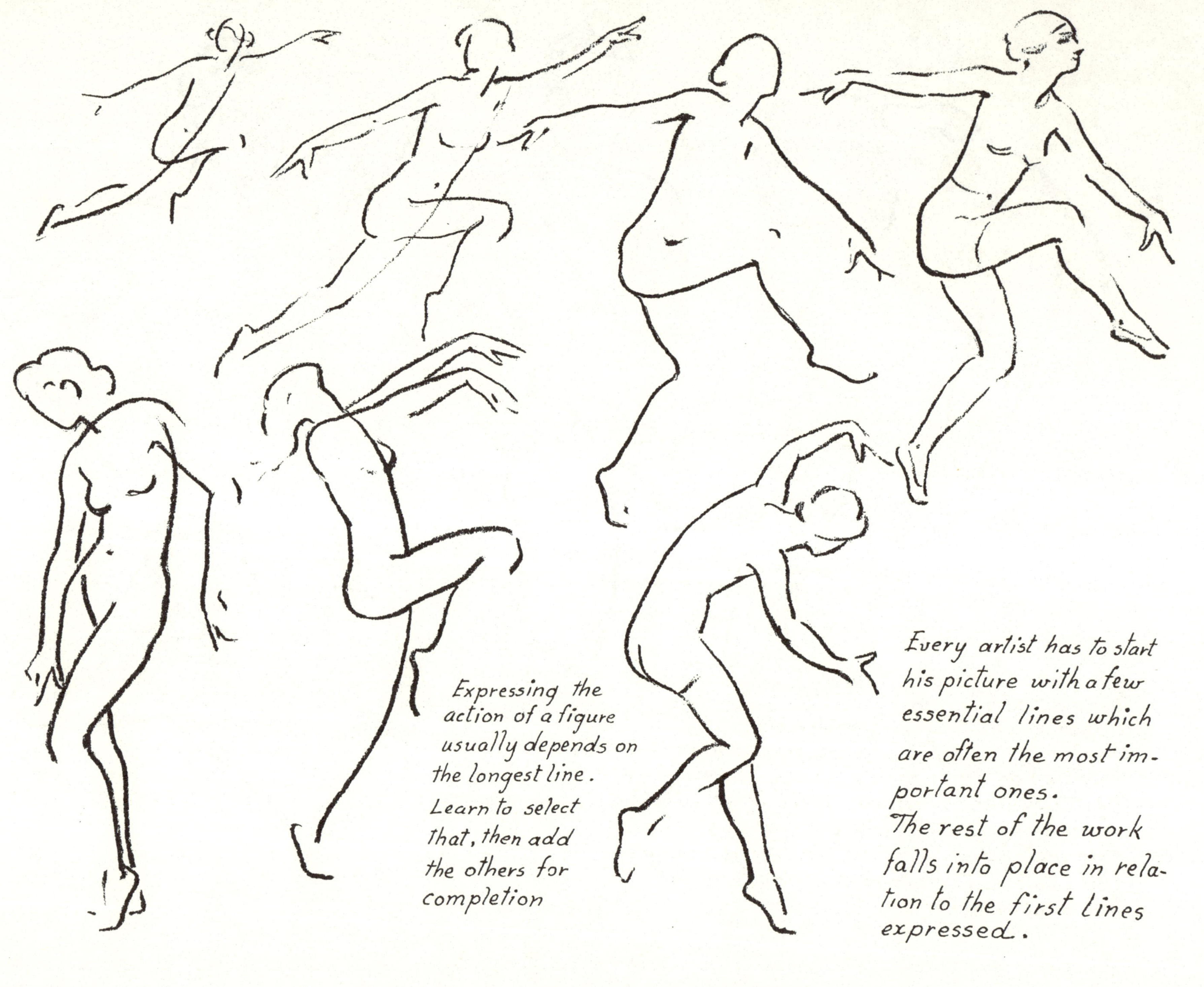

Expressing the action of a figure usually depends on the longest line. Learn to select that, then add the others for completion
Every artist has to start his picture with a few essential lines which are often the most important ones. The rest of the work falls into place in relation to the first lines expressed.

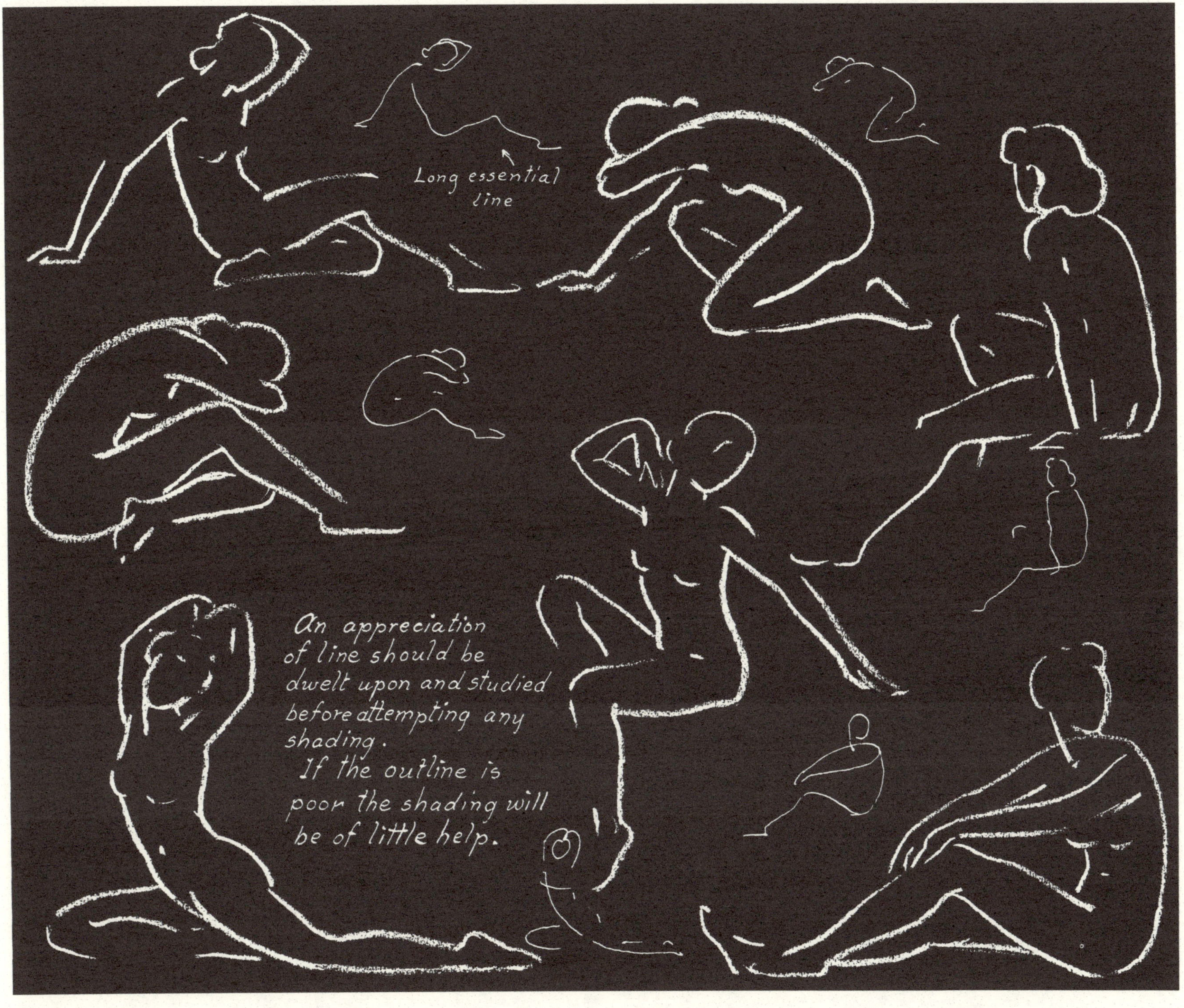
Long essential line
An appreciation of line should be dwelt upon and studied before attempting any shading.
If the outline is poor the shading will be of little help.

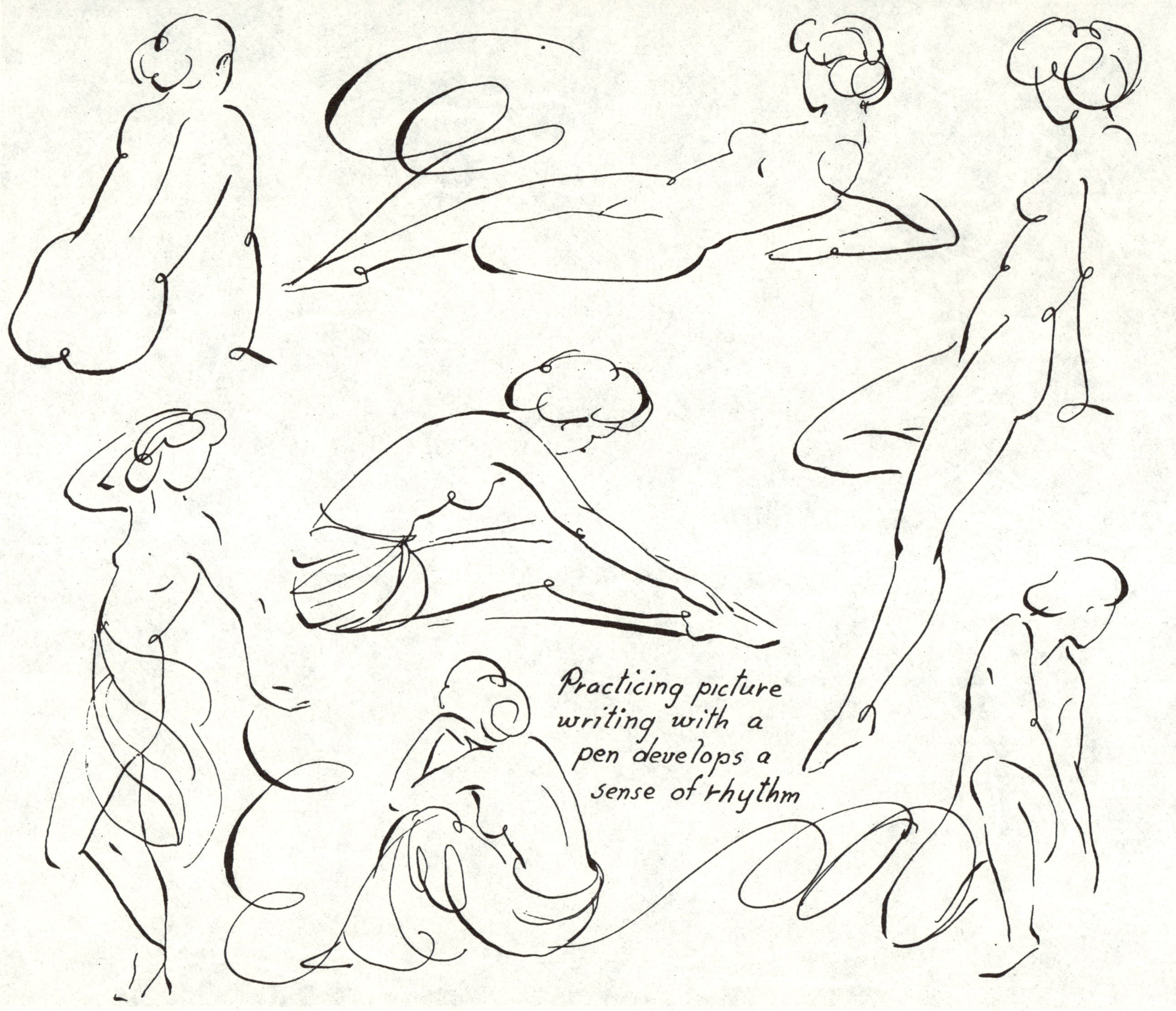
Practicing picture
writing with a
pen develops a
sense of rhythm

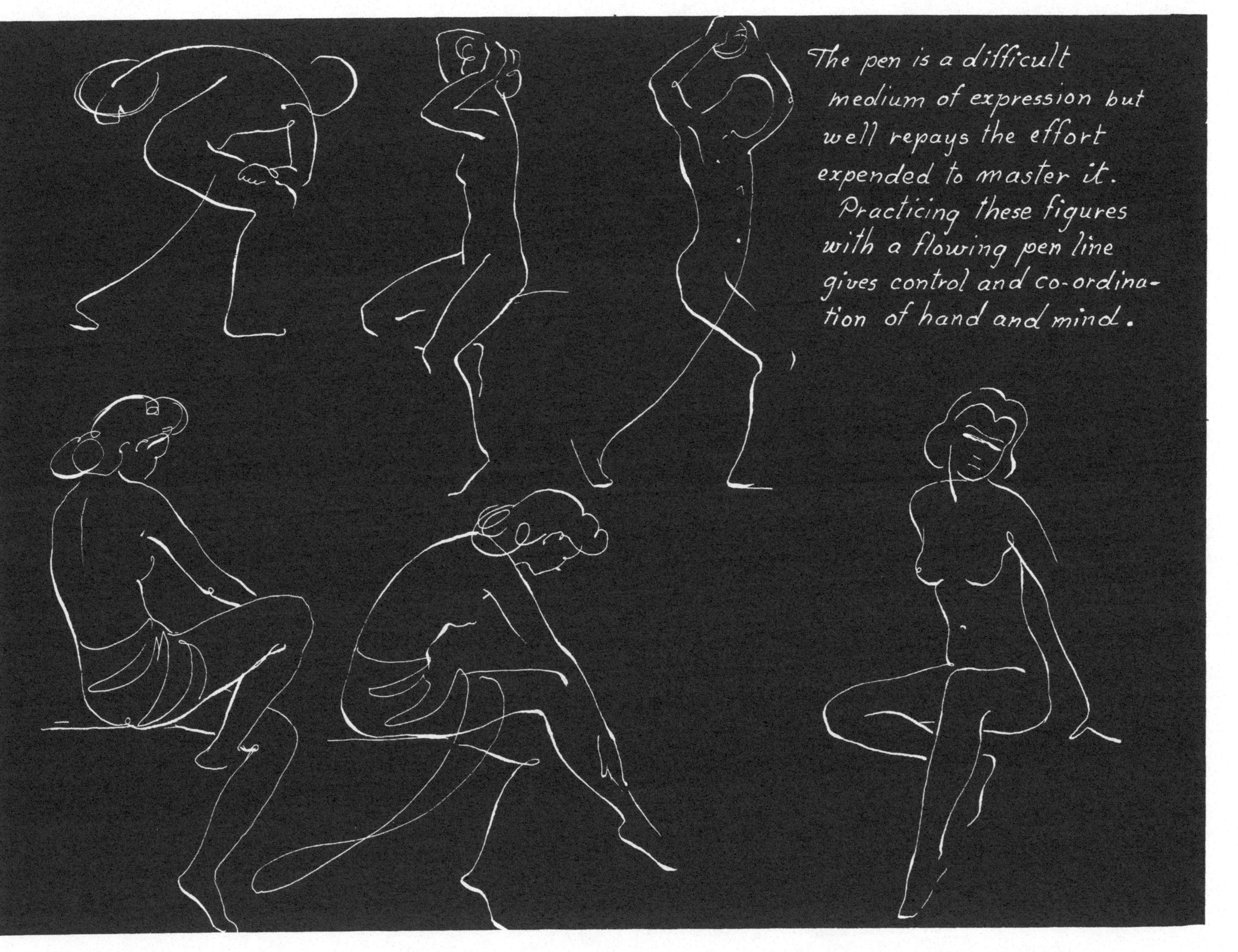
The pen is a difficult medium of expression but well repays the effort expended to master it.
Practicing these figures with a flowing pen line gives control and co-ordination of hand and mind.

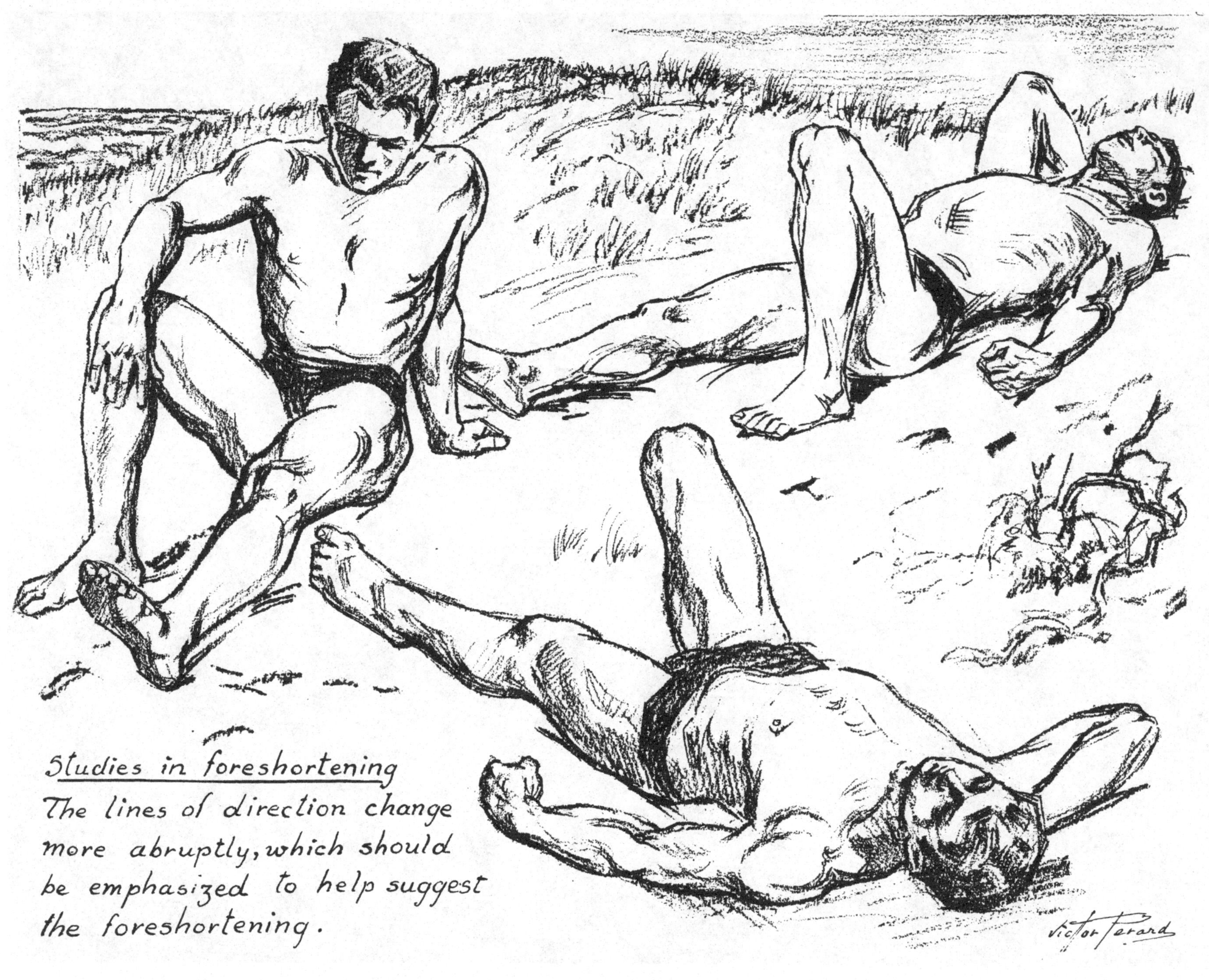
Studies in foreshortening
The lines of direction change more abruptly, which should be emphasized to help suggest the foreshortening.
Victor Perard

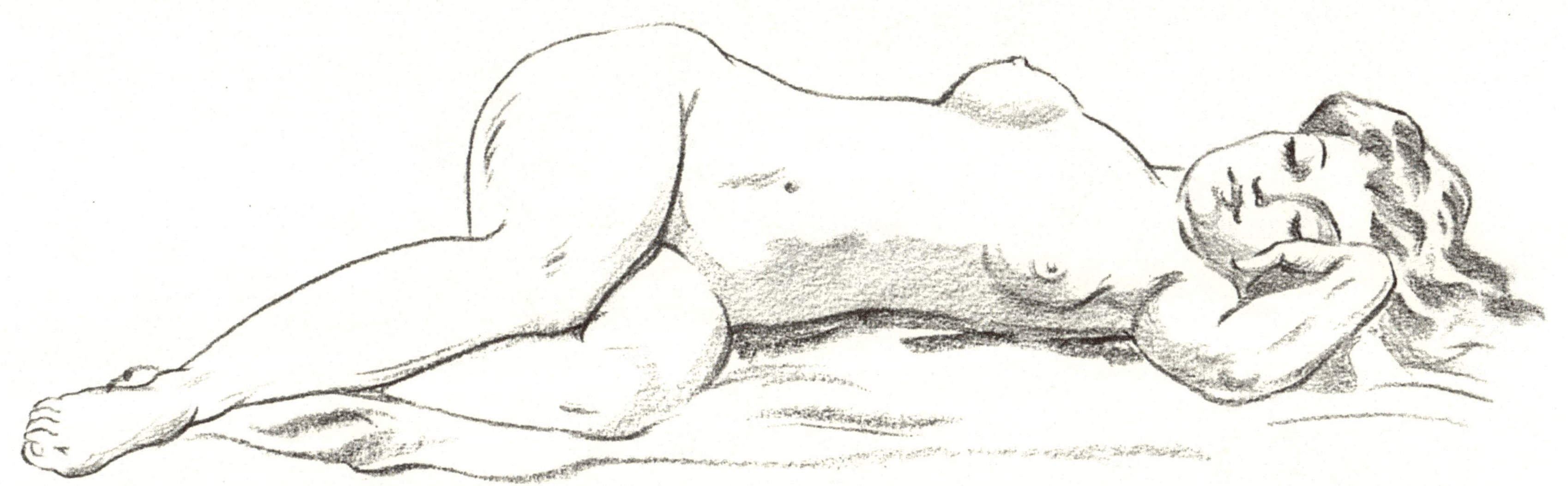

Reclining figures afford an opportunity for the study of foreshortening, which is a difficult problem for the student. In these sketches the outline should be indicated lightly, then the proportions established, and finally gone over with decision and the shadows drawn with broad strokes from the worn-down side of the pencil.

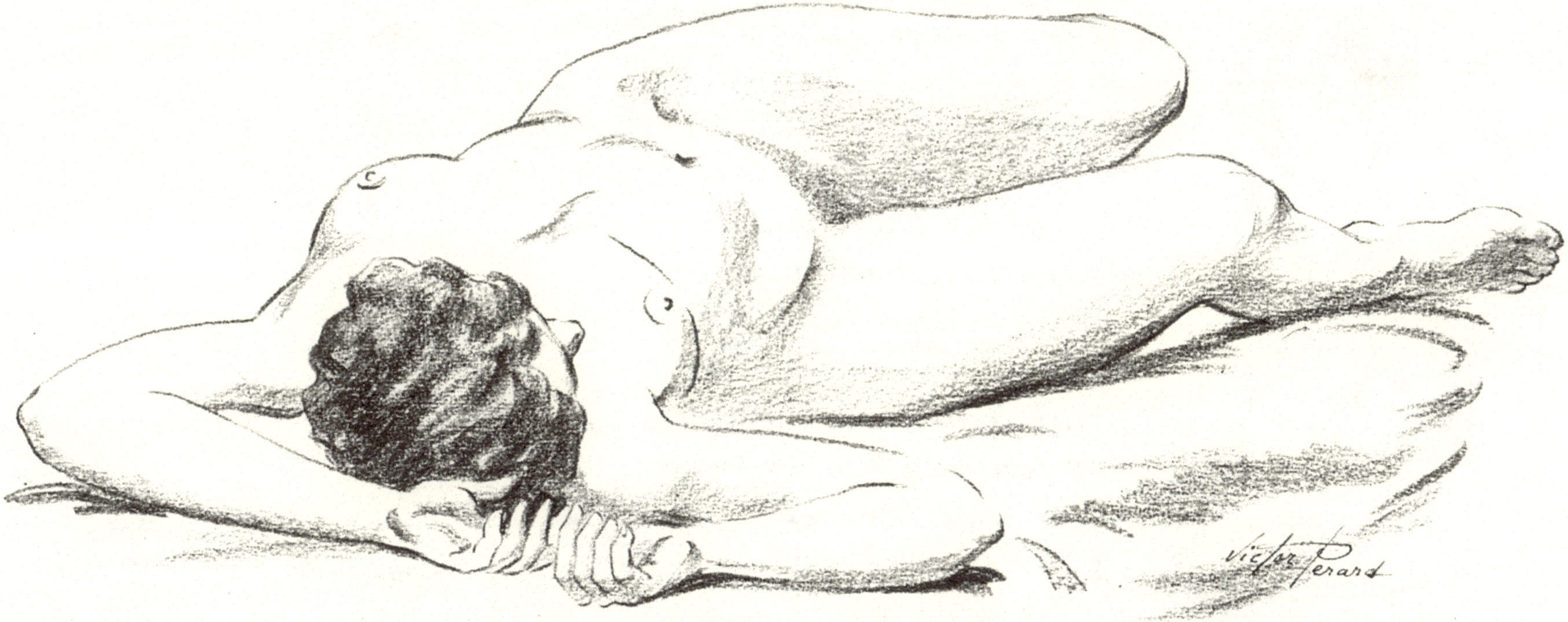

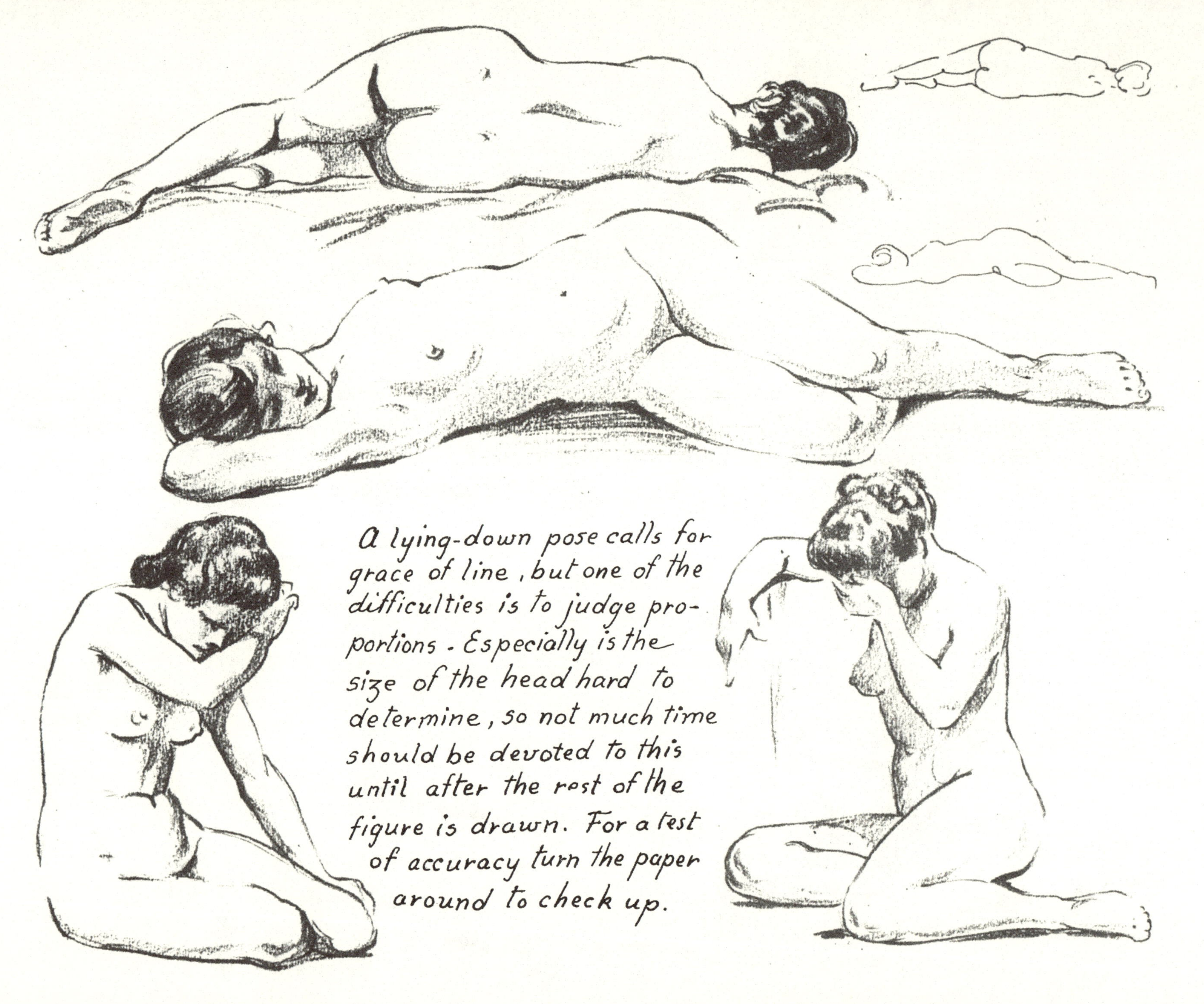
A lying-down pose calls for grace of line, but one of the difficulties is to judge proportions. Especially is the size of the head hard to determine, so not much time should be devoted to this until after the rest of the figure is drawn. For a test of accuracy turn the paper around to check up.

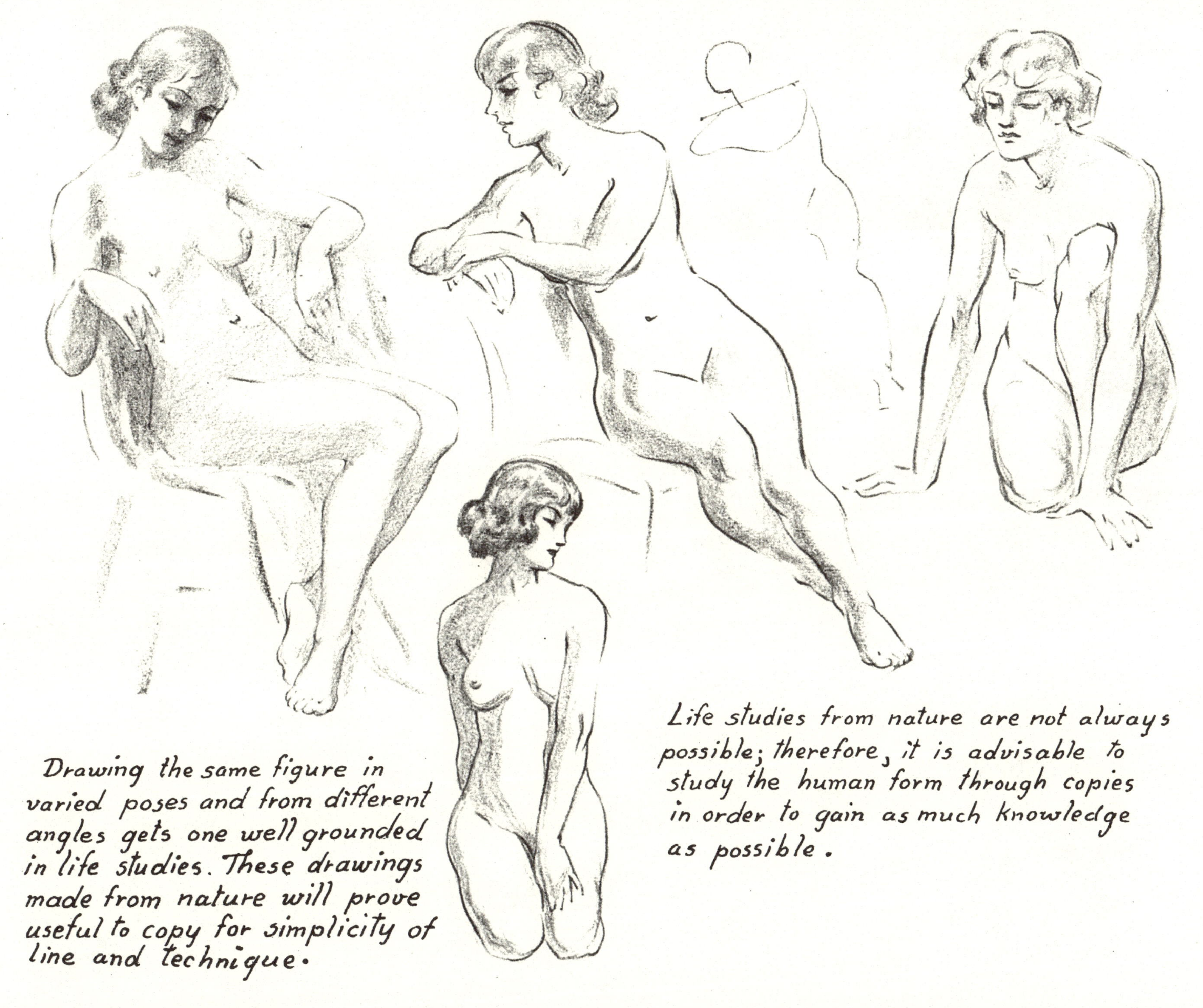

Drawing the same figure in varied poses and from different angles gets one well grounded in life studies. These drawings made from nature will prove useful to copy for simplicity of line and technique.

Life studies from nature are not always possible; therefore, it is advisable to study the human form through copies in order to gain as much knowledge as possible.

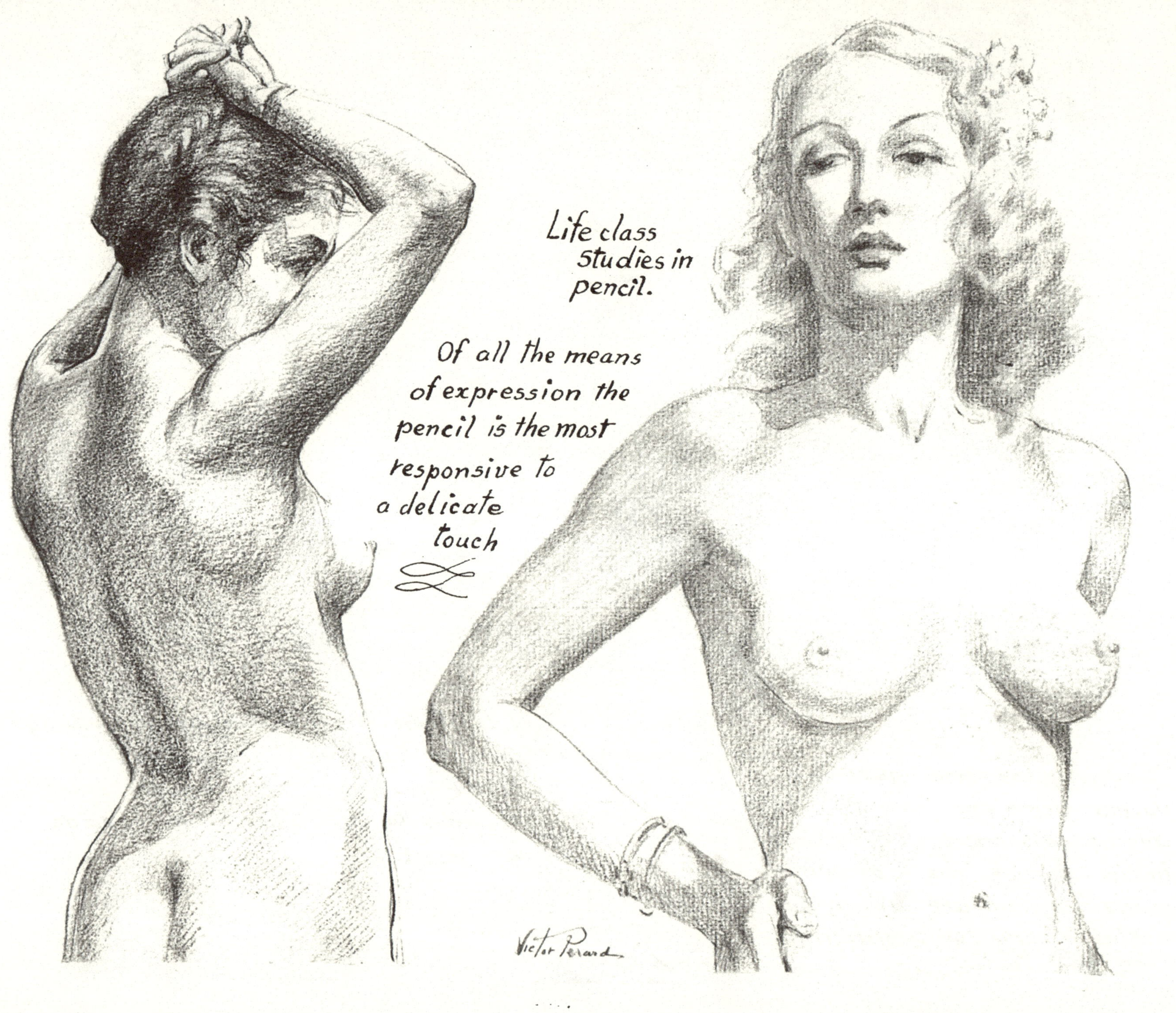
Life class
studies in
pencil.
Of all the means
of expression the
pencil is the most
responsive to
a delicate
touch
Victor Perard

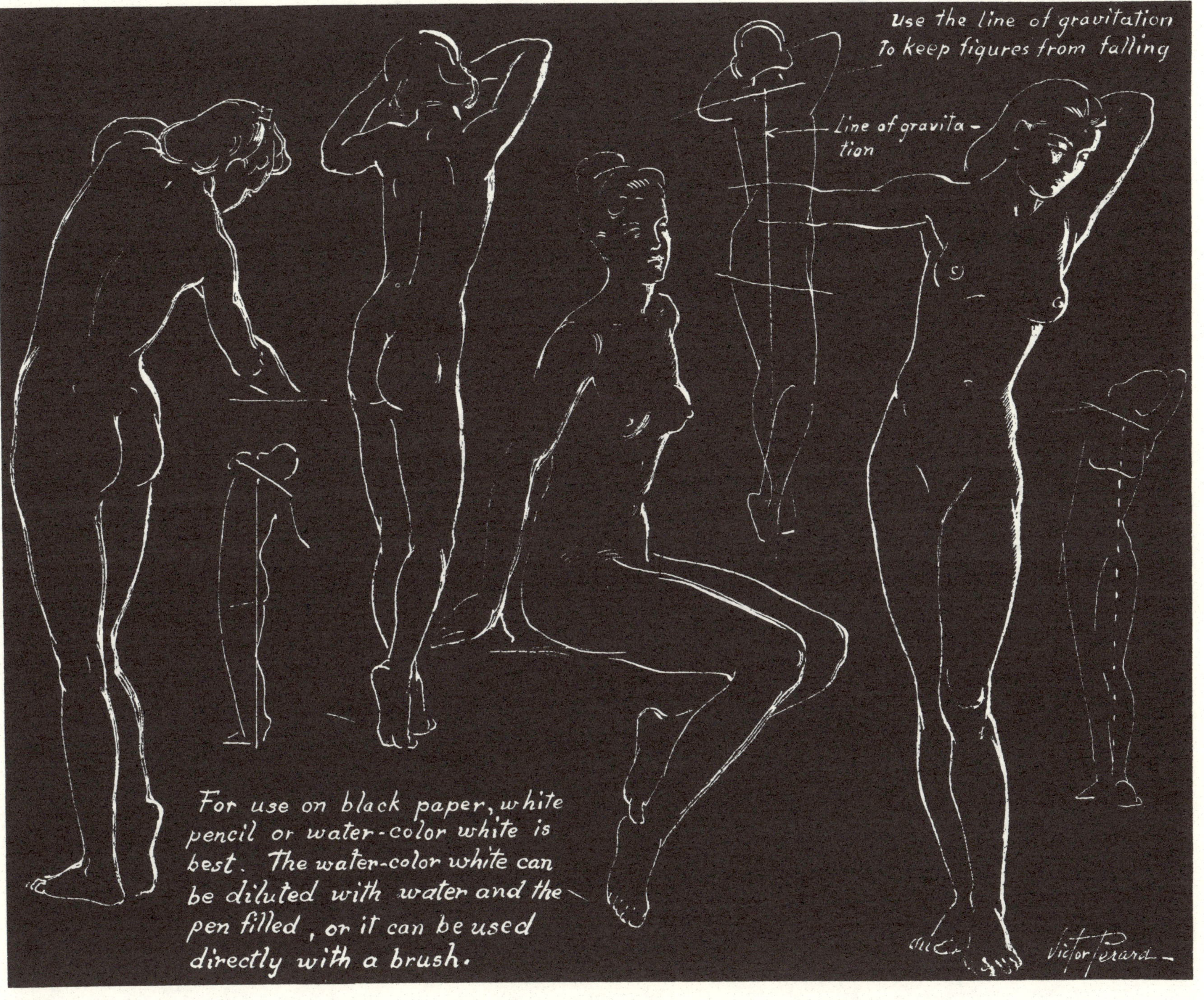
Use the line of gravitation
to keep figures from falling
Line of gravita-
tion
For use on black paper, white
pencil or water-color white is
best. The water-color white can
be diluted with water and the
pen filled, or it can be used
directly with a brush.
Victor Perard

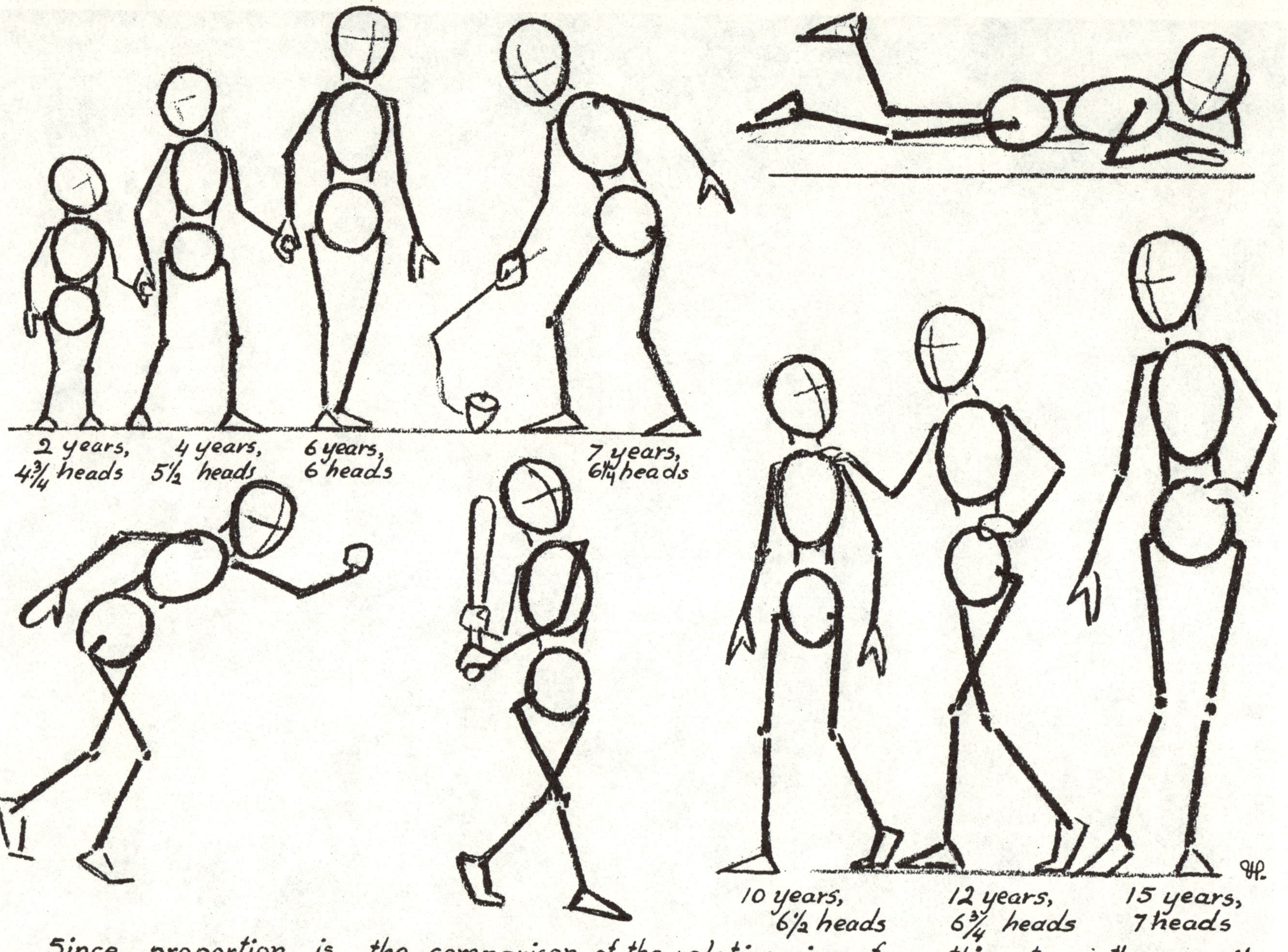

Since proportion is the comparison of the relative size of one thing to another, a unit of measurement must be taken—so we measure heads which is the distance from the top of the skull to the tip of the chin. Children vary considerably in proportions at different ages.